Technology-Enhanced Methods of Money Laundering

Fausto Martin De Sanctis

Technology-Enhanced Methods of Money Laundering

Internet As Criminal Means

Springer

Fausto Martin De Sanctis
3rd Region
Federal Court of Appeals
São Paulo, Brazil

ISBN 978-3-030-18329-5 ISBN 978-3-030-18330-1 (eBook)
https://doi.org/10.1007/978-3-030-18330-1

This Springer imprint is published by the registered company Springer Nature Switzerland AG
The registered company address is: Gewerbestrasse 11, 6330 Cham, Switzerland

Acknowledgments

I want to express my gratitude to the Federal Judicial Center (FJC), notably Mira Gur-Arie, and the Law Library of Congress (LLC), especially Eduardo Soares, both in DC, for having the opportunity to access documents, judicial decisions, courts, and authorities in the United States.

I thank all of the people at the FJC and LLC and the staff of my chambers for their invaluable help and support.

I would like to give special thanks to Viviane do Amaral for her support, affection, and friendship.

Finally, I would like to express my thankfulness to my sons, Thomaz and Theodoro, for their constant motivation for my work, as well as to the Creator for his love over the creation.

Contents

About the Author

Fausto Martin De Sanctis who has a PhD degree in Criminal Law from São Paulo University (USP), is a Member of the Community of Portuguese-speaking Jurists and of the Advisory Board of American University for Legal Studies Programs Brazil, USA, is a Specialist in Civil Procedure from Brasília University (UnB), is Federal Appeals Judge at the Federal Court of Appeals for the Third Region, and is a Writer.

He started the career of the federal judiciary in 1991. Previously, he was a São Paulo State Judge (1990–1991), Public Prosecutor of the Municipality of São Paulo, and Public Prosecutor of the State of São Paulo in the area of the Public Defender's Office. He was a Professor at São Judas Tadeu University for 15 years.

He is General Ombudsman of the Federal Court of Appeals for the 3rd Region and Supervisor of the Monitoring Group of the Federal Penitentiary System.

As the Head of the 6th Criminal Court in São Paulo, specializing in money laundering and financial crimes, for 20 years, he judged complex cases involving financial institutions, several clandestine exchange dealers ("doleiros"), and international drug traffickers, etc.

He is Pioneer in the early sale of goods (before the final decision); in the performance of award-winning or plea-bargaining donations, serving as a basis for regulation of the law; in the allocation of resources to philanthropic entities received in donations (as a form of indemnification to society and show of repentance), donation of works of art for cultural entities and destination to public squares; and in the procedure of telephone interception, adopted by the subsequent legislation.

He received an honorary distinction from the New York State Bar Association (NYSBA) for being considered the forerunner of decisions to prevent and combat corruption and money laundering in Brazil (2016), distinction in commemoration of the 60th anniversary of the departure of the First Contingent of the Suez Battalion toward the Middle East, by the Brazilian Association of UN International Peace Forces (2018); Commendation of the Order of Judicial Merit, in the rank of Grand Officer, by the Labor Court of Appeals for the 2nd Region (2015); Anchieta Medal and Gratitude Diploma of the City of São Paulo (2011); Tiradentes Medal/Rio State Congress—ALERJ (2010); distinctions by the Military Police of the State of São

Paulo (2009) and by the Council for Control of Financial Activities (COAF), Brazilian Financial Intelligence Unit (2008) etc.

He was indicated by his peers in the Association of Federal Judges of Brazil (AJUFE)'s list to occupy a seat in the Brazilian Supreme Court in 2010, 2014, and 2017. His name was included in a list subscribed by the jurists, among them, Miguel Reale Júnior, Modesto Carvalhosa, and Hélio Bicudo, and by 49 class entities and social movements organized for the same purpose on January 25, 2017. He has lectured in Brazil (public and private entities) and abroad, among them the United States (UN/DC, American Congress/DC, Federal Judicial Center -FJC/DC, World Bank/DC, Massachusetts Division of Banks/Boston, Money Transmitter Regulators Association - MTRA/Kansas City, Inter-American Development Bank -IADB/DC, Harvard University/Cambridge, Columbia University/NY, Syracuse University/Syracuse, American University/DC, George Washington University/DC, Georgetown University/DC, Yale University/New Haven, Marquette University/Milwakee); China (Hong Kong University), Russia (Moscow State University), Turkey (Istanbul University), France (The Organization for Economic Cooperation and Development -OECD and Cour de Cassation/Paris), Germany (Heidelberg University/Hannover), Austria (International Anti-Corruption Academy (IACA)/Vienna), Angola (European Union/Luanda), Mozambique (UN/Maputo), Canada (York University – Terrorism, Transnational Crime and Corruption Center -TraCCC/Toronto), Qatar (ONU/Doha), India (Jindal University/Nova Delhi), Malaysia (International Anti-Corruption Conference (IACC)/Kuala Lumpur), Argentina (Grupo de Ação Financeira da América Latina (GAFILAT)/Buenos Aires), Peru (Ministerio de Justicia y Derechos Humanos/Lima), and Mexico (Fiscalía Anticorrupción/Hermosillo).

De Sanctis has written a number of articles published in newspapers and magazines specializing in law and economics, besides books.

His publications include, among others, the following:

Books

International Money Laundering Through Real Estate and Agribusiness: A Criminal Justice Perspective from the "Panama Papers." Cham, Heidelberg, New York, Dordrecht, London: Springer, 2017

Churches, Temples, and Financial Crimes: A Judicial Perspective of the Abuse of Faith. Cham, Heidelberg, New York, Dordrecht, London: Springer, 2015

Economic and Dinancial Delinquency (Delinquência Econômica e Financeira). Rio de Janeiro: GEN/Forense, 2015

Football, Gambling, and Money Laundering: A Global Criminal Justice Perspective. Cham, Heidelberg, New York, Dordrecht, London: Springer, 2014

Criminal Law – General Rules (*Direito Penal – Parte Geral*). São Paulo, Método, Rio de Janeiro: Forense, 2014

Money Laundering Through Art: A Criminal Justice Perspective. Cham, Heidelberg, New York, Dordrecht, London: Springer, 2013

Money Laundering Through Gambling and Soccer: Analysis and Proposals (*Lavagem de Dinheiro. Jogos de Azar e Futebol. Análise e Proposições*). Curitiba: Editora Juruá, 2010

Criminal Liability of Corporations and Modern Criminal Methods (*Responsabilidade Penal das Corporações e Criminalidade Moderna*). São Paulo: Saraiva, 2009

Organized Crime and the Disposal of Seized Assets: Money Laundering, Plea Bargains, and Social Responsibility (*Crime Organizado e Destinação de Bens Apreendidos. Lavagem de Dinheiro, Delação Premiada e Responsabilidade Social*). São Paulo: Saraiva, 2009

The Fight Against Money Laundering: Theory and Practice (*Combate à Lavagem de Dinheiro, Teoria e Prática*). Campinas: Millennium, 2008

Criminal Tax Law: Highlights (*Direito Penal Tributário: Aspectos Relevantes*). Campinas: Bookseller, 2006

Criminality in the National Financial System: Criminal Law and Protection of Brazil's National Financial System (*Punibilidade no Sistema Financeiro Nacional: Tipos Penais que Tutelam o Sistema Financeiro Nacional*). Campinas: Millennium, 2003

Criminal Liability of Corporations (*Responsabilidade Penal da Pessoa Jurídica*), São Paulo: Saraiva, 1999

Articles and Book Chapters

"Football: A Call for Transparency to Curb Corruption." Sociology and Criminology 4:133, OMICS International: Publications, Benefits & Features, 2016.

"Improving Delivery in Development: The Role of Voice, Social Contract, and Accountability." Chapter: "Voice and Accountability: Improving the Delivery of Anticorruption and Anti-Money Laundering Strategies in Brazil." The World Bank Legal Review, vol. 6. Washington, DC: World Bank Group, 2015

"Southwestern Journal of International Law." Chapter: "Requirements for the 2014 FIFA World Cup in Brazil and Requirements of Governmental Bodies to Deter Financial Crimes in the Football Sector." California: Southwestern Law School, 2015.

"Criminal Liability of Corporations" ("Responsabilidade Penal das Corporações"). In *A Book in Honor of Miguel Reale Junior* (*Livro Homenagem a Miguel Reale Junior*). Rio de Janeiro: GZ, 2014

"Popular Action: Using Habeas Corpus in the Context of Financial Crimes" ("Ação Popular: A Utilização do Habeas Corpus na Dinâmica dos Crimes Financeiros"). In *Popular Action* (*Ação Popular*). São Paulo: Saraiva, 2013

"Coherent and Functional Criminal Law" ("Direito Penal Coerente e Funcional"). São Paulo: Revista dos Tribunais, Vol. 919, 2012

"Telephone Tapping and Fundamental Rights" ("Interceptações Telefônicas e Direitos Fundamentais"). In *A Tribute to Afrânio Silva Jardim: Writings and Studies* (*Tributo a Afrânio Silva Jardim: Escritos e Estudos*). Rio de Janeiro: Lúmen Júris, 2011

"The Constitution and Freedoms" ("Constituição e Regime das Liberdades"). São Paulo: Revista dos Tribunais, 2009

"Human Trafficking: The Crime and Victim Consent" ("Tráfico Internacional de Pessoas: Tipo Penal e o Consentimento do Ofendido"). In *Women and Criminal Law* (*Mulher e Direito Penal*). Rio de Janeiro: Forense, 2007

"Crimes Against the National Financial System: A Precursor to Money Laundering" ("Crimes Contra o Sistema Financerio Nacional como Antecedentes de Lavagem de Valores"). In *Money Laundering - Commentary on the Law by Judges at Specialized Courts, In Honor of Gilson Dipp* (*Lavagem de Dinheiro – Comentários à Lei pelos Juízes das Varas Especializadas. Homenagem ao Ministro Gilson Dipp*). Porto Alegre: Livraria do Advogado, 2007

Chapter 1
Introduction

Modern criminals are focusing on the Internet.[1] Since they are increasingly using it to turn dirty money, criminals become more creative and opportunistic money launderers than before. Old methods like to convert, in a casino, their loot into a clean win on the roulette table or redeeming an insurance policy at a discount apparently has gone.

Internet is one of the main sectors attractive to criminals as a means of laundering the proceeds of all types of illegal activity. Most people are familiar with the spam when a high source asks help to transfer significant amounts of money, but first, it is required banking details which promptly will be used to empty accounts and then disappear.

For instance, two scams, in which criminals do actually transferring large amounts of money into an account and then ask the holder to forward it, or offering people jobs in which they can make a substantial income working from home; however, the "job" involves accepting money transfers into their accounts and then passing these funds on to an account set up by the employer.[2]

Also, tax misapplication on Sales, Use Tax, and Games must be a concern because with the rise of virtual worlds, those who cash out, that is, convert virtual wealth to real-world wealth, should be taxed on their gains, especially when there is an activity that occurs entirely within virtual words, what makes it an attraction field for many criminals.

It was not by accident that crime took such an unusual turn. Controls enacted pursuant to recommendations by the Financial Action Task Force—FATF made it necessary to seek out new mechanisms for the laundering of ill-gotten gains.

---

[1] The Internet began in 1969 as a network of four computers located at the University of California at Los Angeles, the University of California at Santa Barbara, the University of Utah, and the Stanford Research Institute. The U.S. Department of Defense funded the initial work through an entity known as the Advanced Research Projects Agency–ARPA. The ARPA Network (ARPANET) was designed to be a decentralized system. See American Bar Association [1, p. 1814].

[2] See MIT—Technology Review [2].

F. M. De Sanctis, *Technology-Enhanced Methods of Money Laundering*,
https://doi.org/10.1007/978-3-030-18330-1_1

Furthermore, the globalization of financial markets and the rapid development of information technology have gradually steered the underworld economy towards new possibilities for the commission of crimes.

Internet is an attractive sector for the practice of money laundering because of the large monetary transactions involved, the general unfamiliarity and confidentiality surrounding it, and the unlawful activity endemic to it due to fake identity or anonymity.

According to Cecily Raiborn, Chandra Schorg, and Christie Bubrig, "laundering money on the Internet entails transferring money electronically from one bank to another, using different names and different locations. The process is repeated until the money becomes clean or untraceable. Three advantages of laundering money on the Internet are that the transactions can be made as often as one wants, with anonymity, and from remote locations."[3] Anonymity is essential to money-laundering activity and becomes undesirable in attempting to control such a process.

The purpose here is to inquire into the scale of the problem and to look into legislative and institutional loopholes that might give power and mobility to organized crime, thereby making it a more deeply entrenched source of unprecedented illicit wealth. The carefree attitude which has been characterized by the industry must be confronted with a realistic understanding of the problem, and must go beyond the adoption of measures taken in isolation or in an uncoordinated manner, lest conflict and instability continue to undermine its credibility and possibly even jeopardize its continued existence.

No one predicted the reach of the World Wide Web, the rise of alternative payment systems, of the massive exploitation of the Dark Web. To Louise Shelley "The spread of the internet was originally interpreted almost entirely as a force for good. The assumption that greater connectivity and greater access to information would lead to more prosperity and greater intercultural understanding was rarely questioned and is still implicit in the way we continue to think about digital transformations. Not enough serious attention is given to dark sides of the globalized digital economy."[6] (see SHELLEY, Louise I. *Dark Commerce. How a New Illicit Economy is Threatening Our Future*. Princeton, New Jersey: Princeton University Press, 2018, p. 03) This analysis seeks to provide a basis for a number of important public decisions, to prompt specialists to speak up in order to keep Internet from being used or manipulated for illegal purposes, and to expound on situational vulnerabilities confronting this market which are not clearly understood by authorities or society at large.

Inasmuch as Internet, like art,[4] is a subject of universal interest, it must not be exempted from criminological scrutiny because of its great social, educational, and cultural importance.

We must constantly reflect on how authorities are defied on a daily basis in their efforts to take steps to prevent money laundering and the financing of terrorism and organized crime. Closer scrutiny is necessary if we are to understand the new global

---

[3] Raiborn et al. [3, p. 37].

[4] See the author De Sanctis [4].

situation that has encouraged the commission of serious crimes and the illegal enrichment of criminals. In other words, we seek solutions that will make effective criminal enforcement possible.

It is important to be mindful that one of the essential criminological features inherent in money laundering, as Pedro Caeiro, citing Jorge Fernandes Godinho and Luís Goes Pinheiro, reminds us,[5] is its necessary links to organized crime, which in turn add considerable diversity to the types of conduct that its prosecution and enforcement may prevent.

Therefore, strong criminal enforcement on the part of government is required from the outset, including investigations into assets of suspects, so that—by confirming their propriety and legitimate ownership—we may do away with the idea that crime pays, albeit despite occasional convictions and sentencing.

The author's purpose is to go beyond a mere introduction to this captivating subject. Considerations will be presented in an effort to further the study of methods likely to add transparency to business dealings and thereby inhibit or curtail unlawful activity. This work seeks to dispel the many mysteries surrounding the business of Internet.

The idea is to connect a number of important dots in the cyberspace, where its business practices are concerned, so as to bring about improvements in crime prevention systems. Our hope is to provide a useful foundation for conducting a critical analysis that is both realistic and practical, and to include an overview of studies already conducted worldwide which touch upon this important and current topic.

The aim here is to provide a reading on this sector, a snapshot of the Internet misunderstands which will provide the groundwork and guidance necessary to give it transparency and a backdrop sufficient for a particularized analysis. Some rigor in procedures for cataloging and investigation are in order, for we ought to remember that the resurgence of organized crime is often the result of a systemic atmosphere of inattention, mutual tolerance, and ethical codes which, however lofty, are in practice applied only selectively. Matters are worsened by the arrogance and permissiveness, if not covert complicity, of portions of civil society (the elite, the press, etc.) that insist on pointing out only the defects that do not suit their purposes.

As combatting crimes through Internet, especially money laundering, is a massive and complex activity, which requires a clear and holistic understanding of the various trends and techniques, criminals can adjust quickly to exploit new opportunities that often allow anonymous high value transactions with little or no paper trail or legal accountability.

An attempt to get a basis for detecting main evolving criminal schemes through Internet, this book is divided into ten chapters. Chapter 1 is the introduction. Chapter 2 deals with overarching topics of cyber-attacks or cybercrimes. Chapter 3 addresses the difficult task of catching online sales financing criminals. Chapter 4 is about social media, and the role of people in it. Chapter 5 seeks to organized online gaming. Chapter 6 addresses forms of payment and the use of NGOs and trusts, and their potential for the movement of ill-gotten gains. Chapter 7 specifically addresses the

[5] Cf. Pedro Caeiro [5].

tax misapplication, which can greatly help to clarify how money-laundering prevention applies to the Internet. International legal cooperation, repatriation, and asset forfeiture are analyzed in Chap. 8. Conclusions are covered under Chap. 9. Final Chap. 10 covers national and international proposals for improving the industry so as to prevent all sorts of crimes on the Internet, like money laundering and the financing of terrorism.

Although this work may, at a glance, appear to cover the entire subject, this is actually far from the case. It has, however, aimed at achieving a logical and practical "completeness" in describing a little or unexplored virtual world, in which cyberspace is used in the commission of serious crimes. The purpose here is to see to it that the use of Internet in the commission of crimes is seldom, if ever, carried to fruition.

References

1. American Bar Association. (2000). Achieving legal and business order in cyberspace: A report on global jurisdiction issues created by the internet. *The Business Lawyer, 55*, 1801–1946.
2. MIT – Technology Review. (2013, October 18). *The secrets of online money laundering*. Retrieved August 14, 2018, from https://www.technologyreview.com/s/520501/the-secrets-of-online-money-laundering/
3. Raiborn, C., Schorg, C., & Bubrig, C. (2003). Guarding against e-laundering of dirty money. *Commercial Lending Review, 18*, 36–39.
4. De Sanctis, F. M. (2013). *Money laundering through art: A criminal justice perspective*. Cham: Springer.
5. Caeiro, P. (2005). Manual distributed in a course sponsored by the OAS and the Brazilian Ministry of Justice and presented to Brazilian judges and prosecutors on October 17–21, 2005. In *Branqueamento de capitais* (p. 4).
6. Shelley, L. I. (2018) Dark Commerce. How a New Illicit Economy is Threatening Our Future. Princeton, New Jersey: Princeton University Press, p. 03.

Chapter 2
Dark Web: Deterring Cybercrimes and Cyber-Attacks

On the one hand, the world is changing since cyberspace has been blanketed all continents. People and their rights (like privacy) are under siege. On the other hand, money-laundering crime laws have become increasingly important in recent years. Many changes have taken place to keep up with the globalization of the economy. Until recently, there were great schisms between East and West and between North and South, and even a Cold War complete with Communist-derived Socialism. As the idea of a market economy gained prevalence, even in countries with no such tradition (such as China), and technological innovations advanced, there grew a need for new managerial practices applied to businesses.

Criminals likewise evolve over time. Despite the positive hopes brought on by the advent of globalization, a cutthroat and destructive competitiveness also developed. There are new and growing fears because we do not know where all of this is headed (though trends look ominous).

The globalization inherent in today's world, with all of its advantages and disadvantages, fosters a transnational and technological criminal enterprise, practiced even by large conglomerates and businesses that necessitate unprecedented cooperative exchanges among nations.

As stated by Ronald Griffin, "…cyberspace technology, when put in the wrong hands, is threatening and unfriendly. Business computers prowl the landscape to compile data about us. Government software spies on people to trap law breakers."[1]

The special field of financial crime, whether committed or not by the Internet, is justified by the simple idea that market rules alone cannot address all of the aspirations emerging within the context of the course of business practices—oftentimes crossing through dangerous, ethical gray areas.

The legal protection of property requires government intervention and social and economic regulation so that the rules of conduct with regard to business practices may be stabilized and hence preserved.

---

[1] Griffin [1, p. 136].

F. M. De Sanctis, *Technology-Enhanced Methods of Money Laundering*,
https://doi.org/10.1007/978-3-030-18330-1_2

Objects of legal protection enjoy a sort of global protection, not just by criminal law, but rather, through the expectation of general stability engendered by rules fostering the proper and honest functioning of markets (of corporations, of private and public roles, of derivative securities, etc.).

This is an area of criminal law designed to fill in loopholes in the definitions[2] of crimes against property owing, in large part, to increases in criminal infractions resulting from the exponential increase of economic activity within the State and of international financial relationships.

Of course criminal law does apply, albeit in a fragmented, subsidiary (last resort) role, with no expectation that its financial branch will function in more than a supporting, symbolic role. Yet when we see that such principles are invoked indiscriminately, without the slightest basis in reason, the result is a systemic lack of protection to the economic order.

The take-away here is that financial crime, as money laundering, is a very current subject, *whether by the magnitude of the material damage it causes, or by its capacity to adapt to, and survive, social and political changes, or even because of its readiness to come up with defenses and to defeat all efforts to combat it.*[3]

Conceptualizing financial crime is no simple task. It does not lend itself to simple measurement by the extent of resulting damages. The classification of financial crimes rests on the collectivized or supra-individual nature of the legal interests or assets that is to be protected.

Reducing intervention to only those alleged facts actually held meritorious is just as imperative as trimming away criminal liability hidebound by excessive formalism. Yet the fact remains that administrative sanctions alone have not sufficed to enforce the basic duties we as citizens are bound by as actors in the economic system.

Criminal law has from the outset concerned itself with protecting the basic institutions of government, and citizens' most basic interests. Over time, however, in addition to being relied upon to provide minimum standards of coexistence, it began to also lend itself to the protection of new social and economic interests. A radical shift in government intervention strategies was enacted to combat the intimidating phenomenon of organized crime which was petulantly working its will on politicians, journalists, judges, businessmen, and so on.

Crimes must be tackled alongside the image of the criminal and the social effects of that type of conduct. The conclusions advanced by Edwin Sutherland defined white-collar crime as crimes committed by an honorable person with social and professional prestige,[4] which may explain why this type of criminal conduct generates little in the way of social reaction. The same can be said about online crimes.

Perhaps this phenomenon is due to the perception of minimal dangerousness of the criminal in the absence of direct violence or confrontation with the victim, or even because no physical harm is even contemplated. This brings us to the idea

[2] In Pedrazzi [2].

[3] Cf. Oliveira [3, p. 69].

[4] In Cavero [4, pp. 276–277].

advanced by Thomas Lynch, that serious crime is more ink-stained than blood-stained.[5] Hence, perhaps, it involves a certain moral neutrality.

According to Dr. José Ángel Brandariz Garcia, imprisoning financial criminals would not even result in the negative social stigma typically expected for those identified as criminals, given their personal and socioeconomic characteristics.[6]

However, it should not be by any means common knowledge that crimes committed online are less harmful to society than crimes committed by other means, given its penetration into our lives and social fabric. In truth, it ends up fostering ordinary criminality (corruption, unfair competition, fraud, etc.). This hampers enforcement efforts if there is widespread ignorance about the harmful effects on society that result from delinquent practice due to the unlimited range of network usage.

Criminals do, in fact, have great potential for engendering crime. They are highly adaptable within society, and often enjoy considerable tolerance within the dark web community, which leads to their increasingly daring and dangerous criminal behavior.

Furthermore, criminals actually run a sort of cost-benefit analysis on the gains to be had from unlawful conduct and possible sanctions (sentences) imposed by the legal system. By running a utilitarian calculation[7] one could easily conclude that getting caught involves little or no consequence, given the complexity and inaptitude of some inneffective criminal justice systems.

Cláudia Cruz Santos argues that *theories of rational choice and situational prevention seem to fit them like a glove. Their assessment of the costs and benefits associated with misconduct might dissuade them from engaging in it, should the opportunities decrease and the possibility of detection and punishment increase.*[8]

The deciding factor is not will, but rather the impracticability of the behavior prohibited by law. No longer can we afford the luxury of complex theorizing over abstract hazards and social harm. Categories of financial crime have to do with increasingly complex regulatory situations, and conduct that is legally intolerable, irrespective of the intentions of the criminal. Those intentions would only come out afterward, after the decision was made to break the rules of conduct binding upon us all.

Financial crime practiced or not through the dark web, given its scope and potential for damage, is consigned to the jurisdiction of the Federal Government—at least in countries such as Brazil and the USA, which rely on a dual justice system.

> A good portion of this jurisdiction is brought to bear upon crimes that are complex, sometimes on account of the suspects or defendants involved—people of great economic or political power who, as a rule, operate within a network having international ramifications—and other times because of the type of financial crime involved, be it corruption, influence-peddling, money laundering, etc. Its seriousness, its harm to society and that

[5] *Apud* Mir and Genovês [5].

[6] In Garcia [6].

[7] Fischer [7, p. 37].

[8] Cf. Santos [8].

> threat it poses to institutions which safeguard the Rule of Law require a different balance between the rights of the accused and other procedural requirements of speedy trials and the duty of the State to prosecute and punish unlawful conduct.[9]

This harmful and unlawful behavior under federal jurisdiction requires recognition of financial criminal conduct as a violation of a negative legal duty, namely, that of refraining from illegitimately harming others or the public order, and of a positive legal duty, that one's behavior be conducive to the greater good of society. This progressive view of legality is increasingly accepted. It does, however, require more complex analysis, involving the said legal duties (both negative and positive) upon which foundation a specific legal and criminal appraisal is constructed.

If we can affirm about a concern of dual justice system about the financial crime, money laundering has a different approach because it can be achieved by ordinary criminals, deserving the same institutional treatment.

The reintegration of criminals into society must therefore center on making them rethink their behavior. If there is indeed any reasoning behind unlawful conduct involving cost-benefit analyses of the outcomes to the offender, a given crime will be committed if and only if the expected penalty is outweighed by the advantages to be had from committing the act.[10] This also applies in case of online crimes, in which, to the point of exhaustion, we see complexity, anonymity, or fake identities.

Several transactions take place over the Internet each day, and with its inherent features, it has been possible to launder illegally acquired funds by criminal organizations. Due to its complexity, the online accounts become more untraceable, and the more untraceable they are, the more dirty money has been used. In terms of criminal matters, rules of evidence often require the prosecution to establish the chain of custody for the evidence it wishes to introduce at trial.

It is important, as stated by Timothy A. Vogel, "procedures for gathering evidence of a cyber-attack take into account these requirements in case a decision is made later to refer the matter to law enforcement for criminal prosecution."[11]

Avoiding detection, money laundering is experiencing some changes as criminals has been optimized payment mechanisms, by micro laundering via sites like PayPal. This has created an increasing difficulty for many law enforcement bodies.

After blanking the world, cyberspace has changed everything, and criminals are using Internet to poach data from other devices, by assuming somebody's identity, and people taking webs to bully others.

For instance, the number of complaints and consumers becoming victims of auction fraud increases annually. Though host auction websites, according to Dara Chevlin, "should be permitted to govern themselves, claiming that their mechanisms are most effective to prevent fraud, the statistics clearly show that their efforts are ineffective in stemming the growing problem of online auction fraud. The scam

[9] Oliveira [3, p. 71].

[10] For more on this, see Sánchez [9, p. 11] and Rodrigues [10, pp. 484–485].

[11] Vogel [11, p. 42].

artists are becoming smarter and using the anonymity of the Internet to their advantage. Several cases have attempted to make eBay accountable for fraudulent activity that occurs on their site because the host auction website makes money at the close of every auction held on their website (fraudulent or not), what incentive does e-Bay have to keep a closer eye on its users? Of course, eBay wants to maintain its reputation. But until host auction sites feel the impact of fraud in their earnings, fraud prevention will not receive the attention and investment of resources that it deserves." The author recommends the imposition of stricter federal regulations on host auction websites.[12]

The transition of crimes to the Internet has created unique challenges for law enforcement. Talking about prostitution on the Internet, Mellissa Farley, Kenneth Franzblau, and M. Alexis Kennedy say that "the prostitution transaction includes not only victim, buyer and trafficker/pimp but the most invisible partner: the online advertiser. When prostitution happened on the street in someone's neighborhood, it was clear whose jurisdiction that was. Enforcement of a range of laws against johns and pimps was sometimes fueled by citizens' concern about prostitution as a neighborhood nuisance rather than concern about prostitution's exploitation and violence. Communities wanted prostitution out of sight and out of their neighborhoods. Because online sex businesses are less visible to the public, victims of sexual exploitation in prostitution are isolated and can be in greater danger from sex buyers." For them, "it is incumbent upon policy makers and law enforcement to enforce existing laws and where needed, to develop new laws and policies that will abolish online (and offline) trafficking and prostitution. While many have been recruited, sold and trafficked into prostitution on social networking sites, the sites can also be turned against traffickers."[13]

Ronald Griffin, citing a case involving business, mentioned the Paradigm Alliance Case. Paradigm and Celeritas were parties to a joint venture and each one placed their business interests in the other's hands on an understanding that they nurture their relationship. One day, long after their relationship was underway, a Celeritas' employee hacked Paradigm's computer. He looted information from the machine and poured the booty into a patent application for new type of software.[14]

It is true that almost every employee is provided with some type of computer access and an email account. The network established on these corporations is increasingly connected to Internet and other companies, raising a new set of threats.

It is interesting to mention here two cases decided in the USA involving the so-called dark web.

Ross Ulbricht, also known as "Dread Pirate Roberts," was sentenced on May 29, 2015 in Manhattan federal court to life in prison in connection with his operation and ownership of Silk Road, a hidden website designed to enable its users to buy and sell illegal drugs and other unlawful goods and services anonymously and beyond the reach of law enforcement between January 2011 and October 2013.

[12] See Clevlin [12, p. 255].

[13] See Farley [13, pp. 1090–1991 and 1094].

[14] Griffin [1, p. 145].

Ulbricht was found guilty of each of the seven charges he faced on February 5, 2015, following a 4-week jury trial. Ulbricht was a drug dealer and criminal profiteer who exploited people's addictions and contributed to the deaths of at least six young people. Ulbricht went from hiding his cybercrime identity to becoming the face of cybercrime. Ulbricht created Silk Road in January 2011, and owned and operated the underground website until it was shut down by law enforcement authorities in October 2013. Silk Road emerged as the most sophisticated and extensive criminal marketplace on the Internet, serving as a sprawling black-market bazaar where unlawful goods and services, including illegal drugs of virtually all varieties, were bought and sold regularly by the site's users. While in operation, Silk Road was used by thousands of drug dealers and other unlawful vendors to distribute hundreds of kilograms of illegal drugs and other unlawful goods and services to more than 100,000 buyers, and to launder hundreds of millions of dollars deriving from these unlawful transactions. Ulbricht deliberately operated Silk Road as an online criminal marketplace intended to enable its users to buy and sell drugs and other illegal goods and services anonymously and outside the reach of law enforcement. Ulbricht sought to anonymize transactions on Silk Road in two principal ways. First, he operated Silk Road on what is known as "The Onion Router," or "Tor" network, a special network of computers on the Internet, distributed around the world, designed to conceal the true IP addresses of the computers on the network and thereby the identities of the networks' users. Second, Ulbricht designed Silk Road to include a Bitcoin-based payment system that served to facilitate the illegal commerce conducted on the site, including by concealing the identities and locations of the users transmitting and receiving funds through the site.

The vast majority of items for sale on Silk Road were illegal drugs, which were openly advertised as such on the site. As of September 23, 2013, the Silk Road home page displayed nearly 13,000 listings for controlled substances, listed under such categories as "Cannabis," "Dissociatives," "Ecstasy," "Intoxicants," "Opioids," "Precursors," "Prescription," "Psychedelics," and "Stimulants." From November 2011 to September 2013, law enforcement agents made more than 60 individual undercover purchases of controlled substances from Silk Road vendors. These purchases included heroin, cocaine, ecstasy, and LSD, among other illegal drugs, and were filled by vendors believed to be located in more than ten different countries, including the USA, Germany, the Netherlands, Canada, the United Kingdom, Spain, Ireland, Italy, Austria, and France. The narcotics distributed on Silk Road have been linked to at least six overdose deaths across the world. These overdose deaths included Jordan M., a 27-year-old Microsoft employee who was found unresponsive in front of his computer, which was logged onto Silk Road at the time, and died as a result of heroin and other prescription drugs that he had ordered from Silk Road. Preston B., from Perth, Australia, and Alejandro N., from Camino, California, both 16 years old, died as a result of taking 25i-NBOMe, a powerful synthetic drug designed to mimic LSD (commonly referred to as "N-Bomb"), which was purchased from Silk Road. Additional victims included Bryan B., a 25 year old from Boston, Massachusetts, and Scott W., a 36 year old from Australia, who both died as a result of heroin purchased from Silk Road, and Jacob B., a 22 year old from

Australia, who died from health complications that were aggravated by the use of drugs purchased from Silk Road.

In addition to illegal narcotics, other illicit goods and services were openly bought and sold on Silk Road. For example, as of September 23, 2013, there were: 159 listings under the category "Services," most of which offered computer hacking services, such as a listing by a vendor offering to hack into social networking accounts of the customer's choosing; 801 listings under the category "Digital goods," including malicious software, hacked accounts at various online services, and pirated media content; and 169 listings under the category "Forgeries," including offers to produce fake driver's licenses, passports, Social Security cards, utility bills, credit card statements, car insurance records, and other forms of false identification documents.

Using the online moniker "Dread Pirate Roberts," or "DPR," Ulbricht controlled and oversaw every aspect of Silk Road, and managed a staff of paid, online administrators and computer programmers who assisted with the day-to-day operation of the site. Through his ownership and operation of Silk Road, Ulbricht reaped commissions worth more than $13 million generated from the illicit sales conducted through the site. He also demonstrated a willingness to use violence to protect his criminal enterprise and the anonymity of its users, soliciting six murders-for-hire in connection with operating the site, although there is no evidence that these murders were actually carried out.

Ulbricht, of San Francisco, California, was convicted of seven offenses after a 4-week jury trial: distributing narcotics, distributing narcotics by means of the Internet, conspiring to distribute narcotics, engaging in a continuing criminal enterprise, conspiring to commit computer hacking, conspiring to traffic in false identity documents, and conspiring to commit money laundering. In addition to the life sentence prison term, he was ordered to forfeit $183,961,921.[15]

On the other hand, the largest marketplace on the dark web—where hundreds of thousands of criminals anonymously bought and sold drugs, weapons, hacking tools, stolen identities, and a host of other illegal goods and services—has been shut down as a result of one of the most sophisticated and coordinated efforts to date on the part of law enforcement across the globe. In early July 2017, multiple computer servers used by the AlphaBay website were seized worldwide, and the site's creator and administrator—a 25-year-old Canadian citizen living in Thailand—was arrested. AlphaBay operated for more than 2 years and had transactions exceeding $1 billion in Bitcoin and other digital currencies. The site, which operated on the anonymous Tor network, was a major source of heroin and fentanyl, and sales originating from AlphaBay have been linked to multiple overdose deaths in the USA. This case was considered a landmark operation because there were multiple servers in different countries, hundreds of millions in cryptocurrency, and a Darknet drug trade that spanned the globe.

AlphaBay was truly a global site and vendors were shipping illegal items from places all over the world to places all over the world. The website, an outgrowth of

[15] The United States Department of Justice [14].

earlier dark market sites like Silk Road—but much larger—went online in December 2014. It took about 6 months for the underground marketplace to pick up momentum, but after that it grew exponentially. AlphaBay reported that it serviced more than 200,000 users and 40,000 vendors. Around the time of the takedown, the site had more than 250,000 listings for illegal drugs and toxic chemicals, and more than 100,000 listings for stolen and fraudulent identification documents, counterfeit goods, malware and other computer hacking tools, firearms, and fraudulent services. By comparison, the Silk Road dark market—the largest such enterprise of its kind before it was shut down in 2013—had approximately 14,000 listings.

The operation to seize AlphaBay's servers was led by the FBI and involved the cooperative efforts of law enforcement agencies in Thailand, the Netherlands, Lithuania, Canada, the United Kingdom, and France, along with the European law enforcement agency Europol.

US law enforcement also worked with numerous foreign partners to freeze and preserve millions of dollars in cryptocurrency representing the proceeds of AlphaBay's illegal activities. AlphaBay's creator and administrator, Alexandre Cazes—who went by the names Alpha02 and Admin online—was arrested by Thai authorities on behalf of the USA on July 5, 2017. A week later, Cazes apparently took his own life while in custody in Thailand.

Because AlphaBay operated on the anonymous Tor network, administrators were confident they could hide the locations of the site's servers and the identities of users. The FBI and its partners used a combination of traditional investigative techniques along with sophisticated new tools to break the case and dismantle AlphaBay.[16]

There are some conducts that demonstrate the suspicion of a criminal practice or of its preparation. For instance, phishing (phone scams), data mining, auction fraud constitute crime, as long as using personal information to assume another's identity to get loans or credit cards or flash drives to download business secrets, and using GPS or computers to locate password-free servers are suspect.

The perpetrator in a cyber-attack can be one of any number of people. While *hackers* is a term generally used for those who attack another device for fun, *crackers* do it for profit. Timothy Vogel reveals that both may be genuinely interested in thwarting the latest in computer security technology, not to profit from it, but rather simply to know that they can best even the most sophisticated of security measures.[17]

In order to avoid these wrongdoings, especially cybersecurity risks, it is important to issue guidance to implement measures designed to effectively detect, prevent, and respond to fraud, and similar behavior, essentially through written policy.

This written policy must provide effective procedures and controls to protect against identified risks; identify and assess the full range of fraud-related and similar

[16] FBI News [15]; The United States Department of Justice [16].

[17] Vogel [11, p. 36].

risk areas, including as applicable, market manipulation; and allocate responsibility for monitoring risks.

In the USA, on September 19, 2012, Senator Johan D. Rockefeller IV, Chairman of the Senate Committee on Commerce, Science, and Transportation, wrote directly to the CEOs of the Fortune 500 companies regarding cybersecurity, in order to provide answers to eight questions pertaining to their companies' cybersecurity practices and their concerns, if any, with certain aspects of the Cybersecurity Act of 2012 that failed to pass the Senate.[18] The Cybersecurity Act of 2015[19] imposed mandatory cybersecurity standards on owners and operators in critical infrastructure industry sectors.[20] On the other hand, the Act classified cybersecurity-related

[18] (1) Has your company adopted a set of best practices to address its own cybersecurity needs? (2) If so, how were these cybersecurity practices developed? (3) Were they developed by the company solely, or were they developed outside the company? If developed outside the company, please list the institution, association, or entity that developed them. (4) When were these cybersecurity practices developed? How frequently have they been updated? Does your company's board of directors or audit committee keep abreast of developments regarding the development and implementation of these practices? (5) Has the federal government played any role, whether advisory or otherwise, in the development of these cybersecurity practices? (6) What are your concerns, if any, with a voluntary program that enables the federal government and the private sector to develop, in coordination, best cybersecurity practices for companies to adopt as they so choose, as outlined in the Cybersecurity Act of 2012? (7) What are your concerns, if any, with the federal government conducting risk assessments in coordination with the private sector, to best understand where our nation's cyber vulnerabilities are, as outlined in the Cybersecurity Act of 2012? (8) What are your concerns, if any, with the federal government determining, in coordination with the private sector, the country's most critical cyber infrastructure as outlined in the Cybersecurity Act of 2012? Rockefeller [17].

[19] See Office of the Director of National Intelligence [18].

[20] Sec. 205. Federal cybersecurity requirements. (a) Implementation of federal cybersecurity standards. Consistent with section 3553 of title 44, United States Code, the Secretary, in consultation with the Director, shall exercise the authority to issue binding operational directives to assist the Director in ensuring timely agency adoption of and compliance with policies and standards promulgated under section 11331 of title 40, United States Code, for securing agency information systems. (b) Cybersecurity requirements at agencies. (1) In general.Consistent with policies, standards, guidelines, and directives on information security under subchapter II of chapter 35 of title 44, United States Code, and the standards and guidelines promulgated under section 11331 of title 40, United States Code, and except as provided in paragraph (2), not later than 1 year after the date of the enactment of this Act, the head of each agency shall—(A) identify sensitive and mission critical data stored by the agency consistent with the inventory required under the first subsection (c) (relating to the inventory of major information systems) and the second subsection (c) (relating to the inventory of information systems) of section 3505 of title 44, United States Code; (B) assess access controls to the data described in subparagraph (A), the need for readily accessible storage of the data, and individuals' need to access the data; (C) encrypt or otherwise render indecipherable to unauthorized users the data described in subparagraph (A) that is stored on or transiting agency information systems; (D) implement a single sign-on trusted identity platform for individuals accessing each public website of the agency that requires user authentication, as developed by the Administrator of General Services in collaboration with the Secretary; and (E) implement identity management consistent with section 504 of the Cybersecurity Enhancement Act of 2014 (Public Law 113–274; 15 U.S.C. 7464), including multi-factor authentication, for (i) remote access to an agency information system and (ii) each user account with elevated privileges on an agency information system. (2) Exception. The requirements under paragraph (1) shall not apply to an

information into Cybersecurity Information Sharing, Federal Cybersecurity Enhancement (including Improved Federal Network Security), the Federal Workforce Assessment, and Other Cyber Matters, as Mobile Device Security.[21]

The Cybersecurity Act of 2017 amended the National Institute of Standards and Technology Act to require the National Institute of Standards and Technology (NIST) to consider small businesses when it facilitates and supports the development of voluntary, consensus-based, industry-led guidelines and procedures to cost-effectively reduce cyber to critical infrastructure. NIST must disseminate, and publish on its website, standard and method resources that small business may use voluntarily to help reduce their cybersecurity risks. The resources must be: (1) technology-neutral, (2) based on international standards to the extent possible, (3) able

agency information system for which(A) the head of the agency has personally certified to the Director with particularity that (i) operational requirements articulated in the certification and related to the agency information system would make it excessively burdensome to implement the cybersecurity requirement; (ii) the cybersecurity requirement is not necessary to secure the agency information system or agency information stored on or transiting it; and (iii) the agency has taken all necessary steps to secure the agency information system and agency information stored on or transiting it; and (B) the head of the agency or the designee of the head of the agency has submitted the certification described in subparagraph (A) to the appropriate congressional committees and the agency's authorizing committees. (3) Construction. Nothing in this section shall be construed to alter the authority of the Secretary, the Director, or the Director of the National Institute of Standards and Technology in implementing subchapter II of chapter 35 of title 44, United States Code. Nothing in this section shall be construed to affect the National Institute of Standards and Technology standards process or the requirement under section 3553(a)(4) of such title or to discourage continued improvements and advancements in the technology, standards, policies, and guidelines used to promote Federal information security. (c) Exception. The requirements under this section shall not apply to the Department of Defense, a national security system, or an element of the intelligence community. See US Congress [19].

[21] Sec. 401. Study on mobile device security. (a) In general. Not later than 1 year after the date of the enactment of this Act, the Secretary of Homeland Security, in consultation with the Director of the National Institute of Standards and Technology, shall (1) complete a study on threats relating to the security of the mobile devices of the Federal Government; and (2) submit an unclassified report to Congress, with a classified annex if necessary, that contains the findings of such study, the recommendations developed under paragraph (3) of subsection (b), the deficiencies, if any, identified under (4) of such subsection, and the plan developed under paragraph (5) of such subsection. (b) Matters studied. In carrying out the study under subsection (a)(1), the Secretary, in consultation with the Director of the National Institute of Standards and Technology, shall (1) assess the evolution of mobile security techniques from a desktop-centric approach, and whether such techniques are adequate to meet current mobile security challenges; (2) assess the effect such threats may have on the cybersecurity of the information systems and networks of the Federal Government (except for national security systems or the information systems and networks of the Department of Defense and the intelligence community); (3) develop recommendations for addressing such threats based on industry standards and best practices; (4) identify any deficiencies in the current authorities of the Secretary that may inhibit the ability of the Secretary to address mobile device security throughout the Federal Government (except for national security systems and the information systems and networks of the Department of Defense and intelligence community); and (5) develop a plan for accelerated adoption of secure mobile device technology by the Department of Homeland Security. (c) Intelligence community defined. In this section, the term "intelligence community" has the meaning given such term in section 3 of the National Security Act of 1947 (50 U.S.C. 3003). See US Congress [19].

to vary with the nature and size of the implementing small business and the sensitivity of the data collected or stored on the information systems, and (4) consistent with the national cybersecurity awareness and education program under the Cybersecurity Enhancement Act of 2014.[22]

The General Data Protection Regulation—GDPR 2016/679 was adopted on 14 April 2016, and after a 2-year transition period, became enforceable on 25 May 2018. Because the GDPR is a regulation, not a directive, it does not require national governments to pass any enabling legislation and is directly binding and applicable in all member of European Union—EU from 25 May 2018, plus Norway, Iceland, and Liechtenstein (European Economic Area—EEA). It is a regulation on data protection and privacy for all individuals within the European Union and the European Economic Area. It also addresses the export of personal data outside the EU and EEA. The GDPR aims primarily to give control to citizens and residents over their personal data and to simplify the regulatory environment for international business by unifying the regulation within the EU.

Superseding the Data Protection Directive, the regulation contains provisions and requirements pertaining to the processing of personally identifiable information of data subjects inside the European Union. Business processes that handle personal data must be built with data protection by design and by default, meaning that personal data must be stored using pseudonymization or full anonymization, and use the highest-possible privacy settings by default, so that the data is not available publicly without explicit consent, and cannot be used to identify a subject without additional information stored separately. No personal data may be processed unless it is done under a lawful basis specified by the regulation, or if the data controller or processor has received explicit, opt-in consent from the data's owner. The data owner has the right to revoke this permission at any time.

A processor of personal data should clearly disclose any data collection, declare the lawful basis and purpose for data processing, how long data is being retained, and if it is being shared with any third parties or outside of the EU. Users have the right to require a portable copy of the data collected by a processor in a common format, and the right to have their data erased under certain circumstances. Businesses whose core activities center around regular or systematic processing of personal data, and Public authorities, are required to employ a data protection officer (DPO), who is responsible for managing compliance with the GDPR. Businesses must report any data breaches within 72 h if they have an adverse effect on user privacy.

The regulation applies if the data controller (an organization that collects data from EU residents), or processor (an organization that processes data on behalf of a data controller like cloud service providers), or the data person is situated in the EU. Under certain circumstances, the regulation also applies to organizations based outside the EU if they collect or process personal data of individuals located inside the EU.

[22] See US Congress [20].

According to the European Commission, "personal data is any information relating to an individual, whether it relates to his or her private, professional or public life. It can be anything from a name, a home address, a photo, an email address, bank details, posts on social networking websites, medical information, or a computer's IP address."

The regulation does not purport to apply to the processing of personal data for national security activities or law enforcement of the EU; however, industry groups concerned about facing a potential conflict of laws have questioned whether Article 48 of the GDPR could be invoked to seek to prevent a data controller subject to a third country's laws from complying with a legal order from that country's law enforcement, judicial, or national security authorities to disclose to such authorities the personal data of an EU person, regardless of whether the data resides in or out of the EU. Article 48 states that any judgement of a court or tribunal and any decision of an administrative authority of a third country requiring a controller or processor to transfer or disclose personal data may not be recognized or enforceable in any manner unless based on an international agreement, like a mutual legal assistance treaty in force between the requesting third (non-EU) country and the EU or a member state. The data protection reform package also includes a separate Data Protection Directive for the police and criminal justice sector that provides rules on personal data exchanges at national, European, and international levels.

Each member state must establish an independent supervisory authority—SA to hear and investigate complaints, sanction administrative offenses, etc. SAs in each member state must co-operate with other SAs, providing mutual assistance and organizing joint operations. If a business has multiple establishments in the EU, it will have a single SA as its "lead authority," based on the location of its "main establishment" where the main processing activities take place. The lead authority will act as a "one-stop shop" to supervise all the processing activities of that business throughout the EU (Articles 46–55 of the GDPR). A European Data Protection Board—EDPB must coordinate the SAs. EDPB must replace the Article 29 Data Protection Working Party. There are exceptions for data processed in an employment context or in national security that still might be subject to individual country regulations (Articles 2(2)(a) and 88 of the GDPR).

Unless a data subject has provided explicit consent to data processing for one or more purposes, personal data cannot be processed unless there is at least one legal basis to do so. They include: to perform a task in the public interest or in official authority; to comply with a data controller's legal obligations; to fulfill contractual obligations with a data subject; to perform tasks at the request of a data subject who is entering into a contract with the controller; to protect the vital interests of a data subject or another person; for the legitimate interests of a data controller or a third party, unless overridden by the Charter of Fundamental Rights.

If consent is used as the lawful basis for processing, consent must be explicit for data collected and the purposes data is used for (Article 7; defined in Article 4). Consent for children must be given by the child's parent or custodian, and verifiable (Article 8). Data controllers must be able to prove "consent" (opt-in) and consent can be withdrawn.

The area of GDPR consent has a number of implications for businesses who record calls as a matter of practice. The typical "calls are recorded for training and security purposes" warnings will no longer be sufficient to gain assumed consent to record calls. Additionally, when recording has commenced, should the caller withdraw their consent then the agent receiving the call must be able to stop a previously started recording and ensure the recording does not get stored.

To be able to demonstrate compliance with the GDPR, the data controller must implement measures which meet the principles of data protection by design and by default. Data protection by design and by default (Article 25) requires data protection measures to be designed into the development of business processes for products and services. Such measures include pseudonymizing personal data, by the controller, as soon as possible (Recital 78). It is the responsibility and the liability of the data controller to implement effective measures and be able to demonstrate the compliance of processing activities even if the processing is carried out by a data processor on behalf of the controller (Recital 74).

When data is collected, users must be clearly informed about the extent of data collection, the legal basis for processing of personal data, how long data is retained, if data is being transferred to a third party and/or outside the EU, and disclosure of any automated decision-making that is made on a solely-algorithmic basis. Users must be provided with contact details for the data controller and their designated Data Protection Officer, where applicable. Users must also be informed of their privacy rights under GDPR, including their right to revoke consent to data processing at any time, their right to view their personal data and access an overview of how it is being processed, their right to obtain a portable copy of the stored data, the right to erasure of data under certain circumstances, the right to contest any automated decision-making that was made on a solely-algorithmic basis, and the right to file complaints with a Data Protection Authority.

Data protection impact assessments (Article 35) have to be conducted when specific risks occur to the rights and freedoms of data subjects. Risk assessment and mitigation is required and prior approval of the national data protection authorities (DPAs) is required for high risks. Data protection by design and by default (Article 25) requires data protection to be designed into the development of business processes for products and services. Privacy settings must therefore be set at a high level by default, and technical and procedural measures should be taken by the controller to make sure that the processing, throughout the whole processing lifecycle, complies with the regulation. Controllers should also implement mechanisms to ensure that personal data is not processed unless necessary for each specific purpose.

The GDPR refers to pseudonymization as a process that is required when data is stored (as an alternative to the other option of complete data anonymization) to transform personal data in such a way that the resulting data cannot be attributed to a specific data person without the use of additional information.

An example is encryption, which renders the original data unintelligible and the process cannot be reversed without access to the correct decryption key. The GDPR requires for the additional information (such as the decryption key) to be kept separately from the pseudonymized data. Another example of pseudonymization is tokenization, which is a non-mathematical approach to protecting data at rest that replaces sensitive data with non-sensitive substitutes, referred to as tokens. The tokens have no extrinsic or exploitable meaning or value. Tokenization does not alter the type or length of data, which means it can be processed by legacy systems such as databases that may be sensitive to data length and type. That requires much fewer computational resources to process and less storage space in databases than traditionally encrypted data. That is achieved by keeping specific data fully or partially visible for processing and analytics while sensitive information is kept hidden.

Pseudonymization is recommended to reduce the risks to the concerned data subjects and also to help controllers and processors to meet their data protection obligations (Recital 28).

The right of access (Article 15) is a data personal right. It gives citizens the right to access their personal data and information about how this personal data is being processed. A data controller must provide, upon request, an overview of the categories of data that are being processed (Article 15(1)(b)) as well as a copy of the actual data (Article 15(3)). Furthermore, the data controller has to inform the data subject on details about the processing, such as the purposes of the processing (Article 15(1)(a)), with whom the data is shared (Article 15(1)(c)), and how it acquired the data (Article 15(1)(g)).

A data subject must be able to transfer personal data from one electronic processing system to another, without being prevented from doing so by the data controller. Data that has been sufficiently anonymized is excluded, but data that has been only de-identified but remains possible to link to the individual in question, such as by providing the relevant identifier, is not. Both data being "provided" by the data subject and data being "observed," such as about behavior, are included. In addition, the data must be provided by the controller in a structured and commonly used standard electronic format. The right to data portability is provided by Article 20 of the GDPR.

A right to be forgotten was replaced by a more limited right of erasure in the version of the GDPR that was adopted by the European Parliament in March 2014. Article 17 provides that the data subject has the right to request erasure of personal data related to them on any one of a number of grounds, including noncompliance with Article 6(1) (lawfulness).

Under the GDPR, the data controller is under a legal obligation to notify the supervisory authority without undue delay unless the breach is unlikely to result in a risk to the rights and freedoms of the individuals. There is a maximum of 72 h after becoming aware of the data breach to make the report (Article 33). Individuals have to be notified if adverse impact is determined (Article 34). In addition, the data processor must have to notify the controller without undue delay after becoming aware of a personal data breach (Article 33). However, the notice to data subjects is not required if the data controller has implemented appropriate technical and organizational protection measures that render the personal data unintelligible to any person who is not authorized to access it, such as encryption (Article 34).

The following sanctions can be imposed: (1) a warning in writing in cases of first and non-intentional noncompliance; regular periodic data protection audits; (2) a fine up to €ten million or up to 2% of the annual worldwide turnover of the preceding financial year in case of an enterprise, whichever is greater, if there has been an infringement of the following provisions: (Article 83, Paragraph 5 and 6), the obligations of the controller and the processor pursuant to Articles 8, 11, 25–39, and 42 and 43, the obligations of the certification body pursuant to Articles 42 and 43; the obligations of the monitoring body pursuant to Article 41(4); (3) a fine up to €20 million or up to 4% of the annual worldwide turnover of the preceding financial year in case of an enterprise, whichever is greater, if there has been an infringement of the following provisions: (Article 83, Paragraph 4), the basic principles for processing, including conditions for consent, pursuant to Articles 5, 6, 7, and 9, the data subjects' rights pursuant to Articles 12–22, the transfers of personal data to a recipient in a third country or an international organization pursuant to Articles 44 to 49, any obligations pursuant to member state law adopted under Chapter IX, noncompliance with an order or a temporary or definitive limitation on processing or the suspension of data flows by the supervisory authority pursuant to Article 58(2) or failure to provide access in violation of Article 58(1).[23]

In short, the GDPR gives people rights with regard to the protection and control of their personal data. With it, people will have direct insight into whether their data was used to generate advertisements, whether the information have been generated to build profiles or whether the companies that collect data have sold this data to third parties.

The user will have the right to access, change, or delete their data that have been provided to companies. It forces the company to delete everything it has on the person if it is requested by the user. By the transnational characteristic of GDPR, any foreign company that has customers, suppliers, or partners allocated in Europe must respect the regulation, otherwise it will be subject to punishments provided by law.

The California Privacy and Data Protection Act (CCPA), inspired by GDPR, has been treated as the most comprehensive privacy law in the United States so far. CCPA takes effect on January 1, 2020 and, like European law, brings a number of challenges to its implementation and compliance. One, among the several already under discussion, is the so-called look back requirement, which determines that companies will have to account for the personal data collected since January 1, 2019, a period of 12 months before the entry into force of CCPA. Another is the short period for adequacy and the expectation of new amendments, since several points of the law still need to be clarified.[24] It is important to say that Brazil, as stated by Rafael Mendes Loureiro and Leonardo A. F. Palhares, "lacks specific regulation on cyber-security; although there are efforts to adopt a binding and integrated regulatory framework. Brazilian legislation on the matter is still evolving."[25]

---

[23] The General Data Protection Regulation (GDPR) [21].

[24] TROJAN, Viviane, JOTA Website, in https://www.jota.info/opiniao-e-analise/artigos/a-nova-lei-de-privacidadee-protecao-de-dados-na-california-ccpa-04052019, published on May 04, 2019, accessed on May 22, 2019.

[25] The current legal framework is a patchwork of laws and regulations, as several soft laws have been adopted, mainly addressed issues in connection with the banking industry. See Loureiro and Palhares [22].

Nicknamed Carolina Dieckmann, the Cyber Crimes Act (12,737, Nov. 30, 2012) criminalizes conduct related to the electronic tool, such as hacking into computers, violating user data, or "tearing down" websites. The project that gave birth to the law (PLC 35/2012) was drawn up at a time when intimate photos of actress Carolina Dieckmann were copied from her computer and scattered throughout the world wide web. The text was claimed by the financial system, given the amount of scams applied by the Internet.

"Computer intrusion" can be punished with imprisonment from 3 months to a year, plus a fine. More harmful conduct, such as obtaining "private electronic communications, trade or industry secrets, sensitive information" from the invasion, could be punished by 6 months to 2 years in prison, and a fine. The same occurs if the offense involves the disclosure, commercialization, or transmission to third parties, by means of sale or free transfer, of the material obtained with the invasion. The law also provides for the increase of penalties from one sixth to one third if the invasion causes economic loss and one to two thirds "if there is any disclosure, commercialization or transmission to any third party of the data or information obtained." The penalties may also be increased by one-third to one-half if the crime is committed against the President of the Republic, Chief Justice of the Brazilian Supreme Court, presidents of the Chamber, the Senate, legislative assemblies and chambers, local chambers or top officials of the direct administration and indirect federal, state, local, or Federal District.[26]

The Brazilian Internet Civil Landmark Act (12,965, April 23, 2014), also deemed the Brazilian Civil Rights Framework for the Internet, established that in the provision of an Internet connection, it is incumbent upon the respective autonomous system administrator to keep records of connection, under a confidential, controlled environment, for a period of one (1) year, and that the Internet applications provider established as a legal entity and exercising this activity in an organized, professional and for economic purposes shall maintain the respective records of access to Internet applications, under secrecy, in a controlled environment and security, for the term of Six (6) months, pursuant to the regulation.[27]

The Brazilian Civil Rights for the Internet, in short, regulates the use of the Internet in Brazil through a series of principles, rights, and duties for Internet users,

[26] The Executive Branch Planalto [23].

[27] Art. 10. The custody and the availability of the records of connection and access to internet applications referred to in this Law, as well as personal data and content of private communications, must take into account the preservation of privacy, privacy, honor, and image of the parties directly or indirectly involved.(…) Paragraph 4 Security and confidentiality measures and procedures shall be informed by the person responsible for the provision of services in a clear manner and in accordance with the standards defined in the regulations, respecting their right of confidentiality regarding business secrets. Art. 13. In the provision of connection to the internet, it is incumbent upon the respective autonomous system administrator to keep records of connection, under a confidential, controlled environment, for a period of one (1) year, pursuant to regulation. Art. 15. The Internet application provider established as a legal entity and carrying out this activity in an organized, professional and economic manner shall maintain the respective records of access to Internet applications, under secrecy, in a controlled environment and of security for a period of six (6) months, pursuant to the regulation. The Executive Branch Planalto [24].

addressing several issues, such as: (1) net neutrality, (2) privacy, (3) data retention, (4) the social function of the Internet, (5) freedom of expression and transmission of knowledge, and (6) obligations related to the civil liability of both users and providers.

According to Rafael Mendes Loureiro and Leonardo A. F. Palhares, Brazil "has adopted international information security management policies. The Brazilian Association of Technical Standards (ABNT) developed NBR ISO/IEC 27001: 2006, which is an identical translation of ISO/IEC 27001: 2005, prepared by the Joint Information Technology Committee (ISO/IEC/JTC 1), Subcommittee on IT Security Techniques (SC 27)."[28] So, best practices and international standards are usually adopted by entities to protect their systems and information.

The legal framework that specifically addresses the protection of personal data, as well as its use and transfer, advanced in the Brazilian Congress on July 2, 2018. Senator Ricardo Ferraço (PSDB-ES) presented his opinion on the House Bill n.° 53/2018 to the Committee on Economic Affairs (CAE), which deals with the proposal. The senator preserved content that was approved by the House in May and made only a few editorial adjustments in the text to suit the House Review procedure: The bill was approved and resulted in Law n.° 13,709, August 14, 2018. It is the Brazilian Protection of Personal Data Act.[29] This Act amends Law n.° 12,965, April 23, 2014, the Brazilian Civil Rights for the Internet.[30] The Brazilian Protection of Personal Data Act is deemed a fundamental step for Brazil's insertion in international forums, as well as providing a secure business environment that will boost the attractiveness and materialization of investments in the order of R$250 billion ($66.50 billion, dollar equivalent to 3759 Reais, Brazilian currency) in digital transformation technologies by 2021, according to a study by Brasscom and the consultancy Frost & Sullivan.[31]

Although properly regulated by the legislation, it does not set forth any rules and regulations that must be followed in order to protect data or information technology systems from cyberthreats. But, companies can be held liable if data is leaked, for instance, a payment of 2% of turnover, provided that if this does not exceed R$50 million or $13.30 million.

Also, there is no obligation requiring the sector to report data breaches to the authorities. However, data breaches that significantly affect users' assets or cause moral damage are usually reported only to data owners. Nonetheless the absent regulation about data breaches, based on the Brazilian Consumer Protection Act, companies must present complete information to their consumers regarding their products and services in order to guarantee their rights to safety and to prevent damage or loss.

According to the Act, personal information such as name, address, email, age, marital status, and financial position obtained by any means: paper, electronic, com-

[28] See Loureiro and Palhares [22, p. 17].

[29] Planalto [25].

[30] Planalto [26].

[31] See Borges [27].

puter, sound, and image are considered personal data (article 5°, I). Also collected are the images taken by video surveillance, the recording of phone calls, the IP addresses (computer identification), and locations obtained by GPS systems.

In the public sphere, the proposal further provides that the user will be informed when the use of his or her data is released for the fulfillment of a legal obligation or by the administration. On the other hand, the rules do not apply if the information is used by a third party, for personal purposes only, or if it is used exclusively for journalistic, artistic, or academic contents (article 23, I).

Data on racial or ethnic origin, religious beliefs, political opinions, membership of trade unions or religious, philosophical or political organizations, data on health or sexual life, and genetic or biometric data when linked to an individual should receive differentiated treatments because they are considered sensitive data (articles 5°, II, and 11 to 13).

In fact, this Act is similar to the General Data Protection Regulation—GDPR of European Union that deals with the processing of personal data. It is the result of a wide public debate. The purpose of the Act was to ensure citizens control and ownership of their personal information, based on the inviolability of privacy, freedom of expression, communication and opinion, informational self-determination, economic and technological development, as well as the free initiative, free competition, and consumer protection. In the justification for the aforementioned Brazilian bill, the head of Justice Department, Minister Eugênio Aragão, said that "the increasingly intense use of personal data in the information society creates an imbalance between the powers of individuals, holders of their own personal data, and the users of such data, precisely because of the amount of personal information that new technologies are able to aggregate and use."

So, the Act sets forth the parameters and limits of the processing of personal data, including when this relationship ends. Considering the transnational nature of the flow of this information, the project covers the processing of personal data carried out in Brazil, such as those carried out abroad, but whose collection has occurred in the Brazilian territory.

Ensuring privacy on the wireless web means complying with laws regarding the collection and use of personally identifiable information. The potential uses and misuses of personally identifiable and location information must be of concern to both consumers and businesses, besides government bodies in order to reduce or to end with cybercrimes or cyber-attacks.

It must be developed wireless applications and business plans that not only comply with current and future legislation relating to privacy and security, but also assuage fears and consumer insecurity. For this, it is important to communicate the terms and conditions of wireless transactions to the customers, obtain customers' assent to such terms, and authenticate that assent by developing a suitable solution for retention of electronic records.

A proposal for a legislation that would address both the cybersecurity standard-setting and information-sharing issues is fully recommended.

References

1. Griffin, R. C. (2012). Cybercrime. *Journal of International Commercial Law and Technology, 7*(2), 136–153.
2. Pedrazzi, C. (1965). O Direito Penal das Sociedades e o Direito Penal Comum. In *Revista Brasileira de Criminologia e Direito Penal* (Vol. 9, p. 133). Rio de Janeiro: Instituto de Criminologia do Estado da Guanabara.
3. Oliveira, E. P. (2011). *Direito e processo penal na justiça federal: doutrina e jurisprudência*. São Paulo: Atlas.
4. Cavero, P. G. (2007). *Derecho Penal Económico – Parte General* (2nd ed.). Lima: Grijley.
5. Mir, J. R. S., & Genovês, V. G. (1987). *Delincuencia de cuella blanco* (p. 71). Madrid: Instituto de Estudos de Política.
6. Garcia, J. Á. B. (2000). *El delito de defraudación a la seguridad social* (pp. 80–81). Valencia: Tirand lo Blanch.
7. Fischer, D. (2011). *Inovações no Direito Penal Econômico: contribuições criminológicas, político-criminais e dogmáticas*. Organizador: Artur de Brito Gueiros Souza. Brasília: Escola Superior do Ministério Público da União.
8. Santos, C. M. C. (2001). *O crime de colarinho branco (da origem do conceito e sua relevância criminológica à questão da desiguualdade na administração da justiça penal)* (p. 175).
9. Sánchez, J.-M. S. (2004). *Eficiência e direito penal. Coleção Estudos de Direito Penal* (Vol. 11). São Paulo: Manole.
10. Rodrigues, A. M. (1999). *Contributo para a fundamentação de um discurso punitivo em matéria fiscal. Direito Penal Económico e Europeu: textos doutrinários*. Coimbra: Coimbra Ed..
11. Vogel, T. A. (2002). Dealing with cyber attacks on corporate network security. *The Practical Lawyer, 48*, 35–46.
12. Clevlin, D. (2005). Schemes and scams: Auction fraud and the culpability of host auction web sites. *Loyola Consumer Law Review, 18*, 223–255.
13. Farley, M., Franzblau, K., & Kennedy, M. A. (2013). Online prostitution and trafficking. *Albany Law Review, 77*, 1039–1094.
14. The United States Department of Justice. (2015, May 29). *Ross Ulbricht, A/K/A "Dread Pirate Roberts," sentenced in Manhattan Federal Court to life in prison*. Retrieved August 3, 2018, from https://www.justice.gov/usao-sdny/pr/ross-ulbricht-aka-dread-pirate-roberts-sentenced-manhattan-federal-court-life-prison
15. FBI News. (2017, July 20). *Darknet takedown. Authorities shutter online criminal market AlphaBay*. Retrieved August 3, 2018, from https://www.fbi.gov/news/stories/alphabay-takedown
16. The United States Department of Justice. (2017, July 20). *Justice News. AlphBay, the largest online 'Dark Marke,' shut down*. Retrieved August 3, 2018, from https://www.justice.gov/opa/pr/alphabay-largest-online-dark-market-shut-down
17. Rockefeller, J. D. (2012, September 19). *Letter from Senator Johan D. Rockeffer IV (D-WV) to Virginia M. Rometty, President and Chif Executive Officer, International Business Machines*. Retrieved June 1, 2018, from https://www.cadwalader.com/uploads/cfmemos/f6e347976c-1cacb03e7d982e936e12cf.pdf
18. Office of the Director of National Intelligence. *The cybersecurity act of 2015*. Retrieved September 2, 2018, from https://www.dni.gov/index.php/ic-legal-reference-book/cybersecurity-act-of-2015
19. U.S. Congress. *The cybersecurity act of 2015*. Retrieved September 8, 2018, from https://www.congress.gov/114/bills/s754/BILLS-114s754es.pdf
20. U.S. Congress. *The cybersecurity act of 2017*. Retrieved September 10, 2018, from https://www.congress.gov/bill/115th-congress/senate-bill/770
21. European Union. *The general data protection regulation (GDPR)*. EU official journal issue, L 119. Retrieved September 10, 2018, from http://eur-lex.europa.eu/legal-content/EN/TXT/HTML/?uri=OJ:L:2016:119:FULL&from=EN

22. Loureiro, R. M., & Palhares, L. A. F. (2018, January). Brazil. In B. A. Powell, & J. C. Chipman (Eds.), *Cybersecurity 2018. Getting the deal through* (pp. 17–21). London: Law Business Research. Retrieved October 3, 2018, from https://gettingthedealthrough.com/area/72/jurisdiction/6/cybersecurity-brazil/
23. The Executive Branch Planalto. *Law 12,737, Nov. 30, 2012*. Retrieved September 12, 2018, from http://www.planalto.gov.br/ccivil_03/_ato2011-2014/2012/lei/l12737.htm
24. The Executive Branch Planalto. *Law 12,965, April 23, 2014*. Retrieved September 12, 2018, from http://www.planalto.gov.br/ccivil_03/_ato2011-2014/2014/lei/l12965.htm
25. Planalto. *The Brazilian protection of personal data act, Law n.° 13,709, August 14, 2018*. Retrieved October 10, 2018, from http://www.planalto.gov.br/ccivil_03/_ato2015-2018/2018/Lei/L13709.htm
26. Planalto. *The Brazilian civil rights for the internet*. Retrieved October 10, 2018, from http://www.planalto.gov.br/ccivil_03/_Ato2011-2014/2014/Lei/L12965.htm
27. Borges, B. (2018, July 2). *Lei geral de proteção de dados pessoais avança no Senado*. Retrieved October 10, 2018, from https://www.jota.info/coberturas-especiais/liberdade-de-expressao/protecao-de-dados-senado-02072018

Chapter 3
Online Gaming: Casino, Lotteries, and Gambling

3.1 Initial Considerations

This chapter will examine the issue related to online gaming, that is, gambling in the sports industry through Internet. The name "gaming" refers to a wide range of activities: gambling, betting, and lotteries. If we could make a definition of gaming, it should include playing of any game of chance or of mixed chance and skill for money's worth.

Gaming industry are one of the attractive sectors to the practice of money laundering due to the large monetary transactions involved and the growing number of people participating in them. As far as other businesses, they have been used by criminals to launder money or to the perpetration of illegal activities with the goal of obtaining illicit gains.

We can no longer treat the problem with bias purely emotional or economic, but work to verify any legislative gaps that provide mobility and dynamism to organized crime, enabling the continuity and unprecedented illicit wealth.

The complexity of the sector and the emotional involvement of the participants end up in prostration of the authorities in this field, which deserves a punctual and accurate appreciation. Taking isolated or uncoordinated attitudes is not simply enough to tackle the problem that can settle in conflicts and instability with serious risk to the involved industry.

It is not possible "in the name of sport" to enable persistent tolerance of criminal practices because surely it eventually annihilates the reputation of gaming. Enforcing property law and popular willing of good practice in gambling and sports will preserve their credibility.

There is a daily concern to reflect the current times, challenging and requiring authorities to take actions against money laundering, organized crime, and tax evasion, especially the need of a different perception of a changing world, which has allowed the perpetuation of a number of serious crimes and illicit enrichment of

F. M. De Sanctis, *Technology-Enhanced Methods of Money Laundering*,
https://doi.org/10.1007/978-3-030-18330-1_3

official agents. In other words, it is important to get an answer that allows for effective prosecution.

For this reason, a sharp criminal intervention by the State is required, at the outset, including the forfeiture of goods and values of criminals once confirmed the unlawful possession or property. Thus, it is be possible to annul any idea that crime is worth, although eventual conviction and imprisonment.

There are obvious risks to contaminate legitimate sectors by determining and administering them with illicit money or by even using them by people who seeks their sole benefit.

Forms of gambling (Casinos), which now and then, are being subject of discussion about its permission or even ruling by Court decisions, in or not favorable to their practices, have demanded specific analysis regarding the remarkable possibility for money laundering. The same can be said about lotteries that are being used for the same purpose.

If, on the one hand, it is possible to check real economic impact when large investments are channeled them with great social membership, business development, and extensive transmission of cultural values, on the other hand, the growth of this industry has been faced with criminal practices, notably corruption, tax evasion, and money laundering.

Misha Glenny, in an important reflection, reveals that:

> Given that the economy has become a powerful force in our world, it is surprising how little systematic effort is devoted to understanding how it works and how it relates to the legal economy. This dark world is not, in any way, other than your partner who lives in daylight; also licit economy often is not as transparent as we think or wish it to be.[1]

The study of gambling activities, casinos, and lotteries is a paramount issue before their vulnerability to criminal exploitation. In Brazil, for instance, it deserved special attention due to the permission of a kind of games called "Bingo," created in order to stimulate sports before his alleged link with known clubs or federations.

However, the use of intensive doubtful payments and the existence of constant movements of large sums of money required especial attention to enforcement authorities and it has been prohibited.

Bank accounts of gambling houses cannot be adequately controlled if those houses allow the transfer or deposit of funds through money changers or extra banking activities or through online untraceable means.

There is still, in many countries, little experience of the authorities to control this line of business, which may pose a high risk factor of money laundering. There would be no effective exchange of information between relevant authorities responsible for overseeing this business practice, nor a clear definition of who would be responsible for sharing information.

This could, certainly, lead to suspicious transaction report of only one or a few isolated acts to the local Financial Intelligence Unit (in the USA, the Financial Crimes Enforcement Network—FinCEN; in Brazil, the Council for Financial

[1] Glenny [1, p. 14].

Activities Control—COAF), which would lead one limited effectiveness. Thus, the set of illicit practices, diluted with various flags casinos, would not lead to knowledge of the entire illegal transaction, because it would only be verifiable by all the selected activity.

To combat the practice of economic and financial crimes, it needs to measure the problem and study the methods used to launder dirty money.

Given the controls that are poorly established and the ease in laundering money (so, its ineffectiveness), the gambling houses are constantly subject to exploitation by criminals through illegal control of operations or the purchase of their own establishments, which would be larceny, fraud, money laundering, etc.

For continuity, customer confidence in this activity is essential, the reason why authorities must allow an honest conduct of games through an adoption of specific rules and required management to ensure a high standard of safety and supervision.

The confidentiality of Suspicious Activity Reports—SARs is protected in the USA. There was some question as to whether this protection was restricted to the Report itself or extended to supporting documentation. At first, only the Report was confidential, but afterward, the Office of the Comptroller of the Currency (OCC) at the Treasury Department decided that supporting documentation was also confidential. This secrecy is so indispensable that, even when subpoenas are issued ordering disclosure of Reports or supporting documentation in several cases, the OCC held that it must be notified by the banking institution. Thus, it might take part in the proceedings and that the disclosure must comply with the Federal Rules of Civil Procedure. There was a suggestion that information be shared among financial institutions to better detect new fraudulent schemes. Through FinCEN and other agencies, the Treasury Department decided to provide information so that they might keep abreast of the trends in that class of crimes, issue statements, and hold meetings and seminars. In no event could the Report be disclosed to anyone supposedly involved, excepting only FinCEN or other appropriate government agencies.

Note that there is a deadline for Suspicious Activity Reports: 30 days from the time the facts are known, but if the suspect cannot be identified, this timeframe extends for another 30 days. No more than 60 days may elapse, however, once the facts become known.

Observe that proper vigilance and Suspicious Activity Reports are deemed essential to ensure that the financial institution has an effective compliance program. Appropriate policies and procedures must be put in place to monitor and identify unusual occurrences by time and place. Reporting systems must include unusual event identifications or alerts (identifying the employee and giving all necessary search information), management alerts (awareness of all methods of identification and evaluation in all business areas), the Report itself and its generation, regardless of size. Monitoring system sophistication must be understood as part of banking risk, with emphasis on what goes into high-risk products, services, account holders, and entities. Financial institutions must therefore have adequate personnel to identify, research, and report on suspicious activities, with due account taken of the general risk level and volume of transactions.

The Financial Crimes Enforcement Network does not have specific instructions to require Internet service providers to report suspicious activity. Due to the nature of the cyberspace, they are not even under general obligation to report cash payments in transactions of $10,000 or more.

A great deal of attention has focused on money laundering due to the highly sophisticated nature of its criminal practices—practices which have been internationally organized and professionally executed for a considerable amount of time.

Organized crime has had a relatively free hand in its efforts to make criminal assets legal. This is made possible by the total or relatively ineffectiveness of current national and international laws, which have not kept pace with the changing situation.

Gilson Dipp points out that organized crime takes advantage of the "inertia of States, and their closely-regulated executive, legislative and judicial branches, which are bound by the principle of territoriality—the idea that the law holds only within its boundaries. This is a hopelessly dated notion. Each State must, without giving up its sovereignty, achieve broad international cooperation. To insist on a nineteenth century conception of sovereignty is to allow organized crime to exercise its will to the detriment of formal sovereignty."[2]

Francisco de Assis Betti views financial crimes as crimes that are generally "marked by the absence of social scrutiny, due to several factors including an excessive attachment to material things such as profit and egotistical zeal among the owners of capital, who are scornful of the lower classes and confident in their own impunity. Most of these crimes are covered up by collusive public officials. When the crimes do come to light, evidence is poorly produced and the facts are difficult to ascertain, given the specialized assessment required, culminating almost always in impunity."[3] Francisco de Assis Betti still adds that it is not always "easy for a criminal to use the proceeds of crime. Profligate spending and the eccentricities that always accompany the easy acquisition of money, and immediate purchases way above one's standard of living, are outward signs of wealth which give rise to suspicion, and are conducive to investigations by either police or internal revenue authorities. Experienced criminals therefore try to come up with arrangements for investing their criminal proceeds and work with others inclined to conceal these assets and obliterate the money trails in order to avoid enforcement efforts."[4]

To the extent that society has realized that serious crime can encompass more than just violent crime, more and more States have ratified international regulatory instruments without restrictions, demonstrating that they are no longer willing to tolerate open-ended criminality within their borders. But, Internet imposed new challenges.

The links between money laundering and organized crime necessitated immediate and aggressive intervention by governments, not least to ensure their very

---

[2] Interview published 11/03/2004 on the *Consultor Jurídico* website. www.conjur.com.br. Accessed 18 August 2018.

[3] In Betti, Francisco de Assis. *op. cit.*, p. 20.

[4] In Betti, Francisco de Assis. *op. cit.*, p. 39.

survival. Observe that money laundering is in essence a derivative crime because the offense is contingent upon an antecedent crime.

Another difficulty with money laundering is that it is not simple to accomplish, nor does it follow any present rule. That was the rule until the Internet appeared making things easier for criminals.

The commission of the crime involves processes that are often complex and sophisticated, with actions taken in a concatenated or scattered manner, all in an effort to make dirty money look legal. One could indeed simply define money laundering as a procedure whereby one transforms goods acquired through unlawful acts into apparently legal goods. However, overriding considerations of legality and legal security do not permit us to make use of such a simple definition.

The crime of money laundering, classically speaking, involves three stages of conduct, namely: concealment or placement, in which goods acquired by unlawful means are made less visible; monitoring, dissimulation, or layering, in which the money is severed from its origins, removing all clues as to how it was obtained; and integration, in which the illegal money is reincorporated into the economy after acquiring a semblance of legality. Added to this is the recycling stage, which consists of wiping out all records of those previous steps completed.

Faced with the complexity of the various forms of conduct and processes comprising online crimes, one is struck by the almost complete impossibility of imposing legal restraints other than through combined means, by proscribing more than one form of conduct, and open-ended means, for the large number of activities described in the Vienna Convention and adopted by most countries calls for intervention for full classification within the limits therein imposed. Additionally, money laundering is always a derivative crime, so that it must necessarily be connected, to a greater or lesser extent, to its antecedent crime. All of these issues give innumerable peculiarities to the criminal practice, peculiarities which must be gradually sorted out by jurisprudence or case law.

In Brazil's case, money laundering was not typified in the main body of the Criminal Code, as was done, for instance, in the USA (in 18 U.S.C. § 1956). This poses an undeniable difficulty, for if the crime in question were codified, it would have to be promptly adapted to the principles and rules of the Criminal Code. Because this system is integrated and hierarchical, there would be no margin for unjustifiable exceptions. Such is the case in France, Italy, Switzerland, and Colombia.

The United Nations Convention against Transnational Organized Crime was convened in Palermo on 11/15/2000,[5] following the United Nations Convention against Illicit Traffic in Narcotic Drugs and Psychotropic Substances of 12/20/1988 (Article 5).[6] Both global regulatory guidelines require the State Parties to make laundering the proceeds of crime itself a crime (Article 6), and provide for the confiscation of "proceeds of crime derived from offences covered by this Convention or

[5] In Brazil, promulgated by Decree No. 5015 dated 03/12/2004, and passed by Legislative Decree No. 231 dated 09/29/2003.

[6] Ratified by Brazil by Decree No. 154 dated 06/26/1991.

property the value of which corresponds to that of such proceeds" (Article 12(1)(a)). Parallel to that is the United Nations Convention Against Corruption held at Mérida in 2003 (Article 31, item 5—confiscation and seizure of money in an amount equivalent to the proceeds of crime).[7]

Items 2, 3, and 4 of Article 12 of the United Nations Convention against Transnational Organized Crime held at Palermo correspondingly assert that "State Parties shall adopt such measures as may be necessary to enable the identification, tracing, freezing or seizure of any item referred to in paragraph 1 of this article for the purpose of eventual confiscation; if the proceeds of crime have been transformed or converted, in part or in full, into other property, such property shall be liable to the measures referred to in this article instead of the proceeds; if proceeds of crime have been intermingled with property acquired from legitimate sources, such property shall, without prejudice to any powers relating to freezing or seizure, be liable to confiscation up to the assessed value of the intermingled proceeds."

Such provisions accurately depict the new world order with respect to combating organized crime, including narcotics trafficking and corruption.

It is sometimes alleged by defendants that the property seized has no links to the crime. It then is up to the judge to properly estimate the amount that flowed from the proceeds of the unlawful conduct imputed, mindful of the need to enforce the requirements set forth in the foregoing Conventions, as well as Article 387, Section IV, of the Brazilian Code of Criminal Procedure, which requires that the sentence be fixed at the "minimum amount required for reparation of damages caused by the infraction, taking into account all losses suffered by the aggrieved party," in order to put the confiscation into effect, that is, to secure definitive forfeiture of that amount for the injured party or to the State as indemnification for damages caused by unlawful conduct.

Under Article K.3 of the Treaty of Maastricht (1992), European Union Member States agreed to adopt a common policy in their domestic efforts, and the 1998 joint action (98/773/JHA) sought to include money laundering as a type of organized crime. This was revoked in part by the Framework Decision[8] of the European Union Council dated 06/26/2001, whereby Member States agreed to not make reservations on Articles 2 and 6 of the European Convention of 1990 (including the rule which provides for money laundering resulting generically from criminal conduct), since

[7] Ratified by Brazil by Decree No. 5687 dated 01/31/2006.

[8] Decision and framework decision (Title VI of the European Union Treaty): With the entry into force of the Treaty of Amsterdam, these new instruments under Title VI of the European Union Treaty ("Provisions on Police and Judicial Cooperation in Criminal Matters") replaced joint action. Framework decisions are used to bring together the legislative and regulatory provisions of Member States. They are proposed on a motion by the Commission or by a Member State, and must be unanimously adopted. They are binding on Member States as to results to achieve, and leave it to national courts to decide on the manner and the means of achieving them. Decisions address all other goals besides the conference committee work on legislative and regulatory provisions of the Member States. Decisions are binding and all measures necessary to carry out the decisions within the scope of the European Union are adopted by the Council through qualified majority vote.

only *serious infractions* can be at issue, and providing measures for confiscation and criminal action on the proceeds of crime having a maximum penalty of greater than 1 year, or crimes considered serious (Article 1).

The Framework Decision of 02/24/2005 (2005/212/JHA) on forfeiture of products, instruments, and property related to the crime allows "extended powers of confiscation" aimed not only at forfeiture of assets of all those found guilty, but also assets acquired by their spouses or companions, or whose property may have been transferred to some company under the influence or control of the guilty parties—for organized criminal practices such as counterfeiting, trafficking in persons or assisting illegal immigration, sexual exploitation of children and child pornography, traffic in narcotics, terrorism, terrorist organizations, and money laundering, provided they be punishable by a sentence of at least between 5 and 10 years of imprisonment, or, in the case of laundering, with a maximum penalty of at least 4 years of imprisonment, and by their nature generating financial income (Article 3, Sections 1–3).

Note that the Palermo Convention provides for international cooperation on matters of confiscation (Art. 13(1)), and expressly provides that the proceeds of crime be allocated to finance a United Nations Organizations Fund, so that it may assist Member States in obtaining the wherewithal with which to enforce the Convention (Arts. 14(3)(a) and 30(2)(c)).

Any illegal proceeds could well be included in the scope of this Convention if one could point to convincing evidence that they might be related to the commission of antecedent crimes and to money laundering. If gambling were indeed being used for purposes of money laundering, those circumstances would justify judicial search and seizure, and possibly confiscation as well.

Leaving illegally obtained money in the hands of criminals—especially members of organized criminal gangs—encourages the reentry of those monies into the underworld, or back into the original illegal business practices occurring prior to, or even after serving a sentence, with the potential for serious harm to society.

To prevent the use by organized crime, it is important to have an adequate understanding of the methods used to launder illicit funds, their vulnerabilities, and the capacity to exchange vital information from foreign authorities.

It is possible to say about the inevitability of the Internet in people's lives and it is not a matter of if but when a bill will be adopted to accurately regulate it.[9]

3.2 Online Casino-Style Games

Intensive payments with cash, possibility of exchanging chips for cash or checks, exchanging operations and intensive search for foreign tourists, who are constantly beneficiaries under certain amenities, such as room and board, make the activities of

[9] See Miller [2, pp. 1–34].

casinos a certain equivalence with the financial institutions.[10] These issues are mainly posed when one is physically in these places.

The Report of the international Financial Action Task Force (FATF[11]), delivered in March 2009, revealed that there are many papers on suspicious activities related to the sector.

It is very easy to convert illicit cash into electronic transactions or cash in these gambles. For example, both in the case of "buy in" as in "cash out" it is possible to exchange values. In the first case, there is a conversion of money into tokens, tickets, or credits in order to start the game. Already, in the second case, the reverse occurs, in other words, the replacement of tokens, tickets, or cash credits in casino checks, claims on accounts, or transfer funds to other casinos.

Likewise, it is possible to convert the ticket called "TITO" (Ticket In/Ticket Out). For instance, the system allows up to a gaming machine accepts bills or tickets with credits printed on it (Ticket In). "TITO" also prints tickets containing credits if the player wishes to settle the game machine (Ticket Out). In this case, the customer can exchange the ticket for cash at the establishment or re-use it on another machine "TITO" to restart the game.

More difficult is the treatment of the issue when it comes across its practice via the Internet.

The possibility of online gambling must give rise to a study of how best to regulate this issue and how to submit to official controls to prevent money laundering. Also there is no control over foreign arms of this method of gambling, which should pipeline the best practices for improving supervision over the transfer of sums of money.

According to John Warren Kindt and Stephen W. Joy "[P]olicy-makers worldwide generally failed to identify the large socio-economic costs associated with Internet gambling, as well as the ability of Internet gambling and other forms of cyberspace gambling to destabilize local national, and even international economies by disrupting financial institutions."[12]

Even when the industry is properly regulated still exists the possibility of major money laundering schemes.

Brazil, despite being one of the most populous countries in the world (more than 220 million people), has a small industry of games. It owned 130,000 machines, including slot machines in about 1500 "Bingos" that operated across the country, reaching its peak in 2006. However, in 2007, many of them were forced to a standstill and many machines were confiscated by the authorities when the practice of

[10] The undeniable movement of people and resources requires strict transparency to prevent the use or management of casinos by organized crime. An important question has been mooted before casinos for associated clients, designed for ocean cruises, causing discussions on jurisdiction in any illicit activity: the place where the ship was registered or in which it operates or visits. Countries there are no specific regulations, which may result in a lack of jurisdictional action, with little scope for criminal activity.

[11] Cf. Financial Action Task Force [3].

[12] See Kindt and Joy [4, p. 111].

corruption in the industry would have been revealed by the operation of the federal police "Hurricane" with alleged involvement of politicians and organized crime in order to keep them open.

Turning to Internet, there has been concern about the checks to ensure the online gaming is not rigged. For instance, in case of casino-style games, when the digital roulette wheel is spun, there is no guarantee that the ball is not deliberately programmed to fall into a number where no players have placed bets. In short, there is a high possibility of cheating by the operator when there is no control over what has been stipulated the minimum payout per number of spins to ensure players have a chance of winning something. Besides that, there is always the possibility for money laundering when, for example, an unscrupulous operator who lures underage gamblers, and those operators who have a disregard for promoting responsible gambling, all of which are very difficult to police online.

A bill aimed at releasing such activities can open a serious precedent for the practice of money laundering if did not come with a great structure for the supervision of gambling. Any legalization of this would certainly increase the availability and accessibility of gaming to the ordinary person while at the same time could well undermine the policies of underage gaming. Internet gaming makes children more exposed to unhealthy gaming habits, especially in case of sites that offer gaming practice modules that do not require money.

It is no possible, without strictly regulation and oversight sufficient mechanisms, to contain organized crime that certainly would set this branch of trade. Gaming regulation must require registration in order for clients to play practice modules.

No justification, as the allocation of revenue to sports, culture, health, safety, opening new jobs and investment, legitimize permission unless that encircle of effective containment of crime.

3.3 Lotteries

It is a vast gambling activity usually controlled by the government and which contributes to the general public. The lottery kicks us right in the "get rich quick" bone. It is a dream getting rich overnight. Although the odds are stacked against lottery wager, there's still something alluring about getting a ticket. After all, someone has to win and someone does win every time. No lottery is a good bet from a mathematics point of view. The odds of winning are so low that even a $1 ticket to a major drawing is a losing investment. Long story short: there are better ways to invest money. The lottery is not a good retirement plan. If you had to choose between buying lottery tickets and investing in your retirement fund, the retirement fund is the obvious choice.

As it depends on lucky, it is a tool interest for criminals. It is that mere specter of a possibility that makes the lottery so successful. A lottery ticket isn't the best investment, but that it is entirely possible to win the big one.

The methods used to launder and use illicit assets are in constant evolution. In order for the standards to remain relevant and effective, the researchers must keep up to date with the latest money laundering and terrorist financing methods, techniques, and trends. It is important to constantly monitor and identify new threats and risks to the financial system and publish the findings in typologies studies. These studies are aimed at raising global awareness and allow an early detection of use and abuse of the systems. They are also instrumental to ensure the development of the most appropriate standards to respond globally to these new and emerging money laundering and terrorist financing risks and threats.

Evidence of money laundering has already been detected through alleged gains in lotteries by people who have rescued dozens or hundreds of awards in different modalities, making millions, which determines the performance of the communication of intelligence financial unit (e.g., the Financial Crimes Enforcement Network—FinCEN in the USA and the Council for Financial Activities Control—COAF in Brazil).

There were cases involving hundreds of awards. In one of them the money invested, result from tax evasion, provided gains totaling over 500 awards only for three people linked to a commercial establishment.

Often, prosecutors requested clarification from the appropriate administration office (in Brazil, the National Superintendence of Lotteries and Games from Caixa Econômica Federal—CEF) such as the drawing dates, amounts, and types of lotteries rescued by a particular investigation. It is very useful to obtain information, including the Income Tax paid and the bank account agency which was paid for each award. This is accomplished by presenting the original ticket that after it is unusable.

Where payments above a certain amount (R$800.00), in Brazil it is required to fill out a Statement of Accrued Income (DAPLOTO), in two copies, one of which is delivered to the customer and another is archived for 5 years with the appropriate department of its administration.

Repeated awards in short period defy the most rudimentary notions of mathematical probability. In the absence of nominal tickets, the *modus operandi* used for money laundering consists of the acquisition of the award ticket from the contemplated real person, exchanging hands of "dirty" money.[13] Such action, however, although mathematically possible near zero, allows application of the principle *in dubio pro reo*.

It remains probable due to the involvement of game house owners or people who sell awarded lottery tickets, responsible for finding and entice winners and even employees of the department responsible for its administration.[14]

---

[13] Cf. Financial Action Task Force [5].

[14] According to statistical data compiled by the Brazilian Financial Intelligence Unit—COAF, the number of Suspicious Activity Reports has been considerable—3051 only in 2018 (until August 08, 2018). Since its inception (1999), the COAF has received 20,915 reports from the Lottery sector, which shows that the possibility of money laundering through lotteries must be taken seriously (in COAF [6]).

Another possibility lies in effective money laundering placing bets in such amounts to cover all the possibilities of success, which leads necessarily to earn less income, but allows money of illicit origin used in games to be converted into provenance known and proven by documents.

So, how well warns Marcelo Batlouni Mendroni, there may be cases in which a person performs how many games he or she needs by getting numerous slips of the game. This is an unknown quantity because there is no identification, and can hit a prize of high value, despite he or she invested higher amount than the prize. With this, the money received would be neat to play.[15]

The hearing of the rewarded person often does not show useful information especially when he or she states that the game existed and with it the consequent gains. Given the secrecy and collusion, corruption of public officials has been established, as well as proximity to politicians. Their practice ultimately contributes to several other criminal procedures, with great social harm.

In the USA, 44 states and the District of Columbia have some sort of lottery. Each state has its own mix of instant win scratch tickets and traditional drawing-style games with large jackpots. The vast majority of states require you to visit a retailer in person to purchase tickets, but a few states have moved to online sales of tickets or at least subscriptions.[16]

The list of states with legal online lotteries is growing by the year and more will almost undoubtedly come online in the near future. Several states have also established lottery sites that don't just sell tickets online, but that also offer instant win games with top prizes worth hundreds of thousands of dollars—all playable from the comfort of home. If you happen to live in Georgia, Michigan, or Pennsylvania, you can check out sites for legal, regulated online lottery games.

More than a dozen states have approved measures that allowing online ticket sales, subscriptions, online scratch card-style games, or both. In these states, you can either buy your tickets in person like normal or visit the official state lottery website to buy lottery tickets online. You can enter state-level drawings from home or even major, multi-state drawings such as Powerball and Mega Millions. Some state lotteries also offer instant win scratch cards online.

According to Hannah Yee Fen Lim, "most online operators, however, just offer online the same lotteries they offer off-line with some operators aggressively advertising and selling tickets on the Internet to players from all around the world. One of the earliest state run lotteries to have an online presence is the UK national lottery which has been online since 2003. In Canada, British Columbia and the four Atlantic provinces have had their lottery operations online since 2006. In the US, some state lotteries, such as Indiana's state lottery, began their internet operations with 'second chance' drawings which used the Internet to give losing tickets another opportunity to win a prize. Players with tickets that did not win a prize could enter their ticket numbers on the Internet for second chance drawings."[17]

---

[15] Cf. Crime de Lavagem de Dinheiro, p. 76.

[16] Sales [7].

[17] Lim [8, p. 79].

Multi-state lotteries are the result of state teamwork. Instead of limiting ticket sales in one state, multi-state lotteries sell tickets in multiple states. With bigger ticket sales come bigger jackpots. Bigger jackpots lead to more ticket sales, which in turn lead to bigger jackpots. It's a powerful cycle that works to generate enormous jackpots.

These lotteries are governed by the Multi-State Lottery Association (MUSL). Thirty-three states participate in the MUSL and share their pools to increase ticket sales and jackpots. Some of the lotteries within the MUSL are spread across all 33 states while others are limited to only a few states. Some of these lotteries even extend beyond the MUSL member states. For example, Mega Millions is played in 43 states, the District of Columbia, and the US Virgin Islands. It is no surprise then that Mega Millions is one of the largest. Powerball is also offered in those same areas. In those lotteries, the jackpots routinely reach more than a $100 million. In more recent years, Powerball jackpots have reached as high as $1.6 billion.[18]

As it turns out, using the Internet for lotteries challenges all the system and has to be analyzed with all its complexity, including reaching across borders by users from other states and other countries.

3.4 Internet Gambling

Illegal betting is prevalent in the world of sport, gambling, and money laundering. Criminals use illegal betting as a means to launder their gains from criminal activities. Therefore, premiums arising from such bets (and here it is possible also to talk about "investments") obtained with dirty money are also illegal and subject to seizure, freezing, and confiscation.

The *modus operandi* of some of these money launderers, as it was seen above, is to acquire lottery tickets from actual awarded people. Knowing awarded people or even lottery owners from where tickets are bought, criminals can apply for the reward of the winner. The scheme is possible only due to collusion between employees or lottery owners and offenders. Thus, the dirty money changes hands. Repeated lottery awards to the same individual in short periods of time challenge the most rudimentary notions of mathematical probability. Although the possibility of several awards to the same person is near zero, the principle of *in dubio pro reo* could always be invoked.

Lottery owners sell lottery tickets through enticing winners. That is why it is important for the government to control and regulate these lottery houses. In Brazil, the responsible government agency would be the Caixa Econômica Federal.

The Financial Action Task Force (FATF) reports that money launderers use football in the following typologies: (1) acquisition and investments in football clubs, (2) international purchase and transfer of players, (3) acquisition and sale of game tickets, (4) bets, and (5) misuse of image rights, sponsorships, and advertising.

[18] See Betting [9].

Hervé Martin Delpierre, who made a documentary titled "24 h chrono," released on May 8, 2013, affirms that the morals of sport are now in doubt. He reveals that of the 15,000 sports betting websites ("paris sportifs")[19] in the world, 85% are illegal. These websites generate more money than sport itself—ten to one hundred times more in certain events. Illicit deals can take place not only about the outcome of a game, but also the number of points or goals, the amount of corners or yellow or red cards, etc.

It is also possible to buy off players, clubs, and referees to fix games. Of the 27,000 football games played each year under the rules of the Union of European Football Associations (UEFA), 7% are suspected of manipulation.[20]

Philippe Kern, founder and director of KEA European Affairs and director of the French think-tank Sport et Citoyenneté ("Sport and Citizenship"), says that a study called "Match-fixing in Sport," led by the European Commission, made recommendations, including criminal penalties, for European countries to take action.[21] The European Commission also published an extensive "White Paper on Sport," detailing money laundering and corruption in the sport sector.[22]

Players themselves, who have time and money in excess, also engage in Internet betting and, as a result, have been targeted for their bets and debts. Hervé Martin Delpierre reveals in his documentary the story of a goalkeeper who ended up in the hands of the Camorra and later received additional threats.

To combat fraud, it is relevant to envision a way to control such gambling websites and the flow of money involved. The European Commission's recommendation to create a crime of "sporting fraud" can also be considered. It is necessary to sensitize players, making them able to resist any pressures and report them to authorities. The economic situation of sport should be sufficiently viable in a way that players are not tempted by organized crime. A mandatory central body of information with the necessary awareness of sports federations and confederations should be the first step to avoid illicit behaviors.

---

[19] Sixty percent of sports betting websites in the world are for football.

[20] Delpierre [10].

[21] Kern [11].

[22] The European Commission's "White Paper on Sport" states the following: Sport organizations are generally aware of these problems and have for some time been discussing them with governmental actors. The need for sport organizations to be transparent was recognized by participants at the conference "Rules of the Game," which took place in Brussels in 2001. In fact, it is one of the key aspects of the conference report. The problem has also been recognized in a number of reports produced by sport organizations, including the "Stevens Report" on Premier League Transfers. One of the reasons why the Independent European Sport Review was launched was that it identified "a range of problems—such as doping, corruption, racism, illegal gambling, money-laundering and other activities detrimental to the sport—where only a holistic approach between football and the EU and national authorities will be truly effective." The review put these problems on record and identified the following key problem areas: "player transfers, payments to agents, investment in clubs and a variety of other commercial deals associated with football, such as sponsorship." European Commission [12].

Gambling conducted via the Internet has drawn a lot of attention. In Brazil, casinos and bingos are considered illegal.[23] Ian Abovitz reveals that "[i]n the United States, courts have traditionally recognized gambling as an area reserved for state regulation pursuant to the Tenth Amendment of the U.S. Constitution. Currently, all fifty states and the District of Columbia conduct some form of gambling regulation, ranging from full legalization in Nevada to blanket prohibition in Hawaii and Utah."[24]

Usually these regulations are designed to generate tax revenue while also providing for the safety of players and operators by limiting the social concerns associated with gambling.

John Warren Kindt and Stephen W. Joy state that "[a] majority of the money generated by Internet casinos went untaxed, created more untaxable money flow, and reduced taxable economic activities."[25]

Although the traditional methods of regulating gambling have been reasonably effective, application to the Internet has proven difficult as the boundless nature and wide accessibility of the medium are widely believed to intensify social concerns.[26]

On October 13, 2006, President George W. Bush signed into law the Unlawful Internet Gambling Enforcement Act of 2006 (UIGEA) ,[27] which prohibits the acceptance of payment of wagers by financial institutions. The UIGEA bans Internet gambling by forcing financial institutions to prevent financial payments of wagers from bank accounts and other financial instruments.[28]

In March 2011, the European Commission opened a public consultation called "On-line gambling in the Internal Market." Its main aim was to identify public policy challenges and market issues referring to the differing regulatory models of national authorities in the European Union.[29] The consultation welcomed views interested stakeholders, including citizens and private and public gambling operators. They were invited to share expertise and contribute data.

According to the *On-line gambling in the Internal Market* from the European Commission, online gambling services are today widely available and used in the European Union. The economic significance of the sector is growing at a very high speed. The advent of the Internet and the growth of online gambling opportunities

---

[23] Law 8.672 of June 7, 1993, called the Zico Act, gave clubs the choice to become companies. In turn, Law 9.615 of 24.03.1998, called Pele Act, revoked Zico Act and was later amended by Law 9.981 of July 14, 2000, called the Maguito Vilela Act, which revoked, in art. 2, the chapter devoted to bingo. Law 10.671 of May 15, 2003, addressed the financial transparency of management, established offenses, and considered sport as a cultural expression of the country.

[24] Abovitz [13, p. 438].

[25] Kindt and Joy [4].

[26] Id.

[27] 31 U.S.C. §§ 5361–5367 (Supp. 2007).

[28] See Blankenship [14].

[29] The Consultation took place March 24–July 31, 2011. See http://ec.europa.eu/internal_market/consultations/2011/online_gambling_en.htm. Accessed June 7, 2018.

are posing regulatory challenges as these forms of gambling services are subject to national regulatory frameworks that vary rather significantly between Member States. These frameworks can be broadly categorized into either licensed operators operating within a strictly regulated framework or strictly controlled monopolies (State owned or otherwise).

A number of Member States have also embarked on a review of their gambling legislation to account for these new forms of service delivery. Furthermore, the growth of online gambling opportunities has given rise to the growth of an unauthorized market, which consists of unlicensed illegal gambling and betting activity, including from third countries and operators licensed in one or more Member States offering gambling services in other Member States without having obtained the specific authorization in those countries.

Online gambling has recently generated an overwhelming interest worldwide. For Anurag Bana, it "is being seen as a potential trading sector that could assist countries with a 'booster shot' in reducing their accumulated fiscal deficits in an effort to encourage domestic and world economies."[30] These developments pose regulatory and technical challenges, and they also give rise to societal and public order issues, such as the protection of consumers from fraud and the prevention of gambling addiction.

As online gambling is a global phenomenon, an effective international regulator should be formed to monitor the management, accountability, efficiency, and sector proportionality of the stakeholders involved in order to sustain market confidence in trading by promoting public understanding in addition to maintaining an appropriate degree of protection for consumers.

According to Jon Mills, "while facilitating commerce and communication, the Internet also facilitates the ability of criminals to elude the laws of any, and every, nation."[31]

That is true that having exploited by entrepreneurs technological advances and consumer demand to build a global gaming market on the Internet, there is an attempt to prohibit it through a monetary control scheme in the USA preventing the use of credit cards and other bank instruments.

Mark D. Schopper reveals that the "*raison d'être* for this legislative effort is purportedly to prevent money laundering."[32]

The Internet provides individuals worldwide with the ability to communicate and exchange information across national boundaries and continents. The project to connect scientists and defense agencies has united the globe with access to information, available anywhere, at any time. And it has also connected criminals and people with criminal purposes.

Moreover, even assuming a high degree of sophistication, supervision, and safety, the Gambling Houses can be seen as something attractive to criminals who do not feel fear for their personal illegal actions. Internet gambling provides the

[30] Bana [15, p. 335].

[31] Mills [16, p. 83].

[32] Schopper [17, p. 303].

unique combination of allowing the public to gamble from the comfort of home, while affording the government the opportunity to limit such gambling, requiring gaming operators to obtain and verify accurate client information. For this, it will be necessary all systems must incorporate a method to confirm identity, age, and location of the player which complies with the legislation in the licensing jurisdiction.

A licensing jurisdiction must include "players to hold an account and/or be registered by the licensed provider; in order to open an account and be registered, players will be required to provide proof of identity, age and place of residence; licensed providers are to require the identification of players each time a player attempts to access the site, using such methods as a personal identification number or password and challenge questions."[33]

Predatory gaming practices and ever-evolving technology has been push countries toward outlawing online gaming. As states Luke Reeves, "legalization and regulation of Internet gambling is possible right now on an intrastate level. While legalizing Internet gaming may not completely eradicate many of the vices associated therewith, undoubtedly legalization could help the industry take some positive steps."[34]

There is a big movement in favor of these activities on Internet and the attempt to prohibit it has failed. As an example, mentioned by Mark D. Schopper when analyzed the scenario in the USA, "more than one million Americans per day log on to the Internet and play casino-style games or make sports wagers for real money. The federal government moves to prohibit this activity. After numerous failed attempts at passing prohibition legislation, the government develops what appears to be an 'effective' method of achieving this goal: a monetary control scheme that would effectively make it impossible for Americans to fund their Internet gambling activities. To this end, the government passes legislation banning the use of credit cards, checks, and electronic funds in Internet gambling."[35]

However, the use of an alternative mechanism already exists in the form of use of electronic money by gamblers, in a completely anonymous via to place bets on the Internet.

The important in this view is to enable the enforcement agent or supervisory body and its team with a well-regulated legislation that makes possible an appropriate administration of the online games. Illegal practice would make the statistics inaccurate and potential revenue figures difficult to establish.

References

1. Glenny, M. (2008). *McMaffia: Crime sem fronteiras* (p. 14). São Paulo: Companhia das Letras.
2. Miller, K. C. (2013). Public policy and the inevitability of internet gambling. *Drake Law Review Discourse, 61*, 1–34.

[33] Gottfried [18].

[34] Reeves [19, p. 506].

[35] Schopper [17, p. 304].

3. Financial Action Task Force. (2009, Mar). Financial Action Task Force – FATF website. Vulnerabilities of casinos and gaming sector. Retrieved August 10, 2018, from http://www.fatf-gafi.org/mwg-internal/de5fs23hu73dsw/progress?id=g0bbqv2M5r
4. Kindt, J. W., & Joy, S. W. (2002). Internet gambling and the destabilization of national and international economies: Time for a comprehensive ban on gambling over the world wide web. *Denver University Law Review, 80*, 111.
5. Financial Action Task Force. Money laundering through the football sector report. Last updated February 1, 2012, Retrieved May 10, 2018, from http://www.fatf-gafi.org/topics/methodsandtrends/documents/moneylaunderingthroughthefootballsector.html
6. Conselho de Controle de Atividades Financeiras – COAF. Brazilian Intelligence Unit, COAF website, Retrieved August 08, 2018, from https://siscoaf.discovery.fazenda.gov.br/coaf/servlet/mstrWeb?src=mstrWeb.3140&evt=3140&documentID=8DC8B1DD11E72FF300000080EF756E0B&Server=161.148.236.17&Port=0&Project=DD-COAF&
7. Sales of lotteries in the United States, in the Statistics Portal. Retrieved August 10, 2018, from https://www.statista.com/statistics/388238/sales-of-lotteries-by-state-us/
8. Lim, H. Y. F. (2011). Online gaming. The state of play in Singapore. *Singapore Academy of Law Journal, 23*, 74–92.
9. Betting USA site. Retrieved June 20, 2018, from http://www.bettingusa.com/lottery/
10. Delpierre, H. M (2018). Du blanchiment d'argent au trucage de matches. Paris en ligne: les mafias truquent le jeu. *Dernières Nouvelles D'Alsace (DNA)*. Retrieved August 10, 2018, from http://www.dna.fr/justice/2012/04/27/les-mafias-truquent-le-jeu
11. Kern, P. The fight against corruption in sport is a major European issue. EurActiv.com. Retrieved August 10, 2018, from http://www.euractiv.com/culture/fight-corruption-sport-major-eur-analysis-515227
12. European Commission. White Paper on Sport. Retrieved May 7, 2018, from http://ec.europa.eu/sport/white-paper/swd-the-organisation-of-sport_en.htm
13. Abovitz, I. (2008). Why the United States should rethink its legal approach to internet gambling: A comparative analysis of regulatory models that have been successfully implemented in foreign jurisdictions. *Temple International and Comparative Law Journal, 22*, 437.
14. Blankenship, M. (2008). The unlawful internet gambling enforcement act: A bad gambling act? You Betcha! *Rutgers Law Review, 60*, 485.
15. Bana, A. (2011). Online gambling: An appreciation of legal issues. *International Business Law Journal, 12*, 335.
16. Mills, J., et al. (2000). *Dickinson Journal of Environmental Law & Policy, 19*, 77.
17. Schopper, M. D. (2002). Internet gambling, electronic cash & money laundering: The unintended consequences of a monetary control scheme. *Chapman Law Review, 5*, 303–330.
18. Gottfried, J. (2004). The federal framework for internet gambling. *Richmond Journal of Law & Technology, 10*(3), 26.
19. Reeves, L. (2013). From Chance to Ka-Ching: A Model for Legalization and Agency Regulation of Internet Gambling in Texas. *Texas Tech Administrative Law Journal, 14*, 487–506.

Chapter 4
Payments Through Illegal and Disguised Means: NGOs, Trusts, Wire Transfers, Cards, and Cryptoassets

4.1 Initial Considerations

Created in December of 1989 by the seven richest countries in the world, (G-7[1]), the Financial Action Task Force (FATF, or *Groupe d'Action Financière sur le blanchiment des capitaux*—GAFI[2]), organized under the aegis of the Organization for Economic Cooperation and Development (OEDC), has a mandate to examine, develop, and promote policies for the war on money laundering. It initially included twelve European countries along with the USA, Canada, Australia, and Japan. Other countries joined afterward (including China in 2007), as well as international organizations (the European Commission and the Gulf Cooperation Council). Brazil joined, initially as an observer and later as a full member, at the XI Plenary Meeting, held in September of 1999.

The following Recommendations from FATF are relevant provisions contained in the 2012 version[3]:

---

[1] USA, Japan, Germany, France, UK, Italy, and Canada, which have since been joined by Russia (G8).

[2] The FATF is an intergovernmental agency organized to promote measures for the fight against money laundering. Its list of 40 recommendations, drafted in 1990, was revised in 1996. Another eight recommendations were drawn up in 2003 (on financing of terrorism) and a ninth in 2004 (also about financing of terrorism). On February 16, 2012, all 49 recommendations were revised, improved, and condensed into 40. These recommendations are not binding, but they do exert strong international influence on many countries (including nonmembers) to avoid losing credibility, because they are recognized by the International Monetary Fund and the World Bank as international standards for combating money laundering and the financing of terrorism. In the 1996 version, they were adopted by 130 countries. In the 2003–2004 version, they were adopted by over 180 countries. It is important to mention that the idea of improving and condensing the recommendations to avoid distortion and duplication, and to also incorporate the nine Special Recommendations on the financing of terrorism into the basic text (40 recommendations), originated in Brazil when it presided over the FATF between 2008 and 2009.

[3] See FATF [1].

F. M. De Sanctis, *Technology-Enhanced Methods of Money Laundering*,
https://doi.org/10.1007/978-3-030-18330-1_4

Countries should identify, assess, and understand the money laundering and terrorism financing risks for the country, and take action to mitigate them (*Risk-Based Approach—RBA*, Recommendation No. 1). Countries should ensure cooperation among policymakers, the Financial Intelligence Units (FIUs) and law enforcement authorities, and domestic coordination of prevention and enforcement policies (Recommendation No. 2). The current text of Recommendation No. 2 (this was in Recommendation No. 31 before) adds legitimacy to Brazil's National Strategy for the Fight against Corruption and Money Laundering (ENCCLA).[4] The crime of money laundering should apply to predicate offenses, which may include all serious offenses, any of a long list, or any offenses punishable by a maximum penalty of more than one year, and criminal liability should apply to all legal persons, irrespective of any civil or administrative liabilities (Recommendation No. 3). No criminal convictions should be necessary for asset forfeiture. Furthermore, with reference to the Vienna Convention (1988), the Terrorist Financing Convention (1999), and the Palermo Convention (transnational organized crime, 2000), the burden of proof on confiscated goods should be reversed (Recommendation No. 4). Countries should criminalize the financing of terrorism (Recommendation No. 5). Countries should implement financial sanction regimes to comply with UN Security Council

[4]According to a study conducted by the Brazilian Federal Justice Council's Judiciary Studies Center on the effectiveness of Law No. 9613/1998, through September of 2001 the Brazilian Federal Police had conducted only 260 police investigations, and most (87%) of the federal judges polled in that study answered that there were no active proceedings in their courts relating to money laundering through 12/31/2000, the date on the survey form (Federal Justice Council, *A critical analysis of the money laundering law*). In 2002 and 2003, with Minister Gilson Dipp of the Appellate Court presiding, and participation from representatives of the Federal Courts, the Office of the Federal Prosecutor, the Federal Police, and the Brazilian Federation of Bank Associations (FEBRABAN), the Council drew up substantive recommendations to improve investigation and prosecution of criminal money laundering by engaging the cooperation of various government departments responsible for implementing the law. It was embryonic to the ENCLA (National Strategy for the Fight against Money Laundering and Recovery of Assets), later renamed the National Strategy for the Fight against Corruption and Money Laundering (ENCCLA). The ENCCLA is made up of the primary agencies involved in the matter, which are the Office of the Attorney General, the Council for Financial Activities Control (COAF), the Justice Ministry's Asset Recovery and International Legal Cooperation Council Department (DRCI), the Federal Justice Council (CJF), the Office of the Federal Prosecutor (MPF), the Office of the Comptroller-General (CGU), and the Brazilian Intelligence Agency (ABin), annually setting policy for all actions to be carried out in the execution of Law No. 9613/1998, on account of private and uncoordinated—if not conflicting—agendas having been observed among government agencies responsible for said enforcement. A meeting was held on December 5–7, 2003, in Pirenópolis in the State of Goiás, to develop a joint strategy for the fight against money laundering. To monitor progress toward the goals set forth in the objectives of access to data, asset recovery, institutional coordination, qualification, and training, and international efforts and cooperation, an Integrated Management Office for the Prevention of and Fight against Money Laundering (GGI-LD) was created in compliance with Target 01 of ENCLA/2004. This Office is comprised of the primary government agencies, as well as the Judicial Branch and Attorney General's Office, conducting both breakout sessions and plenary meetings on various occasions. Every year they define new actions (formerly targets), in hopes that the conclusions arrived at during their work sessions will be transformed into substantive outcomes.

resolutions on terrorism and its financing (Recommendation No. 6), and on the proliferation of weapons of mass destruction and its financing (Recommendation No. 7). Countries should establish policies to supervise and monitor nonprofit organizations, so as to obtain real-time information on their activities, size, and other important features such as transparency, integrity, and best practices (Recommendation No. 8). Financial institution secrecy laws, or professional privilege, should not inhibit the implementation of the FATF Recommendations (Recommendation No. 9). Financial institutions should be required to undertake customer due diligence and to verify the identity of the beneficial owner, and be prohibited from keeping anonymous accounts or those bearing fictitious names (Recommendation No. 10). Financial institutions should also be required to maintain records for at least five years (Recommendation No. 11) and closely monitor politically exposed persons (PEPs), that is, persons who have greater facility to launder money, such as politicians and their relatives (in high posts) (Recommendation No. 12). The 2012 version expanded the definition of PEPs to include both nationals and foreigners, and even international organizations.

Other provisions worth mentioning include: Financial institutions should monitor wire transfers, ensure that detailed information is obtained on the sender, as well as beneficiary, and prohibit transactions by certain people pursuant to UN Security Council resolutions, such as resolution 1267 of 1999 and resolution 1373 of 2001, for the prevention and suppression of terrorism and its financing (Recommendation No. 16). Designated non-financial businesses and professions (DNFBPs), such as casinos, real estate offices, dealers in precious metals or stones, and even attorneys, notaries, and accountants, must report suspicious operations, and those who report suspicious activity must be protected from civil and criminal liability (Recommendation No. 22, in combination with Nos. 18–21). Countries should take measures to ensure transparency and obtain reliable and timely information on the beneficial ownership and control of legal persons (Recommendation No. 24), including information on trusts—settlors, trustees, and beneficiaries (Recommendation No. 25). Financial Intelligence Units (FIUs) must have timely access to financial and administrative information, either directly or indirectly, as well as information from law enforcement authorities in order to fully perform their functions, which include analysis of suspicious statements on operations (Recommendations Nos. 26, 27, 29, and 31). Casinos must be subject to effective supervision and rules to prevent money laundering (Recommendation No. 28). Countries should establish the means for conducting freezing and seizure operations, even when the commission of the predicate crime may have occurred in another jurisdiction (country), and implement specialized multidisciplinary groups or task forces (Recommendation No. 30). Authorities should adopt investigative techniques such as undercover operations, electronic surveillance, access to computer systems, and controlled delivery (Recommendation No. 31). The physical transportation of currency should be restricted or banned (Recommendation No. 32). Proportionate and dissuasive sanctions should be available for natural and legal persons (Recommendation No. 35). There should be international legal cooperation, pursuant to the Vienna Convention (international traffic, 1988), Palermo

Convention (transnational organized crime, 2000), and Mérida (corruption, 2003) (Recommendation No. 36). Countries should provide mutual assistance toward a quick, constructive, and effective solution (Recommendation No. 37), including the freezing and seizure of accounts, even with no prior conviction (Recommendation No. 38), extradition (Recommendation No. 39), and spontaneously taking action to combat predicate crimes, money laundering, and terrorism financing (Recommendation No. 40).

Recommendations 9–23 are the standards most closely associated with the FATF and most directly tied to discussions of regulatory costs, economic growth, and financial inclusion. They include the customer identification and recordkeeping obligations, as well as requirements for filing suspicious transaction reports and conducting enhanced due diligence when opening an account for a foreign political figure or their family members.

Thus, as of the 2012 revision, the Recommendations set forth general guidelines, with details given in Interpretative Notes. The glossary has made it easy to place the standards adopted in proper perspective and also provides important clarifications.

The Interpretative Notes are best described as a sort of common ground made to fit both common law and civil law countries.

One important innovation, albeit not the purpose of the February 2012 review, was pointing out the need for countries to adopt the Risk-Based Approach (RBA). In other words, before applying certain measures, standards must be established to guide public policies for preventing and combating money laundering, terrorism financing, and (this is new) the proliferation of weapons of mass destruction.

Controls that have been required in compliance with the guidelines of the International Financial Action Group—FATF to stop the laundering of values provoked to seek for new mechanisms to launder assets in order to unlink them to the previous crime.

Some Recommendations can have special role for combating illegal gambling and money laundering. Particular attention was given by the FATF for the designated non-financial businesses and professions (DNFBPs), such as casinos, real estate offices, etc., which must report suspicious operations (Recommendation No. 22, in combination with Nos. 18–21). Besides that, FATF established a specific Recommendation to casinos that must be subject to effective supervision and rules to prevent money laundering (Recommendation No. 28).

Moreover, the global financial market and the development of information technologies have gradually driven economy underworld extending the possibilities of the practice of economic crimes.

There have been many initiatives in the war on organized crime. In Mexico, for instance, the war on drugs has had a central focus, with strategies built on the involvement of civil and military agents, setting records for cash forfeitures, drugs apprehended, and extraditions. On September 10, 2007, in the Municipality of Zarzal in the northeastern part of the Department of Valle, the Colombian army captured Diego Montoya, better known as Don Diego, one of the top-ten most wanted criminals on the DEA, CIA, and FBI lists. According to Juan Carlos Garzón, this arrest was probably the most notable achievement in the war on drugs for that year, in which over 57,000 people were arrested, with over 100 extradited to the USA.[5]

Eric Olson shows that there are many similarities between Italian Mafia organizations and Mexican criminal gangs. In his view, "Mexican organized crime is more market focused, less stable, and less durable. Moreover, Mexican criminal organizations are much more willing to attack the state. Additionally, the violence they employ is more gruesome and has different goals, including intimidating their rivals and terrorizing the public. Finally, they seek to shape public perceptions about organized crime by targeting the media either through violence and intimidation or to control the stories that are published."[6]

What was once considered extreme is now commonplace, showing the strength and tenacity of Mexican criminal organizations. *Express* Magazine, a Washington Post publication, printed news of the war between the two main drug cartels in Mexico (Sinaloa and Zetas), which went so far as to display fourteen headless bodies in front of City Hall at the border town of Nuevo Laredo. They also hanged nine people, four of them women, off a bridge in that same town. They left 18 mutilated bodies in a van near Lake Chapala, and used a garbage truck to haul another 49 bodies (with no heads, hands, or feet) near Monterey, Mexico's most important industrial city. The magazine also covered the battle, considered the most spectacular fight for intimidation and propaganda purposes, in front of TV cameras in May 2012, in which many headless bodies of innocent bystanders were publicly tossed about to terrorize civilians and frighten authority figures, such as President Felipe Calderon.[7]

With regard to the Italian mafia, Francesco Messineo observes how they get help from white-collar criminals: "they not only help the Mafia, but also commit crimes in their specific sector. This can be said of all crimes dealing with public bidding processes, even where the hand of the Mafia is not involved, although it generally is, or in such cases as corruption, collusion, and other well-known crimes against the public."[8]

Important initiatives in the war on transnational organized crime also occurred in Brazil. In 2007, Colombian drug Lord Juan Carlos Ramirez Abadia, also known as Chupeta, was arrested in São Paulo and sentenced, with several others, to more than 30 years in prison,[9] and afterward extradited to the USA. Other important actions were taken against the First Command of the Capital (PCC), a powerful criminal organization involved in miscellaneous crimes such as robbery, extortion, and drug

---

[5] In Garzón [2, p. 9].

[6] See Olson [3, p. 9].

[7] Cf. Two Top Cartels at War in Mexico [4, p. 6].

[8] Messineo [5, p. 301].

[9] Record No. 2007.61.81.0011245-7/SP, conviction in 2008 upheld by the Regional Federal Court for Region 3 (São Paulo and Mato Grosso do Sul), Criminal Appeal No. 0001234-26.2007.04.03.6181/SP, heard on 03/06/2012, Rapporteur, Federal High Court Justice Johonsom di Salvo.

trafficking in São Paulo. The police have stepped up their actions in the shantytowns of Rio de Janeiro.

Despite these initiatives, organized crime is still active and adapting itself to enforcement efforts—whether by moving to new territory (Rio de Janeiro) or spreading out its activities in the so-called baby cartels or micro-organizations. It has kept up its strength through well-armed groups assuring its control over extensive regions and the manpower to respond to government enforcement efforts.

In June 2012, police cars were hit by gunfire on the east side of São Paulo. This occurred during a week in which a series of attacks on off-duty police officers culminated in the death of five agents, believed to be a reaction by the criminal gang First Command of the Capital (PCC) to an Elite Squad police operation that killed six people in late May.[10]

Organized crime has indeed defied all stability and government control, and not just in poor suburbs or rural areas. One example occurred in May 2006, when over 80 people were killed, 30 buses set on fire, and a large number of private homes attacked because the government had announced the transfer of PCC leaders to maximum-security prisons.

This happened because one of the most effective instruments for crime fighting is to cut off its financing, that is, to confiscate the proceeds of drug sales and to cut off, limit, or control the flow of money across borders.

Indeed, the movement of money between States through transportation of large sums in cash or electric transfers through bank accounts, added to the possibility of completely uncontrolled transportation of prepaid access cards or stored value instruments, or even black market moneychangers, invariably made up of persons who are well-connected—despite having violated laws against money laundering—must be stopped.

Money Laundering can also occur through the mechanism of fraudulent payments. By say, fixing the price below the market value, or simply leaving out part of the amount payable, the price actually paid will surely be in cash or some untraceable means and delivered to the seller under the table. Then again, when prices are pegged at artificially high levels, the launderer may wish to have illicit financing of his acquisition and, to that end, will resort to fake documentation and anonymity.

Any time such facts or possibilities are known to authorities, all of them mindful that such crime is well-financed, no crime should go unpunished because they will surely lead to increased perpetration by others, and finally to the financing of terrorism.

There is much intelligence work to be done, more than that involved in simply controlling one's borders. Intelligence forces need to work together, because if they are kept apart, each may, in isolation, feel that someone else is responsible for the problem.

We must therefore approach the problem from a technical angle, for there is in many countries an atmosphere that fosters the adoption of solutions that are

[10] Cf. Andre [6].

ineffective, scattered, poorly coordinated, and not cohesive, especially owing to considerable social inequality.

It is not at all uncommon for officeholders to announce, before the elections, their wish to establish strategies for taking the money back out of crime, but little is actually done, other than budget cuts to the detriment of public safety. Indeed, the perception has been that money laundering is a victimless crime, and for that reason it does not claim the attention of society, politicians, and journalists.

According to Janine S. Hiller and DonLloyd Cook, "today it is the development of secure techniques for conducting electronic commerce through encryption or other techniques found in vices such as computer 'clipper chips' that have the same relevance to modern payment systems that the clipper ships had in the nineteenth century."[11] I would add, besides chips, swifts.

The use of an alternative mechanism method of payment is a reality and ensures anonymity what can be deemed as the most powerful and untraceable money-laundering tool ever imagined even by criminals.

Mark D. Schopper reveals, in this way, that "once the alternative payment method 'catches on,' it would be nearly impossible to stop its use without pulling the plug on the entire Internet (and maybe not even then),"[12] which is unthinkable today (I would add).

The American intelligence unit, the Financial Crimes Enforcement Network—FinCEN's new beneficial owner rules took place on May 11, 2018, impacting banks and the program managers and similar companies that help banks to comply with the Bank Secrecy Act, including FinTech companies that provide AML on-boarding and monitoring services. Under the new rules, banks and other covered financial institutions will be required to identify and verify the identity of the beneficial owners of their legal entity customers. These rules added to regulatory burdens, requiring a covered institution to identify each individual who directly or indirectly owns 25% of more of the equity interest of the customer, and one individual with significant responsibility to control or direct the customer. Depending on the entity's structure, this could be one to five individuals. To obtain these individual's names, the bank must require the individual opening the account for the entity to certify who those persons are. The bank must verify the identity of each beneficial owner using procedures that are similar, but not identical, to the customer identification procedures—CIP used by the bank to identify its customers. Perhaps, according to Dan Cohen and John ReVeal, the greatest burden is that the bank must perform this beneficial owner due diligence each time the legal entity opens a new account. Although the BSA does not require new CIP on an existing customer for each new account, these rules require new beneficial owner due diligence for each account.[13]

---

[11] Hiller and Cook [7, pp. 53–54].

[12] Schopper [8, p. 304].

[13] Cohen and Reveal [9].

It is important to highlight that when there is a combination of electronic money and banking institutions that allow, or even encourage, unknown people or businesses to become customers, it is reached a haven for money-laundering activities.[14]

4.2 Using NGOs and Trusts for Illegal Ends

Just as the work of beneficent entities has been important, scandals have stained some of their images and opened the door to an increase in judicial actions against their directors, increasing skepticism in proportion to news coverage of events.

Because their work is philanthropic, and they are generally motivated by altruism and compassion, charities have been immune to legal proceedings. They may be made answerable on account of internal management issues or even external problems (everything from labor suits to fraud, and even money laundering by reason of insolvency, negligence, or poor practices). Its entire board of directors might be held liable for some failure of accounting or diversion of funds.

Nongovernmental organizations, trusts, associations, and foundations tend to be as diverse as a country's population. People are increasingly getting involved in some kind of social or charity efforts. Donations to these social entities have been large. These social entities are accessible since they are governed via the Internet.

Recent disclosures have tarnished the images of certain entities and brought the glare of publicity onto the conduct of some of their managers. A backlash of skepticism has brought about a proportional reaction affecting the volume of donations and volunteer work.

Because philanthropic work is normally motivated by feelings of generosity and empathy, charitable organizations often imagine themselves immune to legal proceedings. Liability could surface based on some poorly handled internal activity, or some other cause occurring outside the organization. This is why the role of the manager is so important.

By the simple fact of their operating with personal and institutional donations, charity organizations are often temples, churches, mosques, NGOs, educational associations, etc., and believe that they are not required to reveal the source of their funds nor to be examined for the large financial transactions they conduct.

The U.S. Congress has, since 1917, allowed deduction of donations to charitable, religious, educational, and other such entities organized as nonprofit NGOs. We cite a 1938 report from the House Committee on Ways and Means in which Eric Thompson explains that tax revenue losses due to charitable donations are offset by easing the financial burden, which, through the resulting benefits, promotes the general welfare.[15]

According to Andrew Cuomo, philanthropic organizations "contribute substantially to our society. They educate our children, care for the sick, preserve our

[14] See Raiborn et al. [10, p. 38].

[15] Thompson [11].

literature, art and music for us and for future generations, house the homeless, protect the environment and much more."[16]

The correctness of granting large tax deductions has been the subject of frequent assessment of its effectiveness, purpose, and potential for abuse. All of this has, according to the author, brought about changes in the law: statutes and regulations governing charitable deductions.

Thus, a philanthropic transfer in the USA must satisfy a complex set of rules to qualify as a tax deduction. These rules are grouped, according to the author cited,[17] into three main requirements: (1) the transfer must be sent to a qualified addressee[18]; (2) it must clearly state the purpose of the donation, that is, not be an exchange of goods or services[19]; and (3) it must consist of a payment or other allowable goods.[20]

The third requirement brings us back to the question of payments.

In the state of New York, for instance, in order to set up a foundation or NGO,[21] a license must be obtained to qualify for tax exemption, and returns must be filed to the State tax authorities, under penalty of being closed down, by means of Form No. 990, dated and properly signed on penalty of perjury, and containing the name and telephone number of the person who keeps books and records for the organization.

The form must be filled out to include a detailed list of all of its activities and management, its revenues, overhead, and liquid assets. It must state the name and purpose of the institution; number of members; whether it has more than 25% of its liquid assets on hand; number of voting members listed within or outside of the entity; number of employees; number of volunteers; revenues from unrelated businesses and taxes paid; contributions and donations; resources invested; benefits paid by and for members; total assets and obligations; basic description of all assistance programs; whether any loans or benefits are granted to or for employees, directors, trustees, or any other persons; the names, hours worked, and job descriptions of all employees and former employees (including directors, trustees, and key personnel); their earnings; and their expenses (including travel or leisure).

For gross revenues of up to $100,000, no external audits are required. From $100,000 to $250,000 the information must be entered by an outside auditor (and documentation reviewed by that professional), who does not, however, check the truthfulness of information obtained. In other words it is not the auditor's job to check donor transactions (to conduct the due diligence). But NGOs with gross annual revenues in excess of $250,000 are required to turn in an outside auditor's report, and that auditor must perform the due diligence.[22]

---

[16] Cf. Cuomo [12, p. 1].

[17] *Id.* p. 242.

[18] Cf. I.R.C. § 170 (c) (2006).

[19] See Mcleman v. United States (24 Cl. Ct. 109, 91-2 USTC 50, 447, 1991).

[20] In I.R.C. § 170 (e) (3) (2006).

[21] Provided they are also recognized as such in the U.S. tax code, also known as the Internal Revenue Code, Section 501 (c); 527; 4947 (a) (1).

[22] Cf. Charities [13].

The Foundation Center, a U.S. center for information on foundations, has published some 29 standards. Brazil, meanwhile, has six unpublished standards (a true case of living in a glass house).[23]

Management and employees of nongovernmental organizations must be answerable for their management and for the protection of the goods and services that benefit us all.

A primary responsibility is to ensure proper accounting for social programs they play a role in, and for funding received from their supporters (public or otherwise). This means they must strictly comply with the law and ethical standards, be committed to the mission of the NGO they represent, protect the rights of their members and, indirectly, of those assisted, and prepare annual reports for their country's federal revenue service and regulatory authorities having jurisdiction—reports that should be available to all interested parties.

They should therefore have technical information at their fingertips to enable them to monitor and record all assets and amounts received, spent, or entrusted to their care.

The website of the National Association of State Charity Officials (NASCO[24]) contains important information on recording and reporting required of NGOs. NASCO members are employees of U.S. government agencies charged with regulating NGOs and their funds.

Marion R. Fremont-Smith, who teaches Public Policy at the John F. Kennedy School of Government, produced an important comparison for Harvard University on the bookkeeping requirements for such organizations. She showed, for instance, that most U.S. states (for example, NY, CA, AK, MO, NJ) require that they have at least three directors.[25]

FATF Recommendation No. 08, in the spirit of clearly delimiting the rights and responsibilities of directors and employees of nongovernmental organizations, encourages countries to establish good policy whereby information on their activities, size, and other important characteristics such as transparency, integrity, openness, and best practices can be had in real time for purposes of supervision and monitoring.

It is not enough to only dimly perceive here a preoccupation with the financing of terrorism, for they could be the means of commission of any number of crimes—including terror-related crimes.

In Pakistan, for example, the Central Bank has placed much stricter controls on NGOs and beneficent societies, ordering a complete review of all of their accounting before the end of 2012, on pain of making them subject to penalties. The purpose was to establish a policy and a set of rules for compliance (to strengthen due

---

[23] According to information provided by Patricia Lobaccaro on 05/16/2012. Ms. Lobaccaro is president and CEO of Brazil Foundation, with office at 345 7th Ave., Suite 1401, New York City.

[24] NASCONET [14].

[25] In the search for greater accountability of nonprofit organizations. Summary charts: State nonprofit corporation act requirements and audit requirements for charitable organizations (document obtained 05/16/2012 from Patrícia Lobaccaro, president and CEO of the Brazil Foundation).

diligence) and to protect them from the risk of money laundering and terrorism financing. All of the country's financial institutions are being required to open accounts in the name of NGOs that match the documents submitted to them. In the event of an organization publicly soliciting donations or the like, accompanied by a bank account number, those financial institutions must promptly take note of and report that account in the event that the account owner of record does not match that of the publication.[26]

Two government intelligence cells were created in India to detect sources of funding used to finance terrorist activity. Analysts there believe that terrorist attacks in India are funded by neighboring countries through NGOs and nonprofits. Up to now they had no way of checking on how funds from abroad, purportedly intended for health and education, would actually be used.[27] In 2010 there were some two million NGOs there, but of that number, only 71 had requested any reimbursement for taxes paid. In 2009 there were 38,600 registered with the government to receive donations from abroad. Some are suspected of being money-laundering channels for the return of illegal cash received from Indian politicians or for terrorism financing, much of it qualifying as investments coming through Mauritius.[28]

NGOs, associations, and foundations lacking proper controls are recognized today as channels for money laundering for organized crime. In fact, the Financial Action Task Force (FATF) has found that sums transferred from NGOs abroad have provided funding for the financing of terrorism on a par with counterfeiting, drug trafficking, extortion, and corruption. This has prompted India, for example, to assemble an umbrella database listing them all.[29]

Money laundering is usually carried out using a layered structure to give the appearance of legality. One such method would be to establish trust companies through which the company manages business for its clients, the beneficiary being one or more holding companies, or a series of companies in several tax havens, to create a separation between the aforesaid holding companies and their ultimate beneficiary. Moreover, the discovery of the real beneficiary would require considerable cooperation on the part of authorities in those tax havens. Some means would have to be established to require the trust to provide its beneficiaries' names whenever requested by the authorities.

It is not even easy to establish who is in charge of the trust, for there is no obligation that that name be revealed. Hence, being its legal beneficiary is an enviable business—which may explain the rather timid recovery of illegal assets.

There are efforts underway in India to publicize the names of organizations (religious NGOs or trusts) requesting tax exemptions. One of India's wealthiest trusts collects huge sums of cash. At the time of writing, there are a number of laws and several states seeking to monitor the activities of these entities. Yet Parul Soni (of Ernst & Young Pvt. Ltd.) believes that federal legislation will be required to achieve

---

[26] Cf. Smith [15].

[27] In Marpakwar [16].

[28] For more on this, see Raja and Samuel [17].

[29] Cf. FATF report in www.gafi-fatf.org, 06/22/2012; Government [18].

bookkeeping transparency and to strengthen the reporting of suspicious activity in that sector.[30]

Trusts, though they may be temples, churches, or mosques, nongovernmental organizations, or educational institutions registered as NGOs, must now reveal the sources of their funds and have their financial transactions closely scrutinized. This is because of new jurisprudence requirements under India's Prevention of Money Laundering Act in 2002.

Indian attorney Bhusham Bahal tells us that the laundering of illegal money has been largely made possible by NGOs operated by powerful businessmen and top politicians, so that this new instrument should prove of valuable assistance to the authorities.[31]

Pakistan has also adopted strict measures to curb money laundering and financing of terrorism by NGOs by putting in place a very broad know-your-customer policy. It requires photocopies of customer photo IDs (identification card or passport), and a copy of the assignment, if done through power of attorney. Companies must produce their charter and bylaws, and a list of directors. Similar documentation is required of individuals, along with audit documents required of clubs, associations, or nonprofit associations.[32]

The trump card in the Indian case is the requirement that sources of funds be revealed, so that know-your-customer policies have to be in place for donations received by the NGOs, as is already the case for financial institutions. They must also provide detailed information on investments and donations received, and anonymous donations are henceforth barred.[33]

In Canada, nongovernmental organizations are as diverse as the population. Many Canadians are involved in charity work, with estimates running to some 36% of the population. Economically, the sector is a major player, inasmuch as two million people are employed within it, with another two billion hours voluntarily contributed. There are over 160,000 NGOs operating nationwide and 85% of the population makes financial contributions to Canadian social entities.[34]

It is important to have a stringent regulatory framework in this field. Talking about NPO, Ricardo Wyngaard states that it recommended, among other, that "enforcement powers under the NPO legislation should provide for the power to sanction office-bearers, impose fines and freeze accounts of NPOs for violation of oversight measures."[35]

Considerable customer due diligence is required. The donor's name or job title is no longer enough (photo ID is preferred). For instance, the donor's purposes and actual financial position must be known (preferably face-to-face), along with his

---

[30] Cf. Soni [19].

[31] See Shah [20].

[32] Cf. Money laundering, terror financing: SECP imposes more conditions. *Business Recorder.* Recorder Report, 09/12/2009. WLNR 17872644. www.westlaw.com. Accessed 23 June 2018.

[33] Again, Palak [21].

[34] For more on this, see Bickerton [22].

[35] Wyngaard [23, p. 23].

signature or the signatures of those acting on his behalf. The source of funding must also be disclosed, and supported by documentation. In the case of a donor company, a copy of the bylaws is required (in order to check the list of directors) from the civil or deed registry having jurisdiction. The true directors of the NGO must be known, again with photo ID, along with the scope of their authority, all of that backed by documentation to properly support the information provided.

4.3 Wire Transfers, Hawala, and Black Market Moneychangers

According to the 2007 U.S. National Drug Threat Assessment, Mexican and Columbian drug trafficking organizations rely in part on money services businesses, particularly wire remitters, to launder drug money.[36]

When people or companies seek to send or receive money from unlawful behavior across national borders, undetected by government institutions, they have come to rely more and more on transfers known as dollar wires or Euro wire, operated by agents known as dollar-changers (*doleiros*) whose activities stretch the legal envelope.

Along these lines, Terry Goddard informs us that in the Arizona Financial Crimes Task Force searches for financial anomalies, disproportionate events unconnected with economic reality. "They immediately saw that Arizona was a huge net importer of wired funds. At the top-ten Arizona wired-funds locations, over $100 were coming in for every dollar wired out. Wire transfers into Arizona from other states, in amounts over $500, totaled more than $500 million per year. Since there was no apparent business reason for this imbalance, the investigators took a closer look."[37]

For example, to preclude the use of fake identities for structuring or fragmentation of operations by companies and individuals in order to keep below the regulatory daily limit of $10,000 which would justify reporting the operation to the authorities, the State of Arizona established Geographic Targeting Orders (GTOs) which require additional identification, such as fingerprints and signatures from all persons receiving wire transfers in excess of $500. Based on such information, twenty-five warrants were issued in 2001–2006 for seizure of wire transfers supposedly made in payment for human smuggling or narcotics trafficking.[38]

The Financial Action Task Force recommends that participating nations obtain detailed information on all parties to wire transfers, both senders and beneficiaries, for monitoring purposes. This would enable the barring of transactions by certain people in accordance with UN Security Council Resolutions 1269/1999 and

---

[36] See Linn [24, p. 138].

[37] Goddard [25, p. 3].

[38] *Id.* p. 4.

1373/2001 on the prevention of terrorism and its financing (Recommendation No. 16).

Hawala means moving money across great distances in a most basic banking service available when some corners of the world haven't been as lucky in joining the global economy. According to Jacob W. Petterchak, "hawala thrives in the Persian Gulf and in diaspora communities where it serves an important economic role in channeling remittances back home. Hawala is an ancient money transfer system that came to play a prominent commercial role. It is a simple system of transferring money without movement through affiliated brokers known as 'hawaladars' using various means of communication."[39]

Today, Hawala become a big business in the United Arab Emirates, and is being applied to some extent via an online money transmitter called TransferWise based out of London. The hawala system is a customary informal channel "for transferring funds from one person to another via an independent broker or agent knows as a hawaladar. As long as there is a sender with some money for a distant receiver, the hawaladar will probably be able to find another hawaladar in close proximity to the receiver and complete the transaction."[40]

This activity, in some way, is similar to clandestine transactions made by exchange brokers, like "doleiros." As a type of Money Services Business—MSB described by the Bank Secrecy Act (BSA), and more specifically as a type of money transmitter, all forms of Informal Value Transfer System (IVTS) may legally operate in any state or territory. Financial regulators historically have emphasized the result rather than the form of the business, unlike some other jurisdiction, like India and Brazil, that takes a hard stance against informal MSBs.

In informal system, the brokers (hawaladars or "doleiros") usually are not registered at the Financial Intelligence Unit and operate without licenses in disagreement to some national authorities, being noncompliant to anti-crimes prevention system. They can be managed through the Internet.

Brazil's foreign exchange legislation spells out a number of issues that are often unheard of, even in the USA.

Take, for instance, Law No. 4131 of October 19, 1962,[41] which requires contracts for currency exchange operations in its Section 7, included by Law No. 11371/2006:

> Article 23 Operations on the free exchange rate market shall be conducted through establishments licensed to conduct foreign-exchange operations, with the intervention of an official broker whenever the law or regulations so provide, both of entities being required to know the client's identity, and how to correctly classify information provided by said client, pursuant to regulations established by Brazil's Currency and Credit Authority.
>
> (...)

[39] See Petterchak [26, p. 108].

[40] *Ibidem*, p. 112.

[41] In www.planalto.gov.br/ccivil_03_leis/L4131.htm. Accessed 16 July 2018.

§ 2 False statements of identity on the form which, in number of copies and following the model established by the Brazilian Central Bank shall be required in each operation to be signed by the client and checked and initialed by the banking establishment and broker therein intervening, shall render the banking establishment subject to charges for infraction, which carry a penalty of a fine in the amount of fifty percent (50%) to three hundred percent (300%) of the amount of the operation assessed against each of the violators. (New language given by Law No. 9069 of 1995)

(...)

§ 7 Completion of the form referenced in § 2 of this article is not required for foreign currency purchase and sale operations of up to three thousand dollars (US$3,000) or its equivalent in other currency. (Included by Law No. 11371 of 2006)[42]

Because of Brazil's currency exchange regulations, remittance companies are required to conduct all of their operations exclusively through financial institutions duly licensed by Brazil's Central Bank, and this also holds for international banking institutions. They must have agreements on file with accredited banks to engage in exchange operations in Brazil, under penalties provided by several regulations, in particular, Law No. 9069 of June 29, 1995 (the *Lei do Plano Real*),[43] which established the real as Brazil's legal tender. It is the currency used to settle all transactions in Brazil.

Its Article 65 provides:

Art. 65 The entry into and departure from Brazil of domestic and foreign currency must be processed exclusively through bank transfers, where banking establishments are required to fully establish the identity of the customer or beneficiary.

§ 1 Excepted from the provisions contained in the heading of this article is the transportation, in cash, of the following amounts:

I—When in Brazilian currency, up to ten thousand reals (R$10,000);

II—When in foreign currency, the equivalent of ten thousand reals (R$10,000);

III—When it can be shown to have entered or left Brazil in accordance with pertinent regulations.

§ 2 The National Monetary Council shall, according to the guidelines from the President of the Republic, regulate the provisions of this article and also provide limitations and conditions for entry into and exit from Brazil of national currency.

[42] The fact that the Central Bank deals more simply with amounts of up to $3000, dispensing with the currency exchange agreement, in no way constitutes a waiver of the requirement that all debits and credits in customer accounts or through financial instruments be recorded so as to allow tracking of assets.

[43] See www.planalto.gov.br/ccivil_03/leis/L9069.htm. Accessed 16 July 2018.

> § 3 Failure to comply with the provisions of this article shall, in addition to sanctions provided in specific legislation and following due legal process, entail forfeiture to the National Treasury of all amounts in excess of those set forth in § 1 of this article.

Legislative Decree No. 857 of September 11, 1969[44] requires the use of national legal tender in all domestic operations, rendering null and void all operations stipulated in foreign currency or which would, in effect, restrict or refuse Brazilian currency as legal tender, but does list several exceptions to the ban.

In this regard, it provides:

> Art. 1—All contracts, securities and documents, and bonds callable in Brazil, which stipulate payment in gold, in foreign currency, or in any way serve to restrict or refuse the cruzeiro as legal tender, are null and void by law.
>
> Art. 2—The provisions of the preceding article do not apply to:
>
> I—Contracts and paper relating to the importation and exportation of goods;
>
> II—Contracts for financing or putting up bonds or guarantees relating to the exportation of nationally-produced goods, sold abroad on credit;
>
> III—Foreign-exchange purchase and sale agreements in general;
>
> IV—Loans and any other obligations in which the creditor or debtor is a person residing and domiciled abroad, excepting only contracts for the lease or rental of real property within Brazilian territory;
>
> V—Contracts for purposes of assignment, transfer, delegation, assumption or modification of obligations referenced in the preceding item, even if both parties to the agreement are residents of and domiciled in Brazil.
>
> Sole Paragraph—Real property lease or rental agreements stipulating payment in foreign currency must, to be enforceable, and be registered in advance with the Brazilian Central Bank.

For its part, Decree No. 23258 of October 19, 1933,[45] provides that the purchase and sale of foreign currency shall be made exclusively in institutions authorized by the Brazilian Central Bank to engage in currency exchange operations, and establishes that:

> Art. 1 All foreign exchange operations conducted between banks, natural persons or legal persons domiciled or doing business in Brazil, with any entities abroad—whenever such operations are made other than through banks licensed to operate in foreign exchange through prior accreditation by examiners on behalf of the Brazilian Central Bank—are considered illegal exchange operations.

This set of codes (Law No. 4131/1962, Article 23; Law No. 9069/1995, Article 65, heading, and Legislative Decree No. 23258/1933, Article 1) makes foreign exchange

[44] In www.planalto.gov.br/ccivil_03/Decreto-Lei/Del0857.htm. Accessed 17 July 2018.

[45] In www.planalto.gov.br/ccivil_03/decreto-1930-1949/D23258.htm. Accessed 17 July 2018.

agreements mandatory (or, for operations of up to US $3000, more simplified forms), thereby establishing Brazilian currency (the real) as legal tender while requiring identification of customers and declaring illegal all foreign exchange operations not conducted through banks accredited by the Central Bank.[46]

By the rules of Brazil's Financial Intelligence Unit (COAF), the item Cash Transfers covers remittances and only applies to the mail and Brazilian postal money orders, both domestic and international, since everything coming from abroad and involving currency exchange operations comes under Central Bank supervision.

There is an official market in the USA which often made use of gray market operators (currency brokers) to allow transfers of money belonging to uninformed foreigners residing in Brazil. To stock its operations, Brazilian currency (reals) usually in cash (from illegal conduct in Brazil) was deposited by the Currency Exchange into the accounts of beneficiaries of wire transfers coming from abroad, while the dollars or euros received from the senders (easy prey) are diverted to redeem and deposit money as part of this bartering in funds. This is the so-called wire operation.

One should bear in mind that whenever the number of immigrants in a given location increases, there is a proportional increase in the gray market transfer of money. Similarly, wherever there is an increase in illegal immigration,[47] it is easier to commit financial crimes.

Another topic of concern is the entry of several factoring companies, which pump money into the accounts of wire transfer beneficiaries in the receiving country, thereby contributing to the offsetting of amounts in furtherance of an illegal black market in unauthorized financial dealings. Quite apart from their main purpose, which is short-term business financing of creditors' claims for goods and services provided on credit, the factor, or invoicer, is only required to keep a record of sales and perform administrative work relating to accounts receivable, receiving no sums and guarding against debtor insolvency.

According to the 1988 Convention on International Factoring held in Ottawa,[48] a factoring contract is a contract between two parties, the client (supplier) and the factor, and the factoring company should perform at least two of the following functions: (1) provide financing for the supplier, including loans and advances on payments; (2) maintenance of accounts relating to the receivables; (3) collection of receivables; and (4) protect against default in payment by debtors. Nothing is said,

---

[46] The International Capital and Foreign Exchange Market Regulations (RMCCI). Retrieved from www.bcb.gov.br/?RMCCI. Accessed 18 July 2018. Consolidate Brazil's currency-exchange regulations. Resolution No. 3568 of 05/29/2008 is the primary regulation. Retrieved from http://www.bcb.gov.br/pre/normativos/busca/normativo.asp?tipo=Res&ano=2008&numero=3568. Accessed 20 July 2018.

[47] For more on the influx of new immigrants who wire money back to their countries of origin, and their profiles, see *Briefing explores the factors that have influenced increases in remitting.* A publication of the Inter-American Dialogue. Accessed Mar 20, 2012, p. 1.

[48] See http://unidroit.org/english/conventions/1988/factoring/main.htm. Accessed 10 July 2018.

therefore, about assisting remittance companies or currency brokers so as to obtain financial compensation on their balances.

Something similar to what occurs in the Black Market Peso Exchange, which has long served international drug traffic, also applies to Brazil, with the establishment of the black market in reals.

According to Resolution No. 13 of the Council for Financial Activities Control, factoring companies are required to report to them, even if not accredited as financial institutions by the Central Bank, which is why they do not apply for licenses or registration. The COAF code is intended, however, to make it possible to identify their owners and directors, perform due diligence on customers, and check whether internal controls are in place.

Central Bank Circular No. 3542 of March 12, 2012, establishes in its Article 1, XI, a requirement to notify the Financial Intelligence Unit if, for instance, the customer does not provide justification for the origin of the money, or where the amount is incompatible with the customer's financial strength (item f); upon the realization of *resources from abroad*, check for financial incompatibility or absence of proper grounds (item g); or should payments occur abroad after deposit of credit in reals into accounts held by persons named in the currency exchange operations, absent in any business or financial links (item j). The U.S. Financial Crimes Enforcement Network (FinCEN) requires banks to perform due diligence on wire transfers to foreign agents or counterparties (31 CFR § 103).

This is why irregular deposits show up in the accounts of recipients of wire transfers with no identification of the depositor, cash transfers to a beneficiary account from a company not authorized by the Central Bank to operate in the currency exchange market, or cash transfers to beneficiary accounts from individuals, for only financial institutions are eligible to receive Central Bank authorization to operate in currency exchange markets.

An occasional such operation may be deemed acceptable if it has, in addition to an investigation as to the origin of funds, proof of deposit through a financial institution accredited by the Central Bank (such as a letter from the bank responsible for settling the operation).

Note that due diligence is not called for when the sending company has its home office in the USA (where that is the source of the dollars).

International remittances are critical to the livelihoods of hundreds of millions of people in the developing world, and mobile technology is one of the most exciting forces shaping how people send and receive them today. Around the world, people are increasingly shifting to digital channels, including mobile phones. The revolution that mobile money brought for domestic payments and cash transfers is now being repeated in international transfers.

This digitization is helping to reduce the costs of sending money internationally, bringing us closer to the achievement of the United Nations Sustainable Development Goal 10. C, as well contributing to the achievement of other UN SDGs, such as reduction of poverty, gender equality, and climate resilience.

Because of its reach and growing use among underserved people, mobile money is uniquely positioned to transform formal remittance markets and to advance financial inclusion. Mobile money providers are at the forefront of domestic payment services in many emerging markets, enabling the recipients of international remittances to pay for goods and services digitally, in turn creating a payments history that could enable them to access credit or insurance in the future. Mobile money has thus established itself as a critical tool for facilitating international remittances while reducing remittance costs and maximizing the impact of remittances on development.[49]

Cases have been observed of payments for drugs through the use of remittances from the USA in a triangle involving Colombia, the USA, and Europe. Euros were brought in by mules (or smurfs) to Colombian currency exchanges, which shipped them to the USA, where they were bundled and sent to Europe, where the receiving company exchanged them for dollars which were then wired to the USA. These operations usually involve immigrants. With the arrival of greater numbers of immigrants in any country, the number of transfers from one person to another increases annually.

On the other hand, some hawala customers may also be subject to prosecution for using unlicensed hawaladars even in otherwise legal transactions. Citing the case *United States v Banki,* Jacob W. Petterchak mentioned the fact of involving "an affluent Iranian-American transferring family money stateside from Iran by way of an unlicensed hawala business in Dubai with access to an American bank account. Given extremely complex sanctions programme in place between the United States and Iran, most business deals and transactions between nationals of the two countries are prohibited."[50]

One of the attractions of these activities is to evade strict licensing requirements on money remitters and foreign exchange dealers formalities. But, it is important for these professionals, hawaladars or "doleiros," to file Suspicious Activity Reports—SARs in case of transactions over certain amount or when the last ones seem suspicious enough, besides making a customer due diligence and complying with national authorities formalities.

For Rachana Pathak, it is imperative to take a "more international, culturally sensitive approach and offer incentives to convince people to switch to a more formalized banking system."[51]

In the USA, the Patriot Act expanded the Treasury's regulatory authority to include informal transfer value systems. Section 359 of the Patriot Act expanded the definition of financial institution to include any "person who engages as a business in an informal money transfer system or any network of people who engage as a

---

[49] GSMA website (the GSMA represents the interests of mobile operators worldwide, uniting nearly 800 operators with more than 300 companies in the broader mobile ecosystem, including handset and device makers, software companies, equipment providers, and Internet companies, as well as organizations in adjacent industry sectors). Mobile Money and International Remittances. Retrieved from https://www.gsma.com/mobilefordevelopment/mobile-money-international-remittances/#! Published on July 24, 2018. Accessed Sept 3, 2018.

[50] See Petterchak [26, p. 120].

[51] Pathak [27, p. 2061].

business in facilitating the transfer of money domestically or internationally outside the conventional financial institution system."[52]

On July 27, 2017, the Financial Crimes Enforcement Network—FinCEN, working in coordination with the U.S. Attorney's Office for the Northern District of California, assessed a $110,003,314 civil money penalty against BTC-e also known as Canton Business Corporation (BTC-e) for willfully violating U.S. anti-money laundering laws. Russian national Alexander Vinnik, one of the operators of BTC-e, was arrested in Greece and FinCEN assessed a $12 million penalty against him for his role in the violations. It was the Treasury's first action against a foreign-located money services business. Among other violations, BTC-e failed to obtain required information from customers beyond a username, a password, and an e-mail address. Instead of acting to prevent money laundering, BTC-e and its operators embraced the pervasive criminal activity conducted at the exchange. Users openly and explicitly discussed criminal activity on BTC-e's user chat. BTC-e's customer service representatives offered advice on how to process and access money obtained from illegal drug sales on dark net markets like Silk Road, Hansa Market, and AlphaBay.[53]

The importance of collaborating with the industry to ensure international remittances (some of them via mobile money) is facilitated safely and securely and consistent with global standards and local policy and regulations.

In this way it is possible to avoid that some sectors of the population use these transactions to launder money, evade taxes, traffic contraband, and fund terrorist activity. And, here again, the international cooperation is essential since MSBs are dependent on collaborative work with multiple countries and jurisdictions.

4.4 Credit/Debit Cards, Stored Value Instruments, and Cryptoassets (E-money)

Credit cards that allow access to an account through magnetic media and a password are quite familiar. However, there are prepayment vehicles that may be transferred and recharged, and quite possibly put to use by money launderers. Very low identification requirements on the part of financial institutions encourage such criminal practices. They do not themselves store value, but do provide access to an account.

It is difficult to draw a distinction between traditional credit cards and the network of prepaid access cards. Stored value cards ought to be clearly classified for the elucidation of government agencies and to facilitate identification of suspicious cards. They are a "pay-before" system that utilizes a credit or debit system.

Such cards are usually not listed among monetary instruments nor are they otherwise subject to customs declarations, although they often exceed the limit

[52] See Shetterly [28, p. 344].

[53] FinCen Website [29].

established for a Suspicious Activity Report—SAR. Authorities appear oblivious to the need to monitor these tools. These innocent cards or instruments can be worth millions, yet authorities are not concerned with them.

The cards closely resemble traditional credit cards, but provide access not to credit at a financial institution, but to a sum of money stored on the card, on a chip, or simply in an account accessible using the card (which sometimes even dispenses with the chip). Increasingly, particularly in the USA,[54] payments are made by this means. There are many different kinds.

The least sophisticated is good for a fixed amount and is activated by a sales clerk. As purchases are made, those amounts are deducted from the card balance until it is exhausted. Such cards are not rechargeable. Typically referred to as gift cards, they are sold at checkouts in U.S. supermarkets. Such instruments make it possible, if carried in hundreds, to send millions of dollars.

Others may be reloaded using a computer or ATM. In these cases, they would represent small bank accounts and the balance does not even show up without proper software and hardware. Large sums can be stored, and easily passed from hand to hand, making these absolutely anonymous.

These types of cards are often not subject to daily withdrawal limits, but only to the total stored value.

Critics have charged that card issuers do not care about online fraud and, according to Andres Rueda, "profit from fraud by charging penalties to merchants hit by fraud and then forcing them to absorb the losses. However, card issuers, with an eye to preserving their stake in a growing market, are introducing measures to deter fraud during online purchases, including the required use of passwords and other forms of authentication."[55] Trying to reduce fraud, card companies and financial institutions are promoting smart cards with 32k chips, capable of holding digital wallets and programmed to allow for different levels of online transaction authentication, or using a secure PIN number or Token connection.

In both the USA and Brazil, no traveler is permitted to carry more than 10,000 (dollars or reals) in cash or cash equivalents (called monetary instruments, such as travelers checks, credit cards, negotiable bills of exchange, bearer checks, or other documents convertible to cash) without declaring them to customs authorities. We should mention here that usually such stored value instruments are not classified, in either country, as monetary instruments for that purpose.

This actual legal loophole allows organized crime a great opportunity to circumvent controls on money laundering, especially across borders or simply through use of the mail.

In money laundering the first phase is known as placement, characterized when the bulk cash proceeds of illegal activity are transferred into financial institutions without attracting undue attention. Since financial institutions strong supervision,

[54] From a volume of just $6.2 million ten years ago, the use of prepaid cards has skyrocketed to over $800 billion in 2008, and is projected to increase to $1.3 trillion in 2009, etc. (according to Goddard [25, p. 9]).

[55] Rueda [30, p. 34].

criminals prefer to cash out money without being exposed to the possibility of detection. Layering is the second phase where multiple layers of artificial transactions are generated to obscure the true origins of the dirty money. At the integrated phase, the money has been successfully incorporated into regular economy. There is also the recycling phase, when an activity is done to guarantee the success of the previous stages.

The phases of money laundering in real world can be, according to Habil Zoltan Andras Nagy and Kitti Mezei, "recognized in the virtual space too. Anonymity is enough for some service requisitions which means a fake name and address are able to hide the real user. Furthermore, most of the financial transactions can be carried out anywhere and anytime. It is supported by the bank sector's interest, on the one hand, the banks help the cash flow with flexible regulations, technical background, client friendly ways, on the other hand, the banks charge the clients with different fees during the transactions which make them interested."[56]

The Financial Action Task Force establishes transparency requirements for beneficiaries of companies, with countries required to obtain reliable and timely information (Recommendation No. 24), including information on trusts, settlors, trustees, and beneficiaries (Recommendation No. 25). Financial Information Units (FIUs) must have timely access to financial and administrative information, either directly or indirectly, as well as information from law enforcement authorities in order to fully perform their functions, including analysis of suspicious statements on operations (Recommendations Nos. 26, 27, 29, and 31).

It recommends restricting or banning the physical transportation of currency (Recommendation No. 32), but says nothing about the cards and forms of payment mentioned here.

Online sites accept debit cards, checks, and wire transfers, the predominant form of payment is credit card, although some large banks and credit card companies have refused to transfer money to offshore accounts because of the potential for fraud. Susan Ormand reveals to her turn that, in case of online gambling, bookmakers are circumventing "these efforts by encouraging bettors to use debit cards or payments services like PayPal, NetTeller, or E-CashWorld."[57]

When money laundering is considered through Internet, it is important to mention about e-money, that is, the financial systems with capabilities to transfer economic value digitally through electronic patterns, applying the Internet's technological advances to commerce.

According to Jonathan P. Straub, "electronic money (e-money) is a byproduct of the Internet and consumer demand for transactional efficiency. E-money facilitates money laundering through unregulated, non-financial entities, making the application of current laundering laws ineffective."[58]

[56] Nagi and Mezei [31, p. 146].

[57] Ormand [32, pp. 451–452].

[58] Straub [33, p. 516].

Cryptoassets[59] or cryptocurrencies, also named virtual currencies, like bitcoins,[60] are digital money issued and transmitted over a network (cryptocurrency network), that is, a network among friends which allows payment by any party to another. These transactions are connected to the Internet, and therefore communicate with other equipment, picking up or transferring signals from different regions. The signals are recorded in a public history listing (called a blockchain) once validated by the system.

By talking about cryptoassets or cryptocurrencies as virtual money and blockchain as a technology draws a line between the two, when, in fact, they are really deeply intertwined. Christina Comben states that "cryptocurrencies are essentially digital assets that can be sent on peer-to-peer basis with no need for a central authority acting as a source of trust (and taking fees). We all know by now that not all cryptocurrencies are created equal. There are plenty of bogus tokens out there. There are also plenty of excellent projects with inane tokens that have nothing to do with their business tokens. Then there are other cryptocurrencies like Bitcoin and Ethereum that are more than just digital forms of money." Taking about blockchain, the same author deems that "going past the notion of a chain of blocks connected to each other, and putting hash pointers and Merkle trees to one side, essentially, blockchains are record-keepers shared over thousands of computers. Any change to one record needs to be accepted by all of the systems contained within the network. All transactions and movements of cryptocurrencies are recorded on blockchains, which cuts out the need for a bank. Cryptocurrencies are a subset of the broader range of applicabilities of blockchain technologies, but they are also extremely tightly connected."[61]

The bitcoin network began on January 3, 2009, with the issuance of the first bitcoins by Satoshi Nakamoto. Owners transfer bitcoins by sending them to another bitcoin address using a client program or website for the purpose. The transfer is accomplished by digital signature and connected to the public encryption key of the next owner. Bitcoin records all data necessary to make the transaction valid in the blockchain.

A bitcoin customer uses a wallet of bitcoin addresses, and is free to create any number of bitcoin addresses. Hence, if user "A" wishes to transfer bitcoins to user "B," he will create a transaction message with instructions to send part of his balance to "B," and the transaction will be validated by "A" using a wallet key. Because

---

[59] A cryptoasset (or cryptocurrency) is a digital asset designed to work as a medium of exchange that uses strong cryptography to secure financial transactions, control the creation of additional units, and verify the transfer of assets. Cryptocurrencies are a kind of alternative currency and digital currency (of which virtual currency is a subset). Cryptocurrencies use decentralized control as opposed to centralized digital currency and central banking systems.

[60] According to Danton Bryans, "bitcoin's inventor, Satoshi Nakamoto, sought to create a system that would solve several issues with traditional fiat currency systems. Cash and Bitcoin transactions are similarly anonymous or pseudonymous, but Bitcoin does not require face-to-face transactions" (see Bryans [34], p. 444).

[61] Comben [35].

of its asymmetric cryptographic method, only owners of a private key can create a valid signature to enable bitcoins to be sent from their wallet.

Using Bitcoins Exchange Services one can buy or sell gift cards and exchange them for bitcoins.[62] Important to mention that bitcoin has been adopted by businesses and organizations with the lack of government intervention. To Danton Bryans "as the U.S. government previously stopped currencies and virtual currencies that the government found to violate U.S. currency laws, and stopped companies that operate under state laws in conflict with federal law, the lack of any such action by the U.S. government indicates that it either tolerates Bitcoin as un unregulated virtual currency or believes that current laws adequately regulate Bitcoin."[63] The same occurs in Brazil.

In the USA, "the first legislative attempt to fight money laundering was the Bank Secrecy Act—BSA, with established reporting requirements for institutions that might be used as money laundering vehicles. In this way, Danton Bryans revealed that BSA effectively made certain institutions accountable for keeping records of transactions in excess of a $10,000 threshold when that institution might benefit from transaction and processing fees due to laundering activities. These requirements gave investigators a paper trail to prosecute launderers and to find possible tax evaders. However, launderers quickly began circumventing the BSA by breaking large transactions into smaller transactions of less than $10,000, using financial service providers outside the scope of the BSA, and using wire transfer systems to circumvent regulators until new regulations passed in 1995. After 1995, financial institutions required to record and report under the BSA included many nonbanking entities classified as money service businesses—MSBs. After a refinement in 2011, this group includes: (1) dealers in foreign exchange, (2) check cashers, (3) issuers of traveler's checks or money orders, (4) providers of prepaid access, (5) money transmitters, (6) the U.S. Postal Service, and (7) sellers of prepaid access. Finally, the 2001 USA PATRIOT ACT ('Patriot Act') extended the already broad definition of money transmitter to any person or business who facilitates money transfer. On March 18, 2013, FinCEN issued interpretive guidance for applying the BSA to virtual currencies."[64]

In 2019, California introduced a bill (n. 1489) to regulate bitcoin and crypto businesses, requiring companies to go through an approval process to conduct crypto-related activities in the state. The scope is to protect consumers against crypto-related scams and frauds while also supporting innovation.[65]

Important to say, in this way, that FinCEN don't treat virtual currencies as equivalent to real currencies and it would treat some users of virtual currencies as money transmitter, but not considering virtual currency users as providers or sellers of

---

[62] See, for example, http://www.bitcoinexchange.cc/aboutcompany.html. Accessed 25 May 2018.

[63] Bryans [34, p. 454].

[64] *Ibidem,* pp. 456–458.

[65] see The Daily Hodl. News and Insight for the Divigal Economy, Feb 28, 2019, in https://dailyhodl.com/2019/02/28/california-introduces-new-bill-to-regulate-bitcoin-and-crypto-businesses-calls-for-50000-penalty-for-violations/, accessed on May 22, 2019

prepaid access or dealers in foreign exchange. Once the user provides money transmission services, that user becomes a virtual currency exchanger, and administrator, or both and must comply with MSB requirements. So, users that merely use the virtual currency for real or virtual goods are not subject to money transmitter regulation, unless that user sells virtual currency for real currency or its equivalent.

On July 18, 2018, U.S. Lawmakers discussed the extent to which the United States government should consider cryptocurrencies as money and the potential domestic and global uses for cryptocurrencies. The Subcommittee on Monetary Policy and Trade Hearing entitled "The Future of Money: Digital Currency" evaluated the merits of any uses by central banks of cryptocurrencies, and discussed the future of both cryptocurrencies and physical cash.[66]

Discussing the legality of virtual currencies and how they should be regulated is an important initiative to regulatory agencies understand how to better incorporate virtual currencies to the traditional economy and how to avoid the problems related to them. The hearing is an attempt to pave the way for future cryptoassets regulation in the USA. Digital assets can be seen whether as an investment vehicle or as rival to cash or other forms of money. Lawmakers in the USA are keeping close tabs on cryptoassets in order to introduce, in the future, official regulation. The hearing in the U.S. Congress does not automatically mean that cryptoassets will be legitimized as a payment method making it legal tender. At least, it is believed that regulators will maintain a positive stance toward cryptocurrencies.

This can lead to the creation of virtual database for issuing electronic money, in which users may check the coins once issued. So instead of withdrawing an amount in bills from a bank, a financial institution could be asked to coin (renew) a block of records identified by a hash value, which can be used for identification and integrity verification, and occasional returns to the bank.

This currency, according to Alaric Snell-Pym, runs into two difficulties. The coins are traceable using their unique serial numbers (much handier than the series of numbers printed on bills) and it is not easy to spot someone using the same coin twice since, consisting as they do of numbers, one could make as many copies as one wished. A number of systems have developed cryptographic techniques to prevent such duplication, complicating the transfer of funds to the point of making it difficult to ensure security.[67]

Problems surface once you notice that it is possible to use different addresses, with one of them used only once for a single transfer. Someone knowledgeable could create new addresses and transfer money amounts to a number of other addresses through several identities or pseudonyms, unless there were some tracking of Internet records, to analyze the transaction from a global perspective. By checking network connections over the World Wide Web, one could verify spending on transactions and know to what addresses they were directed.

E-money can be as anonymous as cash, so there has to be some method or means of breaking that anonymity and tracking the flow of money. There must be some

[66] See U.S. House of Representatives Committee Repository [36].

[67] In Snell-Pym [37].

form of electronic tracking, even easier than for cash money, which simply passes from hand to hand. Cryptocurrencies (like bitcoins) are a transparent means of transacting compared to the existing system. But even though it features the use of fake names or nicknames, identifying its users does not seem all that impossible. Hence, if a trafficker is using a given e-money address, it is possible to download all data on the person using that address and download the entire graph of parties with whom that trafficker has dealings. It might be possible to obtain information on all of his or her clientele. So this medium may not be as anonymous as it appears at first sight.

On the federal level in the USA, there is the Electronic Funds Transfer Act that really deals with consumer transactions. Regulation "E" gives the Federal Reserve the right to regulate those transactions, and the Uniform Commercial Code article 4A deals only with commercial credit transactions. For Valerie J. McNevin, the Office of the Comptroller of the Currency/U.S. Department of Treasury—OCC "promulgated some interpretive rules allowing, for the first time, national banks to sell and market excess capacity in computer equipment and computer lines,"[68] opening up US markets for strong encryption products.

New currencies currently exist and are being further developed due to consumer demand which can be deemed the greatest factor in any commercial success, including payment systems. The negative consequences of widespread use of e-money and its use as a money-laundering tool make it very difficult to regulate due to its necessary international incidence. The use of cryptoassets arouses the interest of governmental enforcement agencies that try to understand how they work and fit the models of understanding and regulation of the current financial system. The Brazilian Internal Revenue Service issued the Normative Instruction 1888 on May 07, 2019, that regulated the obligation of providing information by individuals and legal entities in case of transactions involving cryptoassets, under penalty of fine.[69]

Still, one can easily imagine, as mentioned by Jon Manotis,[70] someone structuring an anonymous bitcoin structure with many branches in order to hide their transactions in case of financial companies refuse to process Internet untraceable transactions. These companies will not want to risk being a part of an illegal activity if they can be deemed involved in it. In case of using cards from foreign bank accounts, there is the possibility to take action against these accounts by the Treasury or Justice Department, using the US Patriot Act.[71]

A police investigation, triggered in Brazil in March 13, 2018, discovered a bitcoin scheme to launder dirty money in a money laundering and bidding fraud schemes in the penitentiary office involving officials linked to the former governor Sérgio Cabral arrested for corruption. Involved in Operation Our bread ("Pão Nosso"), deploying Car Wash ("LavaJato") in Rio de Janeiro, criminals used an

---

[68] McNevin et al. [38].

[69] See Mendes, Guilherme, JOTA Website, in https://www.jota.info/tributos-e-empresas/tributario/receita-federal-in-criptoativos-09052019, published on May 9, 2019, accessed on May 22, 2019.

[70] Matonis [39].

[71] In some way, see Ormand [32, p. 452].

innovative device to launder money, according to the Brazilian Federal Revenue Service. For the first time, the task force in Rio de Janeiro found bitcoin operations. There were four operations, according to Revenue, totaling $80,000 dollars (R$ 300,000) in virtual currency. What has caught Brazilian authorities attention in this operation is that there were operations involving bitcoin. This was really a novelty there. People were trying to sophisticate in some way, maybe trying to fly below the Federal Revenue radar, the Central Bank (Federal Reserve Bank), and Brazilian Financial Intelligence Unit, Conselho de Controle de Atividades Financeiras—COAF. The idea of the criminals was to receive money overseas "using an instrument that is not regulated in most countries" through remittances abroad.[72]

G20 Finance Ministers and Central Bank Governors at their meeting in Buenos Aires on 21–22 July, 2018, recognized the real and growing money laundering and terrorist financing risks from cryptoassets and the urgency of action to address these risks; they reiterated their determination to fight money laundering and terrorist financing, and they called on the Financial Action Task Force—FATF to take further action to counter proliferation financing.

The FATF President, Marshall Billingslea, briefed Finance Ministers and Central Bank Governors on these risks and highlighted the work FATF will be doing under the U.S. Presidency. The G20 asked the FATF to clarify in October 2018 how its standards apply to cryptoassets.

The communique highlights G20 countries' individual and collective commitment to the full and effective implementation of the FATF Standards. Under the U.S. Presidency of the FATF, the FATF prioritizes work on combating the financing of the proliferation of weapons of mass destruction, further strengthening efforts to combat the financing of terrorism and taking action to promote a more consistent and effective regulation of virtual currencies and other cryptoassets.

The FATF recognized the urgent need to clarify how the FATF standards apply to virtual currency providers and related businesses, including for customer due diligence, fund transfers, supervision, and enforcement.[73]

Unlike anonymous cryptocurrencies or e-money which nowadays are impossible to be banned, credit cards and wire transfers for the use of offshores sites made obsolete any domestic monetary control scheme. Innovations needed to be encouraged and allowed to flourish rather than being shut down.

The mere fact that even e-money could be electronically traceable does not preclude its being successfully used for illegal ends, while it has the potential to remove the existing impediments of the traditional payment mechanisms like lack immediacy, security, and anonymity. As more of these types of services become available online, the transactions become more complex and there is greater opportunity for apparently unrelated, off-the-grid value exchanges. Both encryption and electronic money make it almost impossible to prevent serious crimes via the Internet.

Based on a statement of Emery S. Kobor, it is a need to seek to channeling the benefits of technological and geopolitical change to increase access to economic

[72] Coelho [40].

[73] Financial Action Task Force [41].

opportunity, as well as to work to limit opportunities for corruption, financial crime, and terrorism.[74] Also seeing benefits of the emerging technology for beneficial or malicious use, it can be cited Kavid Singh.[75]

The interest in regulating cryptocurrencies stems from the process of tracing cash flows in encrypted mode and this is difficult and more confusing because of the lack of communication between people in the real environment and virtual currency accounts, the existence of obstacles to tracing, such as encryption and anonymizing mixers, and possibilities of creating an unlimited number of accounts. Hence there is a need to well-regulate them.

Allowing account-based or non-account based financial services to be offered by businesses that are not regulated as banks can extend the physical reach of the formal financial system, but requires a new approach to regulation that applies safeguards on the basis of potential risk. The technology represents the transferring of risk, cost, and responsibility on to the consumer, away from banks, and requires global standardization, that is, a global regulatory reform[76] that moves forward into a free market where privacy, safety, and soundness are benefits well-recognized almost exclusively within banking system due to its strong regulation.

As stated by Richard A. Posner, the principal issue for policy is the substantive merit of the law being enforced. The clearer it is that the forbidden conduct is antisocial, the more willing we are to allow the government regulation.[77]

Traditional money-laundering control measures have failed to prevent electronic money laundering. "Existing law enacted to prevent money laundering do not consider the implications of digital money and thus will fail to prevent money laundering through digital payment systems."[78] In fact, by enabling individuals to transfer money without using traditional financial institutions, digital payment systems eliminate the effectiveness of law.

To Jonathan P. Straub, "simply subjecting the e-money transfers to reporting regulations is ineffective because the reporting regulations create an audit trail that only leads to an anonymous transferor. Law enforcement authorities will not have

[74] Kobor [42, p. 316].

[75] See Singh [43, p. 63].

[76] Gail Bronson deems that "a secured transaction of information possesses the following five characteristics: (1) identification of the parties, (2) privacy, (3) authentication, (4) integrity, and (5) non-repudiation. Identification of the parties is the process of verifying the identity of the sender of a message. In public key cryptography, digital signatures provide that identification. Privacy is assurance that communications can be conducted without fear of eavesdropping by unauthorized parties. This is, again, achieved through encryption. Authentication is proof of sender and recipient identity (through digital signatures). A digital signature is an unforgeable piece of data asserting that the named person wrote or otherwise agreed to the attached massage. Integrity of transmitted data is ensured if the data is intact and undamaged, and no one has added or deleted any data from the package during its transmission. Non-repudiation is proof that someone has signed a contract for certain obligations that cannot be denied later. Again, digital signatures are relevant" (see Bronson [44]).

[77] Posner [45, p. 52].

[78] See Hoffmahn [46, pp. 855–856].

the ability to identify suspects because the encryption process creates anonymity for the transferor."[79] He proposes that law enforcement officials must have access to decryption keys to legitimately pursue a suspicious transaction's audit trail because those officials are unable to determine who or what is involved in the transaction since they do not have access to the key used to decode the transmission. So, it would be important to implement a universal encryption key, or create a key escrow agency to hold duplicates of active cryptographic keys.

In the regulation it must be ensured the security of the mechanism whether it is or not considered any payment system. It is relevant to the encryption with authentication through digital signatures that ensures the link between the payer and the payee. So, strong encryption technology can be able to facilitate every phase of money-laundering cycle, since it is possible to avoid financial transaction reporting system, and without the assistance or intervention of third parties such as banks or financial institutions.

Digital currency exchanges, as said by Catherine Martin Christopher, "frequently possess more information about their users, even Bitcoin users, than the Bitcoin software retains. Bitcoin transactions are recorded in the code of the bitcoins themselves, but the only information retained is the recipient's Bitcoin address and the amount of the transfer. Although this transaction ledger is essentially public, considering Bitcoin addresses can be anonymous and disposable, the published information is quite minimal. Other exchange mediums, however, may collect and retain significant amounts of other information; these clues can be used, along with transaction patterns, to identify individuals. Law enforcement should be partnering with such digital currency exchanges to wring what information can be wrung in order to prosecute the launderers and criminal themselves."[80]

Nowadays, the benefits of using cryptoasset (currency) transactions essentially boil down to the fact that they do not incur bank fees or credit card fees. Individuals use cryptocurrency as a weapon in evading taxes by converting their income into virtual currency and transferring the same to an offshore account, adding barriers to the issue. Important to highlight here the statement of Kelsey L. Penrose, who considers the need to ensure the protection of the country's financial system,[81] probably (I add) because of the fear of the capacity of them to revolutionize financial markets.

The importance of institutions (including financial institutions), and their stability, reflects the need for clear rules, reducing uncertainties, and the effectiveness of such rules is decisive for the quality of the economy and for the resulting economic project.

As stated by Angela Walch, citing Janet Yellen, "the costs and benefits of developing new statutes or regulations related to digital currencies should be weighed carefully. New regulation, such as the creation of special licenses for digital currency providers, may work to strengthen the soundness of virtual currency schemes

[79] Straub [33, pp. 530–531].

[80] Christopher [47, pp. 35–36].

[81] Penrose [48, p. 547].

and increase public trust in the products, as some may refrain from investing in or using digital currencies due to a perceived legal uncertainty and/or lack of consumer protection. On the other hand, new regulation would need to be flexible enough to address effectively the evolving nature of digital currency systems and technology *while not stifling innovation*."[82]

In other terms, it is not recommended to overregulate virtual currency and regulators must work to understand it before they regulate. Robert Stokes ponders the danger in regulating virtual currencies since it could be thought of as an over-zealous approach to something which would appear to be of little practical use to a prospective launderer.[83]

Traditional money-laundering schemes and cryptocurrencies laundering schemes, however, are similar in their intents, but are clearly different in their regulations. So, this discrepancy creates a *legal blind spot*,[84] which criminal can easily exploit.

As long as businesses administering cryptocurrencies are a particularly useful example of new money businesses, they may encompass trading in cryptocurrencies, or wallets for such currencies. In accordance with the positioning of Benjamin Lo, "accepting and transmitting anything of value that substitutes for currency makes a person a money transmitter under the regulations implementing the Bank Secrecy Act—BSA. The mere fact that the value transmitted is not represented as physical media, nor issued by a sovereign entity, is not sufficient to exempt of being valuable and substitutable for conventional currency, and that suffices to bring it under the scope of the BSA"[85] or other regulation.

In Europe, cryptoexchanges can be included as financial institutions if they transmit money or representations of monetary value by any means, according to Banking Consolidation (Directive 2006/48/EC, points 4–6 of Annex 1): issuing and acquiring payment instruments and money remittance. Since the definition for payment instruction considers any personalized device and/or set of procedures agreed between the payment service user and the payment service provider and used by the payment service user in order to initiate a payment order, cryptoexchanges fall under it but can be included within the ambit of the Payment Services Directive and also the Money Laundering Regulations, article 4 (13).[86] Point 5 of the Annex, since cryptocurrencies exchanges are not a payment service in this sense (currency is exchanged for what is in effect: a bearer payment instrument): issuing and adminis-

[82] Walch [49, p. 891].

[83] Stokes [50, p. 232].

[84] Term taken from Brian Monroe by Sheng Zhou. See Zhou [51, p. 134].

[85] See Lo [52, pp. 123–124].

[86] "A payment service where funds are received from a payer, without any payment accounts being created in the name of the payer or the payee, for the sole purpose of transferring a corresponding amount to a payee or to another payment service provider acting on behalf of he payee, and/or where such funds are received on behalf of and made available to the payee."

tering other means of payment which are not covered by the Payment Services Directive.[87]

Avoiding crime requires encrypted wire transfers among financial institutions over a secure network in a way that every transaction can be traced and anonymity is almost extinct. Standardize licensing requirements at the Financial Intelligence Unit or directly to the Treasury Department, by acknowledging e-money as forms of international legal currency (which requires cryptocurrency exchangers to abide regulations); including entities dealing in digital currencies as subjects to MSBs' regulations; maintaining identifying records of customers (personal registration through identifying information); detecting the occurrence of an electronic money transfer through tokens programmed to notify law enforcement bodies every time an amount transferred exceeded a certain threshold; programming electronic tokens to keep track of the transactions in which they are used; limiting the number of transactions or its transferability could be used to prevent online crimes, and law enforcement authorities must have access to cryptographic keys because without access to the content of ciphertext, law enforcement bodies cannot determine the transmission's origin, destination, or whether it includes digital money,[88] requiring virtual wallet providers to gather and share information about account holders in order to stop tax evasion.

It is relevant to financial institutions and Designated Non-Financial Business and Professions—DNFBP to design and implement requirement that must be well described to avoid an invitation to fail. Richard K. Gordon recommends that the private sector should report certain client profiling data and records of all financial transactions. To him, financial intelligence should be required to use, to the extent possible, empirical analysis, making results should be far better than the current system.[89]

The governments should keep in mind the possibilities of limiting the value of electronic cash that can be put on smart cards and Internet-based accounts and limiting the number of peer-to-peer transactions. So the governments should work to be sure (1) that electronic cash systems are engineered to produce an audit trail; (2) that the trail can be decrypted on a showing of probable cause by use of the Clipper Chip; and (3) that the trail can be followed by continuing efforts toward international cooperation.[90]

It is essential the clarity of the government's need to be able, under certain circumstances, to gain access to the identities of the people who are behind bank accounts. Crime rate can be reduced by increasing the probability of being caught for money laundering and the precedent crime, increasing the punishment for money

[87] See Stokes [50, p. 228].

[88] Key escrow agencies can provide an important solution to this problem by furnishing law enforcement authorities with cryptographic keys to decode suspicious electronic transmissions within sufficient time to detect online crimes, and money laundering.

[89] Gordon [53, p. 564].

[90] In this way, see Welling and Rickman [54, p. 327].

laundering, and by increasing the transaction costs of money laundering. All these factors must influence a stricter anti-money laundering policy.

E-money products have only just begun to take their place in the global economy as an alternative form of currency and must be addressed by regulators in order to avoid becoming a substantial threat to anti-money laundering worldwide efforts. The regulators need, according to Yen-Te Wu, "to recognize that the essence of financial technology is the integration of emerging technologies and financial services, and need to adopt classified and differentiated management in the regulatory environment and adopt a 'control of neutrality' and 'principle-based supervision' model, in order to not limit market participants' intention of investing in financial technology and the market competition."[91]

It is important the balance among the stability of the existing financial system, financial innovation and a positive interaction between the financial industry and the technology. A supervisory and legal system should not hinder innovation. At least, by assuring the tracking of the money, some progress can be done.

References

1. Financial Action Task Force – FATF. Retrieved June 21, 2018, from http://www.fatf-gafi.org/publications/fatfrecommendations/documents/fatf-recommendations.html
2. Garzón, J. C. (2008). *Mafia & co. – The criminal networks in Mexico, Brazil, and Colombia*. Retrieved 28 September, 2018, from https://www.wilsoncenter.org/sites/default/files/mafiaandcompany_reducedsize.pdf
3. Olson, E. (2012, Mar 29). *Considering new strategies for confronting organized crime in Mexico*. Wilson Center. Retrieved 28 September, 2018, from https://www.wilsoncenter.org/publication/considering-new-strategies-for-confronting-organized-crime-mexico
4. Two Top Cartels at War in Mexico. (2012). *Express*. Washington, DC: a publication of the Washington Post, p. 6.
5. Messineo, F. (2010). Máfia e crime de colarinho branco: Uma nova abordagem de análise. In *Novas tendências da criminalidade transnacional mafiosa*. São Paulo: Unesp Ed.
6. Andre, C. (2012). *Police Car is hit by gunshots on the east side of SP*. Retrieved 2 August, 2018, from www.1.folha.uol.com.br/cotidiano/1109151-carro-da-policia-civil-e-atingido-por-tiros-na-zona-leste-de-sp.shtml
7. Hiller, J. S., & Cook, D. L. (1997). From clipper ships to clipper chips: The evolution of payment systems for electronic commerce. *Journal of Law and Commerce, 17*, 53–98.
8. Schopper, M. D. (2002). Internet gambling, electronic cash & money laundering: The unintended consequences of a monetary control scheme. *Chapman Law Review, 5*, 303–330.
9. Cohen, D., & Reveal, J. (2018). *Beneficial owner new account rules: What FinTech AML program managers and their financial institutions need to know*. Retrieved August 10, 2018, from https://www.fintechlawblog.com/2018/04/beneficial-owner-new-account-rules-what-fintech-aml-program-managers-and-their-financial-institutions-need-to-know/
10. Raiborn, C., Schorg, C., & Bubrig, C. (2003). Guarding against E-laundering of dirty money. *Commercial Lending Review, 18*, 36–39.
11. Thompson, E. (2010). The relationship between tax deductions and the market for unprovenanced antiquities. *Columbia Journal of Law & the Arts, 33*, 241.

[91] Wu [55, p. 252].

12. Cuomo, A. M. *Internal controls and financial accountability for not-for-profit boards*. Charities Bureau. Retrieved August 20, 2018, from http://www.oag.state.ny/bureaus/charities/about.html
13. Charities. New York State. Retrieved 29 August, 2018, from www.charitiesnys.com or www.charitiesnys.com/pdfs/statute_booklet.pdf
14. NASCONET website. Retrieved 2 June, 2018, from https://www.nasconet.org/
15. Smith, M. R. Fremont-Smith. Terror outfit-turned 'charity' JuD set to come under Pak Central Bank scanner. *Asian News International*, 03/13/2012. Retrieved 19 June, 2018, from www.lexis.com
16. Marpakwar, P. State forms cells to detect source of terror funds. *Times of India*. Retrieved 19 June, 2018, from www.westlaw.com
17. Raja D., & Samuel, J. Ten means to put an end to black money issue. *Economic Times* (India). Copyright 2011 Bennett, Coleman & Co., Ltd., The Financial Times Limited. Retrieved November 18, 2011.
18. Government plans 'umbrella law' to tighten scrutiny and regulation of religious trusts and NGOs. *Economic Times* (India). Copyright 2011. Bennett, Coleman & Co. Ltd. 05/03/2011. Retrieved 22 June, 2018, from www.westlaw.com
19. Soni, P. Government plans 'umbrella law' to tighten scrutiny and regulation of religious trusts and NGOs. *Economic Times* (India). Copyright 2011. Bennett, Coleman & Co. Ltd. 05/03/2011. Retrieved 22 June, 2018, from www.westlaw.com
20. Shah, P. *Trusts, NGOs under ambit of money-laundering law*. Business standard, 11/19/2009, 2009 WLNR 23270783. Retrieved 23 June, 2018, from www.westlaw.com
21. Palak, S. *Trusts, NGOs under ambit of money-laundering law*. Business Standard, Mumbai. 2009 WLNR 23270783. Retrieved 18 November, 2009.
22. Bickerton, R. (2010). Good cause. *Canadian Underwriter.* 2009 WLNR 26429376. Retrieved 23 June, 2018, from www.westlaw.com
23. Wyngaard, R. (2012). Policy framework on NPO law. *International Journal of Civil Society Law, 10*(4), 22–23.
24. Linn, C. J. (2007). One-hour money laundering: Prosecuting unlicensed money transmitting businesses using section 1960. *United States Attorney's Bulletin*. Vol. 55, No. 5, Washington, DC.
25. Goddard, T. (2012, Oct 13). *How to fix a broken border: Follow the money*. Tucson Sentinel. Retrieved 28 July, 2018, from http://www.tucsonsentinel.com/opinion/report/101312_goddard_border/how-fix-broken-border-follow-money/
26. Petterchak, J. W. (2017). In defence of hawala: Rethinking regulation of customary banking. *SOAS Law Journal, 4*(1), 107–141.
27. Pathak, R. (2004). The obstacles to regulating the hawala. *Fordham International Law Journal, 27*, 2007–2061.
28. Shetterly, D. (2005). Starving the terrorists of funding: How the United States treasury is fighting the war on terror. *Regent University Law Review, 18*, 327–348.
29. FinCen Website. (2017). *FinCen fines BTC-e virtual currency exchange $110 million for facilitating ransomware, dark net drug sales*. Retrieved September 1, 2018, from https://www.fincen.gov/news/news-releases/fincen-fines-btc-e-virtual-currency-exchange-110-million-facilitating-ransomware
30. Rueda, A. (2001). The implications os strong encryption technology on money laundering. *Albany Law Journal of Science & Technology, 12*, 1–95.
31. Nagi, H. Z. A., & Mezei, K. (2016). The organised criminal phenomenon on the internet. *Journal of Eastern-European Criminal Law, 2*, 137–149.
32. Ormand, S. (2004). Pending U.S. legislation to prohibit offshore internet gambling may proliferate money laundering. *Law and Business Review of the Americas, 10*, 447–454.
33. Straub, J. P. (2002). The prevention of e-money laundering: Tracking the exclusive audit trail. *Suffolk Transnational Law Review, 25*, 515–534.

34. Bryans, D. (2014). Bitcoin and money laundering: Mining for an effective solution. *Indiana Law Journal, 89*, 441–472.
35. Comben, C. *Cryptocurrency vs. blockchain: What's the difference?* See cryptomode site. Retrieved 2 August, 2018, from https://cryptomode.com/cryptocurrency-vs-blockchain-whats-the-difference/
36. U.S. House of Representatives Committee Repository calendar. Retrieved 1 August, 2018, from https://docs.house.gov/Committee/Calendar/ByEvent.aspx?EventID=108581
37. Snell-Pym, A. *Bitcoin security*. Retrieved 3 August, 2018, from http://www.snell-pym.org.uk/archives/2011/05/12/bitcoin-security/
38. McNevin, V., et al. (1997). Financial services: Security, privacy, and encryption. *Boston University Journal of Science & Technology Law, 3*, 99.
39. Matonis, J. *The monetary future at the intersection of free banking, cryptography, and digital currency. Thoughts on bitcoin laundering*. 05/13/2011. Retrieved 8 March, 2018, from http://themonetaryfuture.blogspot.com/2011/05/thoughts-on-bitcoin-laundering.html
40. Coelho Henrique. (2018). *Esquema de fraude no sistema penitenciário do RJ usou bitcoin, diz Receita*. G1. Retrieved 5 July, 2018, from https://g1.globo.com/rj/rio-de-janeiro/noticia/pf-detalha-esquema-do-pao-nosso-que-prendeu-delegado-e-ex-secretario-de-sergio-cabral.ghtml
41. Financial Action Task Force. (2018). *FATF report to the G20 finance ministers and central bank governors*. Retrieved 2 September, 2018, from http://www.fatf-gafi.org/publications/financingofproliferation/documents/g20-fm-cbg-july-2018.html
42. Kobor, E. S. (2013). The role of anti-money laundering law in mobile money systems in developing countries. *Washington Journal of Law, Technology & Arts, 8*, 303–316.
43. Singh, K. (2015). The new Wild West: Preventing money laundering in the bitcoin network. *Northwestern Journal of Technology and Intellectual Property, 13*(1), 36–64.
44. Bronson, Gail et al. Financial services: Security, privacy, and encryption (1997), Boston University Journal of Science & Technology Law. 99, 3.
45. Posner, R. A. (1978). Privacy, secrecy, and regulation. *Buffalo Law Review, 28*(1), 1–52.
46. Hoffmahn, C. D. (1998). Encrypted digital cash transfers: Why traditional money laundering controls may fail without uniform cryptography regulations. *Fordham International Law Journal, 21*, 799–860.
47. Christopher, C. M. (2014). Whack-a-mole: Why prosecuting digital currency exchanges won't stop online money laundering. *Lewis & Clark Law Review, 18*(1), 1–36.
48. Penrose, K. L. (2014). Banking on bitcoin: Applying anti-money laundering and money transmitter laws. *North Carolina Banking Institute, 18*, 529–551.
49. Walch, A. (2015). The bitcoin blockchain as financial market infrastructure: A consideration of operational risk. *New York University Journal, Legislation & Public Policy, 18*, 837–893.
50. Stokes, Robert. Virtual money laundering. The case of bitcoin and the linden dollar. Information & Communications Technology Law, vol. 21, n° 3, 2012, p. 221-236.
51. Zhou, S. (2014). Bitcoin laundromats for dirty money: The Bank Secrecy Act's (BSA). Inadequacies in regulating and enforcing money laundering laws over virtual currencies and the internet. *Journal of Law Cyber Warfare, 3*, 103–142.
52. Lo, B. (2016). Fatal fragments: The effect of money transmission regulation on payments innovation. *The Yale Journal of Law & Technology, 18*, 111–147.
53. Gordon, R. K. (2011). Losing the war against dirty money: Rethinking global standards on preventing money laundering and terrorism financing. *Duke Journal of comparative & International Law, 21*, 503–565.
54. Welling, S. N., & Rickman, A. G. (1998). Cyberlaundering: The risks, the responses. *Florida Law Review, 50*, 295–327.
55. Wu, Y.-T. (2017). FinTech innovation and anti-money laundering compliance. *National Taiwan University Law Review, 12*, 201–258.

Chapter 5
Online Sales

Commerce over the Internet has grown significantly, and it is common for consumers to buy goods, benefiting themselves by reducing search costs and providing easily accessible information about seller reputation and product quality.

On the other hand, businesses, with the rapidly evolving worldwide market due to Internet, must open their doors to fundamental change, while consumers must put faith in the new electronic stores. Because of ease, convenience, and speed in online negotiations, electronic commerce became commonplace.

To Maricel P. Montano, "the 'explosive growth' of the Internet has increased the ease with which businesses can be formed and engage in commerce. E-commerce enables sellers from any location to sell goods or services to any other location without maintaining an actual physical store."[1]

Important to mention that by greasing the wheels of commerce, the Internet has provided significant reductions in cost and greater access to more products for more people around the world, and a dark side of it has emerged.

Unscrupulous and nefarious individuals are aware about the benefits of this market for them who want to keep their illegal activities in full anonymity.

For instance, they have entered this market, eager to sell tainted, expensive, and poor quality drugs or prescription pharmaceuticals to anyone with a credit card and the willingness to pay. Besides of being an illicit and increasingly easy means of profit, it has become a foundation for additional criminal activity.[2]

The need to attract more interested in negotiating and seizing the opportunities are well synthesized with what happened at the dinner of English star David Beckham.

In fact, in 2007, he was in New Zealand with his team (LA Galaxy) to play an exhibition match against local team (Wellington Phoenix). While in Wellington he dined at Nando's restaurant in Courtenay Place. Moments after he had finished his meal, a mystery customer swiped the football star's cutlery. The haul included a

[1] Montano [1, p. 386].

[2] See Liang and Mackey [2, p. 126].

F. M. De Sanctis, *Technology-Enhanced Methods of Money Laundering*,
https://doi.org/10.1007/978-3-030-18330-1_5

half-eaten corn cob, a knife and fork with pieces of food still on them, a glass, and a half-filled soft drink bottle. The items were subsequently listed on online auction site Trade Me for sale. It is unclear what amount(s) the seller actually received for these items. The soft drink bottle at one stage had allegedly attracted a bid of NZD 5000. The partially gnawed corn cob failed to attract a bid after being listed for sale for the bargain-basement price of NZC 80. However, as stated by Andrew Maples, it also attracted much comment on the Trade Me website, looking for more corn left.[3]

It is clear that this website (and similar ones) has increased in the volume of trading through online sales and auction sites providing them a low cost, easy, and convenient method of marketing items Websites have provided unparalleled opportunities for people to market their wares and sellers to make more money with no taxation on their profits. Besides the fact of misappropriation of goods that were stolen from the restaurant, authorities must have concern about the underreporting of income from it due to the absence of a comprehensive capital gains tax.

Also, some laws proscribe online frauds, having the Federal Trade Commission—FTC sued to halt a pyramid scheme operated on a company's website,[4] the Securities and Exchange Commission—SEC has pursued a number of fraudulent online marketing schemes.[5]

Also there is a non-protection of personal data because of some not reliable websites, besides considering the number of spam emails and other electronic solicitations that have the potential to entice individuals who may not have had the original intention of purchasing online. There is no way to guarantee the quality of goods that are being purchased, even if they are real or counterfeit.

Online sellers can, according to Maricel P. Montano, "easily register to sell goods on websites by providing very little information to the online platforms. For instance, eBay's registration form asks only for the seller's name, address, telephone number, email address, and date of birth. Moreover, as one researcher found, by performing a search of the Internet using the search engine Google, none of the online trading platforms notified sellers that a Form 1099 would be filed with the IRS, nor did they request that the sellers provide their Taxpayer Identification Numbers—TINs."[6] An Internal Revenue Service—IRS Form 1099 is one of the several IRS tax forms used in the USA, a type of information return that must be filed with the IRS, reporting various kinds of business transactions, other than wages, salaries, and tips (for which Form W-2 is used instead). The form is used to

---

[3] Maples [3, p. 58].

[4] See Shipley [4, p. 23].

[5] 16 The Computer Lawyer 27 (April 1999): summarizing four enforcement actions filed by the SEC on February 25, 1999 against 13 individuals and companies across the country for committing fraud over the Internet and deceiving investors; 17 The Computer Lawyer 31 (February 2000): summarizing a civil fraud action filed by the SEC against 3 residents of Southern California for manipulating the price of stock by spreading false information on Internet financial message boards.

[6] Montano [1, p. 390–391].

report payments to independent contractors, rental property income, income from interest and dividends, sales proceeds, and other miscellaneous income.[7]

Policymakers should well address the problem, being aware and taking actions about these issues, due to unfettered Internet illicit goods sales threatening financial system, public health, tax order, private property, and consumer law.

In the USA, the Food and Drug Administration—FDA is the primary federal agency tasked with addressing the issue of online drug sales, and regulates this industry through enforcement of the Federal Food, Drug, and Cosmetic Act—FDCA, and the Internet Drug Sales Action Plan—IDSAP. The FDA's plan primarily seeks to reduce illegal Internet sales of prescription drugs by: (1) expanding enforcement efforts through increasing monitoring and criminal or civil enforcement actions; (2) partnering with other state and federal agencies and other organizations such as the National Association of Boards of Pharmacy—NABP and Federation of State Medical Boards to more effectively enforce federal and state laws against illegal online sales; and (3) engaging in public outreach to better inform consumers about the dangers of Internet drug sellers.[8] So, the FDA has broad authority to regulate the practice of selling prescription drugs when the sale is done without the supervision of a licensed professional, when connected with health care fraud, and when it involves unapproved, counterfeit, adulterated, or illegal drugs. Getting the Internet pharmacy licensure requires a collection of appropriate clinical information and patient data that otherwise may not be reported or documented for application, renewal, suspension, and termination. Besides this, it would be possible to have the help of the Medical Community in self-policing through guidelines or programs in an attempt to address the issue of rogue online pharmacies.[9]

As stated by Florencia Marotta-Wurgler, "an additional wrinkle in the online world is the widespread use of browsewraps and 'pay now, terms later' (PNTL) contracts. In the former, sellers present their contracts as hyperlinks at the end of a webpage or somewhere in their site with relatively little notice to consumers; in the latter, sellers do not make their contracts available to consumers until *after* they purchase the product. Obviously, lack of notice or delayed disclosure makes it costlier for consumers to become informed about the relevant terms and decreases their ability to comparison shop on this dimension."[10] That is why prescribing mandatory terms, being suspicious of terms of sellers with market power, or requiring increased contract disclosures, and being aware about the risks imposed by online payments are concerns to be addressed by all actors: sellers, consumers, and government bodies. The purpose here is making consumers well informed about contract terms and less vulnerable to seller exploitation.

The issue of illicit Internet sales is also related to financial transactions with all the concerns surrounding the latter ones: the use of chips (covered by private number contracts) and swift (international wire service with stands for Society for

[7] See Internal [5].

[8] Liang and Mackey [2, p. 144].

[9] See Taylor [6, p. 244].

[10] Marotta-Wurgler [7, p. 12].

Worldwide Interbank Financial Telecommunication), in other words, payment orders transmitted electronically over an Internet account. Communications on the Internet must be secure and its users must have confidence in that security. As Janine S. Hiller and Don Lloyd Cook say "officials in government have frequently argued that 'unbreakable' encryption should not be exported and that key recovery techniques should be required because of the danger that pornographers, pedophiles, terrorists, drug dealers and other criminals will use this technology as a means to evade detection."[11]

An important example here is the European law. According to Richard Eccles, talking about the Article 101 of the Treaty on the Functioning of the European Union—TFEU, it "treats selling on the Internet as 'passive' as opposed to 'active sales'. Generally, under the EU competition law regime for vertical agreements, restrictions on active sales can be permitted under the exceptions criteria of Article 101 (3) whilst restrictions on passive sales are almost always prohibited."[12] This means that a restriction on passive selling, including a restriction on Internet selling, is treated as by its nature infringing the competition rules, without needing to demonstrate that it actually has anti-competitive effects. So, a regulatory international system over the Internet must be deemed limited.

A simple, but effectively, tax regime must be conceived by reducing the number of taxing jurisdictions and eliminating the risk of compliance cost growth, allowing online sellers continue without fear of an exhaustive burden of compliance.[13] On the other hand, consumers must be aware that purchasing from unauthorized dealers voids warranty protection[14] and, for that, can get some benefit when buying from authorized dealers what it is important to protect trademark and copyright.

Many issues arise when utilizing electronic commerce and the attendant payment systems. Talking about credit card use for payments, security and cryptography, methods of insuring necessary authenticity, non-repudiation, and information privacy or secrecy is an important topic that impacts all of the Internet payment methods. Although theoretically there is no need for particular software to effect a credit card transaction since the information may be simply transmitted over the computer network between the buyer and seller, in practice, some security measures must be taken to deter the unauthorized interception of this information. In this way, Janine S. Hiller and Don Lloyd Cook state that "a buyer may use encryption to directly forward credit card information over the Internet, but this process may not be practical if the seller does not have the same encryption, and it does not protect the buyer against the fraudulent, impostor merchant."[15] So, it is important to provide a means of payment in response to the development of the new technology methods.

[11] Hiller and Cook [8, p. 87–88].

[12] See Eccles [9, p. 4].

[13] Giving states access to revenues to which they feel entitled but with they are unable to collect.

[14] To Robert W. Payne, "warranties are a key element to your armor against unauthorized dealers." See Payne [10, p. 1].

[15] See Hiller and Cook [8, p. 76].

A single set of rules will bring legal certainty for sellers and buyers in the legal regulation rules and thus help businesses expand their activities to foreign online markets and increase consumer trust through a high level protection.[16] On the other hand, it is important to pay attention to the Online Behavioral Advertising—OBA, sometimes known as profiling or behavioral targeting, used by online publishers and Internet marketers to increase the efficiency and effectiveness of their advertising campaigns. According to Steven C. Bennett, OBA works "by collecting data on a user's behavior on the Internet including browsing habits, search queries, and website viewing history,"[17] making the Federal Trade Commission—FTC and the Department of Commerce—DOC more concerned about the need for intensive regulation.

Notwithstanding the fact that the developmental trajectory and use of the Internet are fragmented on a global level, the creation of a uniform regulatory framework is to Robert M. Kossick crucial to the future growth of e-commerce. So, e-commerce regulations should be harmonized to assure (1) the principle of non-discrimination with respect to the recognition of data messages as writings; (2) technology neutral recognition of signatures; (3) flexible, commercially responsive, and uniform public key infrastructure provisions with respect to certification authority—CA qualifications, binding procedures, certificate lifespans, certificate revocation lists, cross-jurisdictional certificate recognition standards, and the privacy related studies and liabilities of CAs and subscriber; and (4) party freedom to establish transaction specific agreements regarding, *inter alia*, writings, signatures, and certificates.[18]

In other words, a coherent package of legislative changes must be developed by introducing online sales in order to uniform application of future acts, taking into account consumer preferences, business practices and that online sales can affect competition,[19] especially in the retail area, by the reduction of the documentation costs and the impact on distribution costs, the geographical extent of activity area and the asymmetric information. Online transactions must be recognized and create a security interest, that is, an interest in personal property that secures an obligation and arises in favor of the buyer payment rights.

References

1. Montano, M. P. (2010). Can widening the scope of information reporting to include income derived from online sales help to narrow the expanding tax gap. *Southern California Law Review, 83*, 379–423.

[16] In this way Svetlana S. Racheva and Sergey V. Romanchuk. See Racheva and Romanchuk [11, p. 103].

[17] See Bennett [12, p. 899].

[18] Kossick [13, pp. 281–283].

[19] See Stefanescu [14, p. 72].

2. Liang, B. A., & Mackey, T. (2009). Searching for safety: Addressing search engine, website, and provider accountability for illicit online drug sales. *American Journal of Law & Medicine, 35*(1), 125–184.
3. Maples, A. (2012). Online sales and auction sites, isolated transactions and the income tax act 2007 (NZ). *Journal of Australian Taxation, 14*, 57–88.
4. Shipley, D. E. (2001). Liability issues facing online businesses. *The Arkansas Lawyer, 36*(1), 20–30.
5. Internal Revenue service website - IRS.gov. Retrieved July 4, 2018, from https://www.irs.gov/forms-pubs/about-form-1099misc
6. Taylor, E. (2008). Illegal human growth hormone markets: Issues in controlling online drug sales and advertising. *The Journal of Legal Medicine, 29*, 237–253.
7. Marotta-Wurgler, F. (2011). Some realities of online contracting. *Supreme Court Economic Review, 11*, 11–23.
8. Hiller, J. S., & Cook, D. L. (1997). From clipper ships to clipper chips: The evolution of payment systems for electronic commerce. *Journal of Law and Commerce, 17*, 53–98.
9. Eccles, R. (2015). Online sales and competition law controls. *International Journal of Franchising Law, 13*(3), 3–10.
10. Payne, R. W. (2014). Dealing with unauthorized online dealers: Sales of genuine products. *Business Law Today, 2014*, 1–3.
11. Racheva, S. S., & Romanchuk, S. V. (2016). Legal perspectives and obstacles for unified digital contract rules of online sales in the European Union within the digital single market strategy context. *InterEULawEast: Journal for International and European Law, Economics and Market Integrations, 95*, 95–106.
12. Bennett, S. C. (2011). Regulating online behavioral advertising. *The John Marshall Law Review, 44*, 899–962.
13. Kossick, R. M. (2011). The internet in Latin America: New opportunities, developments & challenges. *Florida Journal of International Law, 13*, 263–288.
14. Stefanescu, T. (2014). Competition and online commerce. *Romanian Competition Journal*, 72–82.

Chapter 6
Social Media

The use of social media has reached some ubiquity with Internet access and social media applications on most cell phones and other mobile devices. The ability of businesses to reach the public, also through Internet postings, potentialized the risk of public-relations mishaps. Cathryn Rudolph reveals that some entities feel leery of social media.[1]

Social media has entered the mainstream as a source for personal information about others, and many people have taken notice.

According to Agnieszka McPeak, "as social media technology morphs and develops at an astonishing rate, the rules defining its ethical bounds evolve at a snail's pace. As a result, the advent of new technology like social media tests the adequacy of the existing legal ethics rules."[2]

On the other hand, when we talk about mass media, it can be said that it is a powerful source of information, through which the information and psychological impact on both a wide audience and an individual is carried out. The danger in this case is the fact that "the information containing the propaganda of aggression, harmful models of social behavior to society (criminal awareness of committing specific crimes), affects both the person's awareness, including legal one, i.e. presses gradually and in doses, and the moral and ethical criteria. Thus, in terms of the development of information society consideration of mass media deserves separate attention as a determinant of crime, it is primarily about information and psychological impact of television (hereafter—TV) on the criminal situation."[3] Similar consideration can be done taking into account the Internet, I would add.

In an environment of persistent manifestations of violences for some Internet users, anonymity potentializes examples of future behavior. Under certain circumstances people with latent aggression follow this model. If the demeanor, although aggressive, is socially successful, the aggressor can reach the objective, and then, it

[1] Rudolph [1, p. 187].

[2] See Mcpeak [2, p. 847].

[3] Bailov and Sakhuta [3, p. 15].

F. M. De Sanctis, *Technology-Enhanced Methods of Money Laundering*,
https://doi.org/10.1007/978-3-030-18330-1_6

becomes the standard conduct. So, there is a need of the state control and legal regulation, not only at the legislative but also at the level of the mass media, forming the legal awareness of citizens by establishing the necessary restrictions on broadcasting harmful information in terms of criminal situation.

For a good social media policy, it is important to introduce goals for its usage, and all the actors must agree to comply with these goals, using it on behalf of the publication and for personal purposes. In this sense, the statement of Cathryn Rudolph is important, for whom "a law review's social-media policy should be tailored to suit the needs of the particular publication, but the overall framework should remain similar to the typical framework used by other entities."[4]

The policy should include the designation of who has authority to use social media on behalf of someone and provisions about harassment, and discrimination, with sanctions. Users must be aware that the anti-discrimination and anti-harassment provisions apply to their social media usage as well as when on behalf of someone.

Considering that Internet provides access to an incredible array and variety of cultural products from around the world, as a means of homemade self-published books, songs, and videos, an analysis about copyright issues is relevant.

According to Daniel Gervais, "a driving force of our copyright regime is arguably an assumption that changes in the way that cultural products are created and disseminated will be translated into human progress."[5] There has been progress in distance education due to the inherent low costs, besides books can be more easily accessed and worldwide information-sharing or culture provides any kind of manifestations and considerations.

Filters, often in the form of search engines or a driven social media, govern and may prevent from seeing other cultures or being exposed to unwanted content and viewpoints or may lead to presentations that distort or make fun of other cultures. "The Internet, like may technological tools, is thus a double-edged sword: it greatly increases access to and availability of information and cultural productions, and makes available simple, inexpensive tools to promote culture, cooperation, joint action and consensus building. By the same token, the overabundance of information and culture can easily produce a tunnel vision effect." Gervais does not recommend a one-size-fits-all copyright regime, what the author calls a "fundamental error". He conceived four categories of authors: authors who just share works, scholars, creators without professional support, and professional authors.[6]

So, Internet, the new environment, leaded to a major paradigm shift in the notion of authorship. Because of the need of perfection of new culture development tool, copyright rules must be adapted, separating professionals from nonprofessionals, knowing that the first ones need financial flows to make a decent work.

That is why social media created a new frontier of constitutional issues, especially when the difficulty in defining the boundaries between free expression and

[4] Rudolph [1, p. 188].

[5] Gervais [4, p. 388].

[6] In that sense, Gervais [4, p. 390].

criminal acts is taken into account. The First Amendment to the United States Constitution is so described "Congress shall make no law respecting an establishment of religion, or prohibiting the free exercise thereof; or abridging the freedom of speech, or of the press; or the right of the people peaceably to assemble, and to petition the government for a redress of grievances."[7] In the same way, the Brazilian Constitution: "Art. 5 Everyone is equal before the law, without distinction of any kind, guaranteeing to Brazilians and foreigners residing in Brazil the inviolability of the right to life, liberty, equality, security and property, as follows: IV—the manifestation of thought is free, and anonymity is forbidden."[8]

This Constitutional command guarantees freedoms concerning religion, expression, assembly, and the right to petition. It guarantees freedom of expression by prohibiting Congress from restricting the press or the rights of individuals to speak freely. According to Daniel S. Harawa, "while there has always been tension as to where to draw the line between free expression and criminal acts, in the age of social media this tension is unprecedented."[9] So, protected and criminalized online speech must be rethought.

All social media activity, although the First Amendment, has no constitutional protection, in case, for instance, of advocacy intended and likely to incite imminent lawless action, obscenity, defamation, child pornography, fighting words, fraud, threats, speech integral to criminal conduct, and speech presenting a grave and imminent threat. To Daniel S. Harawa the government has the power to prevent.[10]

That's why it is relevant to define the line between online speech and criminal activity as social media became part of basic human expression. One way to do so would be to look at the motive of the speaker and whether he or she had actual criminal intent, and then whether the speaker took some action in furtherance of that intent. Besides this, it is not possible to consider that people say things online that they would never say in person, since social media make bigger facts with unlimited repercussions. When there is just social media activity with nothing more the speech does not constitute a clear danger. Social media became a method of engaging in bigger and larger social dialogue, an informal way to redefine democracy, that is, a tool to express concerns and happiness.

Unimportant issue related to the subject is about the access of sensitive information based on the First Amendment right. Derigan Silver deemed that the first controversy began just 10 days after the attacks "when Chief Immigration Judge Michael J. Creppy issued a directive mandating closure of all 'special interest' immigration hearings. In December 2001, a Michigan immigration judge held a closed hearing to decide if Rabih Haddad, who had overstayed his tourist visa and was suspected of having connections to al-Qaeda, could be deported. Several media

---

[7] U.S. Const., amend I. Cornell Law School website, Legal Information Institute, in https://www.law.cornell.edu/constitution/first_amendment, accessed on August 2, 2018.

[8] 1988 Brazilian Constitution, article 5, item IV. Government website, Planalto, http://www.planalto.gov.br/ccivil_03/constituicao/constituicao.htm, accessed on August 2, 2018.

[9] Harawa [5, pp. 367–368].

[10] Ibidem, p. 380.

organizations, along with members of Haddad's family and the public, sued, contending the closed proceeding was unconstitutional. Both a federal trial court and the U.S. Amendment right of access established in *Richmond Newspapers, Inc. v. Virginia* (448 U.S. at 573) applied, even though the immigration hearings were not actually court proceeding but administrative, quasijudicial proceedings. The courts held that the Creppy directive requiring blanket closure of all 'special interest' hearing was unconstitutional.

A few months later, however, in a case involving closed deportation hearings in Newark, New Jersey, the Third Circuit issued a contractor decision, ruling 2–1 that there was no constitutional right of access to such proceedings. In 2003, the U.S. Supreme Court refused to hear an appeal in the case, thereby failing to resolve the conflict between the two circuits. Five years later, the Court's 2008 ruling that foreign detainees at Guantánamo Bay have the right to challenge their imprisonment in civilian courts opened the door for more battles over government secrecy. In more than 100 cases brought as a result of the ruling, the Justice Department filed unclassified documents under seal, thereby restricting access to judges, lawyers and government officials. The secrecy, the government said, was necessary because some unclassified documents mistakenly contained classified information. On June 1, 2009, a federal district judge ruled the wholesale sealing of unclassified documents violated the public's First Amendment and common law right of access to judicial records. Unfortunately, these battles have continued well into 2010. In April, a federal appeals court judge abruptly closed the courtroom just 1 min after arguments began in the case of a Guantánamo Bay detainee."[11]

For the cited author, although censorship, in its most basic form, deals with prior restraints on the press, because of the judiciary's traditional antipathy toward prior restraints—even when national security information is involved—and the ease of dissemination brought about by the Internet, preventing the media from accessing information has become an alternative to outright media censorship.

The arbitrary closure of courtrooms and the removal of an entire case from a public docket are only possible to make effective terrorism trials and for a narrow amount of time. That is why the judiciary must provide, in common place, access to terrorism trials.

Important to mention that constraints do not exist for social media. Any person can post anything online with little fear of repercussion. The environment of social media is conceptually anonymous and can encourage inflammatory and shocking behavior. To act outside normal inhibitions and participate in caustic and less ethical activities, individuals create names or new identities, hampering efforts to control these actions.

Anonymity can be deemed an important value for free speech: "only by preserving a space where we, and especially those individuals already burdened with repressive regimes, can speak anonymously—and thus freely—can we ensure that all of us will be among the winners in the ongoing battle between surveillance and

[11] See Silver [6, pp. 144–145].

freedom,"[12] but cannot be out for some surveillance.[13] Although pervasive, surveillance is needed because electronic communications cannot be considered anymore exclusively a private space. It is possible to say that there is in the present days a systemic secrecy crisis, which forces to an interdisciplinary approach and the maintenance of traditional supervisory powers.

The public–private blur is one of the ambiguities that obscures the essential nature of Internet. Data protection can be considered an obstacle to effective counter-terrorism and counter-money-laundering measures. Equally important is the domestic–international face of it. What is certain is the fact that combating online crimes imposed to authorities, both domestic and international, a dramatic shift from the traditional view and approach to the problem.

All these must encourage to find a balance between the right of security and the right to privacy, by keeping in mind that for the preserving of the democratic values, both of them are fundamental.[14] It is not time to simplify an extraordinarily complex and complicated set of issues. Sometimes, there are different perceptions of the same risk, making another prioritization of the values that is believed to be protected with a genuine understanding. But talking about terrorism threats, for a good outcome, usually from international cooperation, it is important to have a unified struggle.

The Internet is a rich source of opinions, in posts, comments, as well as in platforms like Facebook, Twitter, blogs, and message boards. According to Jeremy Prichard, Paul Watters, Tony Krone, Caroline Spiranovic, and Helen Cockburn, "on just one day in early June 2015 it was estimated that there were more than three billion internet users collectively using almost a billion sites, sending more than 200 billion emails, making nearly four million blog posts, sending more than 750 million Tweets, and almost 1.5 billion Facebook accounts were active."[15]

The social media as evidence is relevant. With people posting anything and everything, trial lawyers have a greater ability than even before to paint a picture of a person as they are in real life. Facebook photos of a plaintiff snow skiing or sledding were found although she claimed to have a post-accident sensitivity to cold. Another example is given by John G. Browning, for whom a personal injury plaintiff who claims to be unable to participate in sports and physical activities post-accident would have a hard time contesting the relevance of Facebook photos of him running a local half marathon or lifting weights.[16] For the use of social media

[12] In this way, Froomkin [7, p. 159].

[13] For instance, the US government used several electronic surveillance programs to monitor al-Qaeda's Internet use. The government reportedly used Carnivore, a computer program that can read a suspect's email and other electronic data on a real-time basis, and print or store the information for FBI agents to view or save as electronic evidence for prosecution. The government also used Echelon, a global eavesdropping system that links supercomputers throughout the world to automatically search through the millions of intercepted messages for ones containing pre-programmed keywords of fax, telex, and email addresses (see Sidhu [8, p. 388]).

[14] In this way, Siserman [9, p. 422].

[15] Prichard et al. [10, p. 218].

[16] See Browning [11].

content, if the evidence is not obtained by pursuing the device directly or using any of the available forensic tools, authentication should be recommended. Authentication of social media content requires some evidence (1) that the content came from an account associated with the purported author, and (2) of author identity, in order to avoid fabrication and manipulation.

Gwendoly Waters recommend departments to designate a social media manager to handle specific core functions in order to protect people, besides ongoing training on current issues to avoid the hazards of social media.[17]

In this content, unfortunately, the proliferation of computer viruses and malicious software, fraud, hacking, and copyright piracy, and the circulation of obscene and hateful representations, reconfiguring the landscape of crime threats and patterns crime, are usual. A particular concern exists due to extensive use of social media by vulnerable people like children and youth people, making them socially visible and accessible to others.

Dealing with all these risks is compelling authorities to ameliorate them through a range of preventive measures. To those measures it is relevant to include the fostering of greater awareness of potential risks on the part of users, providing more transparent information about the use of personal information by social media providers, provision of enhanced privacy tools to help users better manage their online presence, and more effective regulation and oversight of data-gathering practices by third parties, be they individuals, business of state agencies.[18]

Certainly, the lack of guidance by regulators or judiciary may give bad users of Internet more leeway in escaping liability by invoking qualified immunity in terms of the First Amendment (free manifestation of thought). Social media itself may serve essential functions with regard to speech and news dissemination that signal a need for speech protection beyond that held by individual social media users, at least in the criminal realm.

Talking about the speech on social media that supports terrorist groups, VanLandingham states that it is important to be "mindful to ensure prosecution and hence suppression of ideas do not impede the very democratic discourse our nation is based upon."[19] It is need to criminalize social media companies' failure to police their public websites for threats that may violate anti-terror statutes. Also, compliance programs for social media companies should be established to ensure that their own agents do not violate any anti-terror provisions.[20]

Facebook faced $1 billion in liability in a New York federal court for allegedly providing a communication platform to terrorists in Israel and the Occupied Palestinian Territories. The case was brought on behalf of more than 20,000 families and victims of attacks by Hamas, the Palestinian group that controls Gaza.

Widely available cyber terrorist sermons, instructional videos, blogs, and interactive websites raised complex expressive concerns, and the protection of free

[17] In this sense, see Waters [12, p. 4].

[18] See Yar [13, p. 217].

[19] Vanlandingham [14, p. 56].

[20] Also Klein and Flinn [15, p. 112].

speech has never been an absolute bar against regulation of low value expressions, such as calls to violence and destruction.[21]

The Communications Decency Act of 1996—CDA was the first notable attempt by the United States Congress to regulate pornographic material on the Internet. Section 230 of the Communications Decency Act was not part of the original Senate legislation, but was added in conference with the House, where it had been separately introduced by Representatives Christopher Cox (R-CA) and Ron Wyden (D-OR) as the Internet Freedom and Family Empowerment Act and passed by a near-unanimous vote on the floor. It added protection for online service providers and users from actions against them based on the content of third parties, stating in part that "no provider or user of an interactive computer service shall be treated as the publisher or speaker of any information provided by another information content provider." Effectively, this section immunizes Internet users from liability for torts committed by others using their website or online forum, even if the provider fails to take action after receiving actual notice of the harmful or offensive content.

This Section 230 of the Communications Decency Act of 1996 can force companies into a censorship role if lawsuits cannot be prevented by the law. According to William Roberts, citing Robert Corn-Revere, "to the extent the suits allege that social media platforms should be held responsible for the postings by third parties that they consider to be beyond the pale, then Section 230 was designed to provide immunity in just that situation."[22]

In fact, the presence of terrorist speech on the Internet has tested the limits of the First Amendment. Given the magnitude of the problem, Alexander Tsesis proposed empowering government agencies to seek warrants, obtain injunctions, and hold criminally accountable the creators, instigators, and facilitators of cyber terror, in a realistic approach to combat terrorist incitement, threats, and material support without violating First Amendment principles. He is against the idea for data protection or data mining, for corporate self-policing, and for banning on encrypted or public source communications that would prevent the use of important communication tools, which can serve legitimate business and private purposes as well as to obfuscate criminality.[23]

A regulation should enforce registration disclosure and develop mechanisms to reveal the true personal identity, as follows: (1) implementing an user ID system, that is, establishing an universal Internet user identification, a unique identification number for each individual upon completion of a brief registration process by an applicant; (2) providers must store user traffic data for a long period although the cost and privacy concerns; (3) the user account must be barred from establishing a new account after a predetermined number of violations; (4) authorities should create a centralized monitoring and enforcement division in order to track online activities and identify illicit operations and threat nodes that require immediate enforcement action, also having the power to take any measurable action against

[21] See Tsesis [16, p. 651].

[22] Roberts [17, p. 29].

[23] Ibidem, pp. 691–692.

noncompliant providers, as well as imposing fines for negligent providers; and (5) a consolidated blacklist of individuals and entities banned from using, benefiting, or profiting from the Internet alerting people about bad users should be established.[24]

In short, it is relevant to make more difficult for bad users to exploit the Internet by implementing significant prevention and enforcement-oriented reforms, targeting surveillance (because the amount of information generated), and without a lack of coordination with service providers and authorities. It is more than time for us to have an effective global response, an international legislative response, by reexamining privacy standards to protect the majority of users, also from intrusive and often unnecessary surveillance by intelligence agencies, and cutting off Internet support of social media for illegal activities.

Communication, of course, is protected by the freedom of speech right unless it is in furtherance of some criminal conduct. The right protects an individual who transmits, without doing more, the message, that is, a passive ideological statement, but when it becomes an incitement to imminent unlawful action or a threat, neither of which is protected. That is why a valid subscriber information would discourage some of such communications.

The regulation should not be focused only on what governments should do, but also on a burden on users and providers on Internet. In this process of modifying existing laws and creating new ones, it is relevant to maintain a delicate balance between protecting freedom of speech and protecting citizens from online crimes, taking advantage of the growth of criminal nexus by tracking criminals rather than crimes.

References

1. Rudolph, C. (2013). Unleashing law reviews onto social media: Preventing mishaps with a social-media policy. *Thomas M. Cooley Law Review, 30*, 187–191.
2. Mcpeak, A. (2014). Social media snooping and its ethical bounds. *Arizona State Law Journal, 46*, 845–897.
3. Bailov, A. V., & Sakhuta, P. V. (2016). Mass media as crime determinants. *The Journal of Eastern European Law, 24*, 14–17.
4. Gervais, R. (2015). Authors, online. *Columbia Journal of Law & The Arts, 38*, 385–396.
5. Harawa, D. S. (2014). Social medial thought crimes. *Pace Law Review, 35*, 366–397.
6. Silver, D. (2011). Media censorship and access to terrorism trials: A social architecture analysis. *Notre Dame Journal of Law, Ethics & Public Policy, 25*, 143–186.
7. Froomkin, A. M. (2017). Lessons learned too well: Anonymity in a time of surveillance. *Arizona Law Review, 59*, 95–159.
8. Sidhu, D. S. (2007). The chilling effect of government surveillance programs on the use of the internet by Muslim-Americans. *University of Maryland Law Journal of Race, Religion, Gender & Class, 7*, 375–393.
9. Siserman, C. (2013). A global perspective on the protection of privacy and related human rights in countering the use of internet for terrorist purposes. *Masaryk University Journal of Law and Technology, 7*, 401–422.

[24] Ideas taken from Benjamin R. Davis (see Davis [18, pp. 177–184]).

10. Prichard, J., Watters, P., Krone, T., Spiranovic, C., & Cockburn, H. (2015). Social media sentiment analysis: A new empirical tool for assessing public opinion on crime. *Current Issues in Criminal Justice, 27*(2), 217–236.
11. Browning, J. G. (2016). *Introducing social media evidence*. Advocate Texas, Chapter 15, 21–22.
12. Waters, G. (2012). Social media and law enforcement: Potential risks. *FBI Law Enforcement Bulletin, 1*, 1–5.
13. Yar, M. (2012). E-Crime 2.0: The criminological landscape of new social media. *Information & Communication Technology Law, 21*(3), 207–219.
14. Vanlandingham, R. E. (2017). Jailing the Twitter bird: Social media, material support to terrorism, and muzzling the modern press. *Cardozo Law Review, 39*, 1–56.
15. Klein, S., & Flinn, C. (2017). Social media compliance programs and the war against terrorism. *Harvard National Security Journal, 8*, 53–112.
16. Tsesis, A. (2017). Terrorist speech on social media. *Vanderbilt Law Review, 70*, 651–708.
17. Roberts, W. (2016). Terrorists on social media. *Washington Lawyer, 31*, 26–29.
18. Davis, B. R. (2006). Ending the cyber jihad: Combatting terrorist exploitation of the internet with the rule of law and improved tools for cyber governance. *CommLaw Conspectus, 15*, 119–186.

Chapter 7
Tax Misapplication: Sales and Use Taxes and Games Taxation

Usually, millions of consumers engage in online transactions as varied as purchasing books to downloading music to printing out movie tickets. In addition to being a convenient way to order and compare prices, online sales have another benefit to consumers: most are tax-free. Besides it, there is a competitive disadvantage to traditional brick-and-mortar stores.[1]

One of the foremost tax challenges in online transactions certainly relates to financial operations, including sales[2] and use tax compliance.[3] While the sale taxes are collected by the entity that is selling the good (usually a retailer), a use tax is paid directly to the taxing state by the user of the good (end-user or consumer).

To Eric Menhart, enforcing a use tax is a problem and needs education of consumers, because most of them have no idea how to do the calculation and very few even know that any such tax is due.[4] That makes easier collecting sales taxes over regulated retailers on Internet transactions. He reveals that the U.S. Congress first got involved in the issue of Internet taxation in 1998, when it passed the Internet Tax Freedom Act—ITFA, a moratorium on state and local taxes on Internet access. The ITFA did not prevent local sales taxes from being collected by state, but did prevent multiple or discriminatory taxes on electronic commerce by defining such fees as taxes on interstate commerce. The ITFA defines a discriminatory tax as "any tax imposed by a State or a political subdivision thereof on electronic commerce that is not generally imposed and legally collectible by such State or such political

[1] See Menhart [1, pp. 23–24].

[2] A tax levied on the retail price of merchandise and collected by the retailer.

[3] According to the U.S. Supreme Court, a use tax is a tax on the enjoyment of that which was purchased, that is, "a tax imposed on the use of personal property and especially property purchased in another state; specifically: a one-time tax imposed on the exercise or enjoyment of any right or power over tangible personal property that is incident to the ownership, possession, custody, or leasing of it" (Merriam-Webster's Dictionary of Law, see https://www.merriam-webster.com/legal/use%20tax, accessed on August 2, 2018).

[4] See Menhart [1, p. 25].

F. M. De Sanctis, *Technology-Enhanced Methods of Money Laundering*,
https://doi.org/10.1007/978-3-030-18330-1_7

subdivision on transactions involving similar property, goods, services, or information accomplished through other means."

For retailers, lacking substantial tax resources, navigating the different sales and use tax laws of different jurisdictions—determining the applicable state and local tax rates, ascertaining the correct tax base, collecting tax from customers, filing the appropriate returns, and remitting proper payment—is a nearly insurmountable task.

For Brian Howsare, talking about this challenge, "in order to minimize the scope of this task and make sales and use tax compliance manageable undertaking, it is imperative for retailers to know exactly with states' sales tax laws bind them. That is, retailers must know which states can legally require them to collect tax and file returns, and which states cannot." According to him, based on the Supreme Court jurisprudence, state legislatures are not permitted to impose taxes or take any other action that would impede commerce among the states due to the Commerce Clause of the United States Constitution (Congress has the power to regulate commerce among the several states). In 1992, the Supreme Court ruled in *Quill Corp v. North Dakota*, requiring an out-of-state vendor to collect and remit sales tax on the sale of goods to an in-state customer.[5]

Under New York's tax code, every vendor of tangible property must collect sales taxes. The definition of "vendor" includes businesses that solicit in-state business through paid employees, independent contractors, agents, or other representatives. However, a 2008 amendment to New York State Tax Law substantially modifies the legal definition of "vendor" to include those businesses that solicit transactions through a commissioned and in-state independent contractor or other representative. The commissioned contractor or representative directly or indirectly refers potential customers, whether by a link on an Internet website or otherwise, to the seller. Cumulative gross receipts from in-state commissioned sales by all residents with this type of an agreement with the seller must be in excess of $10,000 during the preceding four quarterly periods. According to Jennifer Heidt White, Amazon and Overstock each sued the Department of Taxation and Finance by arguing that the 2008 amendment was unconstitutionally overbroad and burdensome. The New York County Supreme Court rejected their claims, concluding that the statute was carefully crafted to limit the tax collection obligation to only those sellers doing more than $10,000 worth of business, thanks to commissioned-affiliate solicitation of in-state sales.[6]

In short, under NY current law, Internet retailers like Amazon and other remote sellers, while subject to sales tax collection responsibilities for in-state transactions, are not required to collect and remit use taxes on purchases by out-of-state customers.

To Scott T. Allen, "a company selling its products out of state can be required to collect use taxes only in jurisdictions where it has a substantial nexus to the state. States have typically relied on physical presence in asserting nexus, although some

[5] Howsare [2, pp. 151–152].

[6] White [3, pp. 38–39].

states have claimed authority to impose use tax collection on vendors based on other factors, such as whether company representatives in the state solicit business." This author also mentioned the U.S. Supreme Court decisions, in *McLeod v. J.E. Dilworth Co.* and *General Trading Co. v. State Tax Commission* cases, to highlight that under commerce clause, taxes on goods sold by traveling salesmen and shipped into a state from another state are unconstitutional if applied to the original sale but constitutional if applied to the use of the good after it enters the taxing state. This distinction between sales and use taxes, according to him, remains intact today as only use taxes can be constitutionally applied to remote purchases. With a reasonable tax legislation (allowing states to impose use tax collection liability on remote vendors if they implement certain simplification measures, such as having a single agency that administers sales and use taxes, a single tax return and audit procedures for sales and use taxes, a uniform tax base, and rules that relieve vendors from liability for errors made in reliance on information provided by the state, and exempting all businesses that gross $1 million or less in annual remote sales), the disparate use tax liability between remote online retailers and their brick-and-mortar counterparts would be reduced considerably under the legislation. Internet shoppers would have fewer opportunities to evade use taxes, and consumer behavior would no longer be distorted by the tax advantage that online retailers currently possess. A system in which businesses—already equipped to deal with the paperwork that accompanies sales and use tax collection—rather than consumers have the responsibility to report taxes to states is far easier to administer and ensure compliance.[7]

Internet retailers have been growing as they have built distribution centers in several places to permit same-day delivery, allowing respective states to require them to collect and remit sales and use taxes on purchases within their borders. A webserver, in the context of an online retailing operation, that takes a customer's orders, processes payment, and delivers a digital product to the end consumer can be in some way compared with a traditional retailer because the latter one makes a number of decisions involving functions, such as ordering and maintaining inventory and negotiating terms with suppliers.

According to Andrew W. Swain and Nathaniel T. Trelease, taxing authorities developed attributional nexus from the U.S. Supreme Court's decisions in *Scripto v. Carson*, in which the Court upheld Florida's imposition of its use tax on a Georgia retailer based on the retailer's use of independent contractors (jobbers) to solicit sales in the taxing state. In *Tyler Pipe Indus. V. Dep't of Rev.*, "to establish the requisite connection between the in-state entity and the remote retailer, the in-state entity's activities must establish and maintain the remote retailer's market. Taxing jurisdictions traditionally have used attributional nexus as a technique to subject remote mail-order retailers to a state's taxing jurisdiction." In *Border Online, LLC v. State Bd. of Equalization*, "a limited liability company ('LLC'), sells books, CDs, videos, magazines, and other tangible goods over its Internet website. The LLC was formed under Delaware law and is headquartered in Michigan. Online sold its products to customers throughout the nation, including California, delivering its products

[7] See Allen [4, pp. 940, 944, and 960].

to customers using a common carrier. During the tax years in question, Online did not maintain a place of business in California, own or lease property in the state, locate employees in it, or hold bank accounts there. Online did not collect sales taxes associated with its sales to California customers." In order to attribute an agent's in-state physical presence to an out-of-state retailer, the company's in-state activities must be significantly associated with Online's ability to establish and maintain a market in California.[8]

So, it is important for policymakers to develop measure to design, test, and implement sales and use tax system that simplifies sales and use taxes for all out-of-state or remote commerce, including Internet transactions in order to avoid under-reporting and tax evasion. Talking about games taxation, taxes should not be levied against sources which are not considered income; so, game or virtual worlds (computers simulated 2D or 3D environment, ranging from the simple to the complex) should not be taxed for being a game when the purpose of it is the game itself, and not for items that may be acquired in the game: taxing income and excluding that which is not. In other words, instead of focusing on finding and prosecuting the wrongdoers, policymakers should put more emphasis on trying to tax them.

A big concern has thus arisen and derived from this issue: if virtual assets are legal subjects of taxation in the specific case of in-game communities in which virtual assets have values corresponding to the real world.

Scott Wisniewski cited the *Glenshaw Glass* case, in which the U.S. Supreme Court interpreted "gross income" as consisting of "undeniable accessions to wealth, clearly realized, and over which the taxpayers have complete dominion," what is called "realization." This realization requirement is currently understood as on operation requirement which "has less to do with economic theory and more to do with finding an administrable legal concept of gross income," noting that there were, according to *Einsner v. Macomber*, only two types of sources from which income could arise: labor and capital.

The Court then held that increases in wealth in the form of additional capital did not become income until the new wealth was "severed from the original capital." In effect, new capital income did not become legal income until its holder "cashed out" and converted the paper gains into currency: the realization event. However, this notion of realization was severely weakened in the *Helvering v. Bruun* case. The taxpayer leased land to a tenant who built a building upon it. When the tenant defaulted on the lease, the taxpayer took back the land, now with the building on it. The taxpayer then claimed that since the termination of the lease had not severed the building from the land, the taxpayer had not gained any new asset, but merely materialized a paper gain—in effect the land upon which the lease had been based had appreciated in value. The Court found this argument unpersuasive, finding that the appreciation in value due to the building was realized income which must be reported as such. Thus, realization events now began to take on a scope based more upon an appraisal of the actual conditions at operation in a transaction.[9]

---

[8] Swain and Trelease [5, pp. 37 and 40–42].

[9] See Wisniewski [6], items 23 and 24.

So, the realization requirement does not rely on formalistic notions but it is now met so long as the taxpayer and the Internal Revenue Service—IRS is capable of easily determining the disposition of a good into taxable income. If an individual is recognized as possessing property rights, it is clear then that a realization event has occurred, differently if he or she is recognized as license rights.

As stated by Vito Tanzi, when he talks about Technological Developments and the work of fiscal agents, "it would be prudent for many countries, and especially for those with high tax burdens, to begin preparing themselves for what could prove to be significant downward pressures on tax levels in futures years," making policymakers and tax administrators to face a challenge in the coming years that might change the way in which taxes have hitherto been levied and collected.[10]

Tax authorities, on one hand, have to transpose the traditional physical presence for taxation focused on activities that occur at the place of production, adapting concepts, in order to align the general legal rule, and, on the other hand, consider the digital environment, due to the existence of a new model, to preserve and not interfere in the values of cyberspace.

Arthur J. Cockfield concludes that "if tax authorities fail to develop tax rules that can effectively tax e-commerce transactions, they may resort to alternative strategies in order to protect their revenue bases."[11]

So, taxation in this context has to be focused on how best account covering transactions that occurs solely in virtual world. Adam S. Chodorow suggests that the Internal Revenue Service—IRS "adopt a hybrid approach to basis accounting in virtual worlds, where basis is traced for virtual items and pooled for currency, thus taking the best of both approaches and balancing administrative concerns with the conceptually accurate result for both nonfungible and fungible assets."[12]

The question here begins with whether virtual property belongs to gamers or game creators, and can be more easily overcome by common law systems adapting traditional property theories since civil law countries need to engage in careful analysis and study before legislating because a true owner must be designated.[13]

Given the complexity of the Internet phenomenon itself, allowing many online crimes, including tax evasion and money laundering, Hinterseer believes that "controlling it will inevitably require a coherent, comprehensive, and holistic set of interlocking laws, regulations and policies".[14]

The lack of an adequate and understandable legislation that allows, besides monitoring activity on the part of the Financial Intelligence Unit, taxing by the Internal Revenue Service is recommended. The belief that crimes on Internet is a relatively small risk (highly specialized market, highly visible, and with many complexity) compared to other physical environments combined could make the law a dead

---

[10] Tanzi [7, p. 1282].

[11] Cockfield [8, p. 403].

[12] Chodorow [9, p. 328].

[13] In this way, see Steinberg [10, p. 420].

[14] Cited by Morgan [11].

letter, a sort of institutionalized make-believe which does not properly merit the attention one would expect from enforcement authorities.

Furthermore, establishing the same requirements for operations performed inside the virtual world, if no adapted to it, can engage in domestic or international cash transfer services or tax evasion, what compels to record the amounts transferred, form of payment, transaction date, purpose of the wire transfer, name, individual or corporate taxpayer ID, where applicable, of both sender and receiver and addresses for both.

These requirements would give a false impression that any money laundering occurring in that sector could actually be detected. There is also a need to require Internet providers (in the broadest sense of the word) to turn in Suspicious Activity Reports upon acceptance of such illegal funds as may be detected (applying the willful blindness doctrine).

Considering that taxation is not just a means of financing government and it is also a very visible component of the social contract underlying the state, tax evasion lies in substantial part in reforming governments to ensure that they uphold their side of the social contract. In this sense Richard Gordon and Andrew P. Morriss deem that, "there are trade-offs to be made on virtually every margin in the design to tax systems and ignoring them is a recipe for dysfunction. Improving international tax systems is more likely to result from continuing 'to eliminate tax preferences,' 'a better approximation of tax depreciation to the actual depreciation of assets,' and continuing 'the process of base-broadening and rate-moderating that started in the second half of the 1980s."[15]

Many of the illegal activities have proliferated because of the increasing use of anonymous remailers, and consequently, without tax compliance.

According to Maricel P. Montano, "the 'nature of the network'—the Internet—as a rapidly evolving borderless global forum consisting of a multitude of anonymous users contributes to one of the core problems of enforcing tax laws with respect to e-commerce: asymmetric information."[16] One aspect, as Leandra Lederman explains, "of the asymmetry problem is that the taxpayer knows the facts regarding the relevant transactions he or she engaged in during the tax year-or at least has ready access to that information but does not necessarily volunteer this information on his or her annual tax return."[17]

Another aspect is that the U.S. government, so far, has no solution to prevent or restrict offshore tax evasion by using cryptocurrency. Offshore tax evasion is subdued under the Foreign Account Tax compliance Act—FATCA, which requires foreign financial institutions to report the financial assets of American account holders to the Internal Revenue Service—IRS. However, the FATCA does not require virtual wallet providers, specialized storage service for cryptocurrency, to report American account or virtual wallets to the U.S. government as it does banks or

[15] Gordon and Morris [12, p. 119].

[16] Montano [13, p. 390].

[17] Cited by Montano in Ref. [13, p. 391].

credit unions. Therefore, the IRS should define cryptocurrency as being subject to the FATCA restrictions to avoid tax evasion using offshores virtual wallet providers.[18]

It is important to mention that the FATCA now is a worldwide system. The Common Reporting Standard—CRS, developed in response to the G20 request and approved by the OECD Council on 15 July 2014, calls on jurisdictions to obtain information from their financial institutions and automatically exchange that information with other jurisdictions on an annual basis. It sets out the financial account information to be exchanged, the financial institutions required to report, the different types of accounts and taxpayers covered, as well as common due diligence procedures to be followed by financial institutions. So, the G20 also should define cryptocurrency as being subject to the CRS.[19]

In short, it is relevant having a system of taxation of all income from whatever source derived, including, but not limited to: (1) compensation for services, including fees, commissions, or additional benefits, and similar items; (2) gross income derived from business; (3) gains derived from dealings in property; (4) all income from auctions, traditional or online, and consignment sales unless certain exceptions are met; and (5) also a well-designed reporting system.

Underpayment, underreporting, and nonfiling must be able to enable tax policy decisions, avoiding tax gaps, and making efforts by increasing voluntary compliance, reducing opportunities for evasion and money laundering, and simplifying the administration of the tax laws. In this way, having an overall compliance requires third-party reporting or withholding, such as wage, salary, and tip compensation reported by employers through adequate forms.

For that, it is clear that other countries may be useful in evaluating whether this new reporting requirement can be an effective means of addressing noncompliance by taxpayers engaged in online sale, that is, being a global phenomenon, international approach is mandatory. Thus, it is imperative to shape tax policy through effective information reporting of the income.

A unified regulatory tax regime is relevant to avoid overtaxing sales by state taxing authorities since it is possible to glimpse that the states, in the eagerness to increase the values of taxes (their budgets), can become more aggressive in their attempts to collect sales taxes from online transactions. The ideal would be to treat online sales as similar as possible to physical transactions without creating a substantial burden affecting activities disproportionately. That is why an effective regime must be conceived by reducing the number of taxing jurisdictions and eliminating the risk of compliance cost growth.

The goal should be increasing in the legal liability of the sales administrators as the primary method by which to balance anonymity concerns through personal accountability and tax compliance.

---

[18] In this way, see Valeriane [14, pp. 864–865].

[19] OECD website [15].

References

1. Menhart, E. (2007). Taxing the internet: Analyzing the states' plan to derive online sales revenue. *Journal of State Taxation, 25*, 23–34.
2. Howsare, B. (2017). The new normal for sales and use tax in the United States: Will a state challenge to supreme court precedent overhaul sales and use tax compliance for online retailers. *Pittsburgh Tax Review, 14*, 151–171.
3. White, J. H. (2008). Safe haven no more: How online affiliate marketing programs can minimize new state sales tax liability. *Shidler Journal of Law, Commerce & Technology, 5*(1), 36–49.
4. Allen, S. T. (2013). Adapting to the internet: Why legislation is needed to address the preference for online sales that deprives states of tax revenue. *Tax Lawyer, 66*(4), 939–960.
5. Swain, A. W., & Trelease, N. T. (2006). Online retailers netted by nexus: The borders online case. *Intellectual Property and Technology Law, 35*(1), 37–42.
6. Wisniewski, S. (2008). Taxation of virtual assets. *Duke Law & Technology Review, 7*, 1.
7. Tanzi, V. (2001). Globalization, technological developments and the work of fiscal termites. *Brooklyn Journal of International Law, 26*, 1261–1282.
8. Cockfield, A. J. (2002). Designing tax policy for the digital biosphere: How the internet is changing tax laws. *Connecticut Law Review, 34*, 333–403.
9. Chodorow, A. S. (2010). Tracing bias through virtual spaces. *Cornell Law Review, 95*, 283–328.
10. Steinberg, A. B. (2009). For sale – One level 5 barbarian for 94,800 won: The international effects of virtual property and the legality of its ownership. *The Georgia Journal of International and Comparative Law, 37*, 381–420.
11. Morgan, J. S. (2003). Dirty names, dangerous money: Alleged unilateralism in U.S. policy on money laundering. *Berkeley Journal of International Law, 21*, 802.
12. Gordon, R., & Morris, A. P. (2014). Moving money international financial flows, taxes and money laundering. *Hastings International and Comparative Law Review, 37*, 1–120.
13. Montano, M. P. (2010). Can widening the scope of information reporting to include income derived from online sales help to narrow the expanding tax gap. *Southern California Law Review, 83*, 379–423.
14. Valeriane, E. M. (2016). IRS, will you spare some change: Defining virtual currency for the FATCA. *Valparaiso University Law Review, 50*, 864–911.
15. OECD website. *Model mandatory disclosure rules for CRS avoidance arrangements and opaque offshore structures*. Retrieved September 2, 2018, from http://www.oecd.org/tax/exchange-of-tax-information/model-mandatory-disclosure-rules-for-crs-avoidance-arrangements-and-opaque-offshore-structures.pdf

Chapter 8
International Legal Cooperation, Confiscation/Repatriation of Assets, and Virtual World

8.1 Initial Considerations

International cooperation is the only means to counter global online crimes, including money laundering. To Stephen Jefferey Weaver,[1] global money laundering can impact countries at home, and "therefore requires collaborative efforts to fully protect domestic interests." So, it is relevant to continue honing informational sharing across countries to reconstruct the transactions by audit trail. That is why a series of reporting requirements in a global system recognizes the importance of reconstituting the sequence of transactions.

December 2008 brought headlines that shocked the world: prominent banker Bernie Madoff had not been providing legitimate investment services, but running a fraudulent operation (a chain or Ponzi scheme). Over the course of several years, Madoff gulled thousands of investors who had shelled out over $65 billion. In March 2009, he pled guilty to nine counts, including financial fraud, money laundering, and perjury. In June of that same year he was sentenced to over 150 years in prison.

Madoff was given more than just a custodial sentence. Prosecutors sought forfeiture of all of his revenue from the scheme, a total of some $170 billion. They were trying to recover this amount, alleging that Madoff's assets and those of his wife were acquired with the proceeds of crime and should therefore be confiscated by the government. Their aim was to deprive him of four houses totaling some $22 million, a Steinway piano worth $39,000, and silverware worth some $65,000.[2]

The U.S. Department of Justice confiscated some $1.737 billion in 2011, which was $191.1 million more than in 2010 ($1.545 billion). Its purpose was to deter crime by disrupting, damaging, and dismantling criminal organizations through the use of the forfeiture sanction.[3]

---

[1] Weaver [1, p. 464].

[2] In Henriques [2, B6].

[3] The United States Department of Justice [3, p. 10, 12].

F. M. De Sanctis, *Technology-Enhanced Methods of Money Laundering*,
https://doi.org/10.1007/978-3-030-18330-1_8

Depriving financial criminals such as white-collar criminals, drug and weapons traffickers, racketeers, and members of other criminal syndicates of their ill-gotten proceeds and instrumentalities of their trade not only achieves important law enforcement objectives but also provides an effective means of recovering funds for victim restitution.

The confiscation of such resources by the State also strengthens public safety in general, by allowing for federal investment in state and federal police forces, and in education to prevent serious crime.

All of the money or assets transferred to the State will certainly result in special crime-fighting and prevention programs, as well as combined efforts on the part of the states and the federal government and its agencies, culminating in proper enforcement methods to curtail crime. The ideal is to create a safe place for freedom, security, and justice. This is no small feat, for it necessarily implies a joint effort on the part of the police, prosecutors, and the courts to obtain property illegally acquired. Forfeiture, confiscation, and repatriation require cooperation. Learning from decisions made in the searching out and seizing of the proceeds of crime will result in improvement of the work and training of public agents, and in the adoption of new measures to fight crime.

Despite the vast quantities of goods routinely seized and confiscated, unlike today the subject had not held the attention of scholars—unlike other issues such as the length of prison terms, the growing number of inmates, and the quality of penitentiaries and prisons.[4]

When assets are confiscated, the message that gets sent to organized crime is that financially, crime no longer pays, and is not in the best interests of its practitioners. It drives home the message that some types of behavior really are prohibited, and that to insist on engaging in them is to pay the price.

It would be better if confiscated assets could be put on exhibit, with a plaque explaining that each property was confiscated by the Justice Department.

Here, despite the enormous effort it takes to convince and garner commitments from several national and international government agencies, it is incumbent upon the judge to reconcile the interest generated by the free exposure resulting from a simple exhibition, without losing sight of the duty to preserve.

The specialized Sixth Federal Criminal Court of São Paulo, Brazil, on money laundering attempted to put the above proposal into practice in urging government agencies to see to the preservation of the asset, and also to direct it to a public space, even if on a provisional basis. The property here was an artwork.

The understanding was that the exhibit, albeit temporary, would lend the judicial decision added cultural value, to allow persons of all backgrounds—even though they may use the public mass transit system—to witness works of artistic and historical value.

It was in this spirit that the judge in charge of the Sixth Federal Criminal Court of São Paulo (the current author) engaged the daughter of artist Galileo Ugo Emendabili, Fiametta Emendabili Barros de Carvalhosa, in negotiations for some

[4] In this way, McCaw [4, p. 183].

twenty months, and likewise persuaded state and municipal governments to further the public interest while reconciling it with the private interest of the author, until arriving through meetings at decisions which made all of this possible in July 2008, namely:

> The sculptures titled [Goddesses of Engineering: Muse of Engineering and Muse of Sculpture] are now under the stewardship of the State Secretariat of Culture at the Casa Brasileira Museum, pursuant to a court order making possible the public display of seized works of art.
>
> By virtue of the decision handed down on 10/03/2006 (folios 3887–3889), which ordered the removal of the sculptures from the Casa Brasileira Museum for permanent exhibit at a public park, their installation at Luís Carlos Paraná Park was suggested by the state and municipal governments, and that transfer was ordered to take place within 30 days, then later postponed on 11/22/2006 for another 60 days.
>
> Meanwhile, the sculptor's daughter (…) made clear her wish to obtain sponsorship to install the sculptures at the location indicated by the municipal government, but in accordance with a design she herself suggested.
>
> A year and five months have elapsed since that removal decision, and there has been no word of the granting of that sponsorship. To the contrary, the State Secretariat of Culture has disclosed the existence of an "impasse."
>
> She nonetheless has made it known she favors immediate transfer, pursuant to that judgment on 03/07/2008, along the lines proposed by the City, with the proviso that the installation ought to be done, if possible, as she proposed, that is, as outlined by her engineer (…), in Art Deco style (folios 5092–5121).
>
> There is no justification for further delay of free public access to these beautiful creations by the renowned sculptor Galileo Emendabili on account of an argument over the base upon which these works of art are to be mounted.
>
> The reader should be aware no opposition was encountered while these works of art by sculptor Galileo Emendabili stood abandoned behind closed doors, deteriorating in a private warehouse.
>
> Thus, let the word go forth to the State Secretariat of Culture, to the Department of Historic Patrimony and to the Subprefecture of the Diocese that existing resources be allocated for immediate transfer of the aforesaid sculptures to the indicated locale, in order to provide free and general public access, with such transportation to be handled so as to not damage the artworks but rather, honor the requirement of protection for those pieces. If this is forthcoming, the restoration of those sculptures should be accomplished in very little time.
>
> Without prejudice to this measure, the artist's daughter may continue to seek backing so that her petition may finally be granted, that is, the completion of her design, already approved by the body politic, and that she be permitted to supervise the transfer of the statues.
>
> (...)

Serve notice to the Office of the Federal Prosecutor.

São Paulo, March 10, 2008.

FAUSTO MARTIN DE SANCTIS

FEDERAL JUDGE

Transcribed here are the Minutes of the Meeting allowing the public exposition:

Minutes of Meeting

On the 13th day of May of the year 2008, at 11:30 AM in the Hearings Room of the aforesaid Court, present were the Right Hon. Federal Judge, DR. Fausto Martin de Sanctis, along with the Adjunct Secretary for the State Secretariat of Culture, Mr. Ronaldo Bianchi, the Director of the Department of Historic Patrimony, Mr. Walter Pires, representative of the Secretariat of Boroughs, Mr. José Paulo Mortari, the architect for the Department of Historic Patrimony, Mrs. Rafaela Bernardes, State's Attorney, Counsel for the Culture Secretariat, Dr. Jussara Delfino, and Fiammeta Emendabili Barros de Carvalhosa, and with regard to the sculptures [Goddesses of Engineering: Muse of Engineering and Muse of Sculpture], the following was decided by Common Accord: (a) Restoration and transportation—the Government of the State of São Paulo (State Secretariat of Culture), shall move forward within 90 days; (b) Base to resemble the design presented by the daughter of sculptor Galileo Emendabili and illumination—to be the responsibility of the São Paulo City Government, within 90 days. Nothing further, notice given to all in attendance.

After work was begun at the public park, it was determined that the Clerk of the Court be present for the photographic record, and the court was notified as to the absence of information under temporary protection, so that the state's attorney's office motioned and the court ordered placement of specific plaques on both sides of the base, reading as follows: "Sculptures seized by order of the São Paulo Federal Court, Sixth Federal Criminal Court, in Record of Proceedings No. (…)."

Confiscation differs from pecuniary penalties because of the implicit perception that the violation determines the payment. But when assets are forfeited, the amount varies in accordance with the proceeds derived from criminal behavior. The greater the proceeds from crime, the larger the confiscation. Defendants in comfortable financial circumstances ought to be subject to forfeiture of assets not trivial to them. In other words, ill-gotten goods are taken in proportion to criminal behavior.

Pecuniary fines and confiscation are measures independent of one another, yet incorrectly distinguished by many jurists. Because they are calculated differently, they cannot be added together for the purposes of establishing the penalty imposed, for that would reduce the penalty.

The system as a whole works best when confiscation is kept as one of the solutions among the several outcomes of sentencing. The clear message sent by proceeding with such measure is that unlawful behavior is in fact prohibited.

In addition to criminal cases, there is also the possibility of administrative or civil confiscation. Financial Action Task Force Recommendation No. 04 makes it clear that no prior criminal conviction is required for the forfeiture of assets.

This is something that occurs frequently in the USA (actions *in rem*, that is, proceeding against the thing itself) whenever the property or its possession is related to criminal activity.[5] As these claims are framed, ownership or possession is considered illegal, in which case the interested party may intervene to prevent loss to the government. In such cases it is incumbent upon the government to prove beyond a reasonable doubt that the asset is actually subject to forfeiture, inasmuch as the thing and its possessor are both somehow connected to crime.[6]

In the case of fungible goods such as cash, showing the connection between the asset and the crime is quite complicated.[7] In harmony with this, there is also the United Nations Conventions against Organized Crime (Art. 12(a)) and against Corruption (Article 46), which operate on the idea that the confiscation is indeed collectable, even in the event of the death of the accused or expiration of the statute of limitations.

To Catherine McCaw, civil and criminal confiscations are not mutually exclusive. Were the Government to file both actions, each on its own grounds, and lose one, this in no way precludes continuing to seek confiscation on the remaining action.[8]

The symbolism in the forfeiture of personal property is striking. People promptly perceive that the outcome is as upsetting, if not more so, when having to face, in addition to imprisonment, loss of the equivalent of the proceeds from crime.

Hence, confiscation has become a priority strategy in the fight against organized crime. However, inasmuch as criminal activity has become transnational (online crimes are essentially international), and criminal investments have increased incredibly outside of national boundaries, a vast network has emerged to make use of the proceeds of crime, and has taken root in loopholes or legal hurdles in the way of crime-fighting efforts.

Criminals often work off an interpretation established in case law. This is what justifies shoring up asset forfeiture even though the assets may have been transferred to some third party who nevertheless ought to have perceived that these were the proceeds of unlawful conduct, or had been transferred precisely to avoid confiscation (establishment of a good-faith third party).[9]

No burdens should be placed on police and state's attorneys' efforts to temporarily freeze or solicit the freezing of assets liable to disappear if nothing is done, and all such measures are, to be sure, subject to consideration by the courts. Nor is any such interference warranted when the assets are located abroad.

---

[5] Cf. United States v. Bajakajian, 524 U.S. 321, 330–31 (1998) and United States v. One-Sixth Share, 326 F.Wd 36, 40 (1st Circ. 2003).

[6] 18 U.S.C. § 983 (c) (1) (3).

[7] 18 U.S.C. § 984 (a) (2): *Except as provided in subsection (b), any identical property found in the same place or account as the property involved in the offense that is the basis for the forfeiture shall be subject to forfeiture under this section.* 18 U.S.C. § 984 (b): *No action pursuant to this section to forfeit property not traceable directly to the offense that is the basis for the forfeiture may be commenced more than 1 year from the date of the offense.*

[8] McCaw [4, p. 195].

[9] See Confiscation [5].

Governments ought therefore to allow the freezing, seizure, confiscation, and repatriation of assets in order to facilitate the fight against organized crime, itself a global business, in such a manner as to force the criminals to change their ways.

Financial Action Task Force—FATF Recommendation No. 30 establishes the possibility of conducting freezing and seizure operations, even when commission of the antecedent crime may have occurred in another jurisdiction (country), and add to this the implementation of specialized multidisciplinary groups or task forces, thereby showing the importance of international cooperation to vitalize all necessary efforts to assist States in their mission to fight crime.

According to Fletcher Baldwin Jr., in examining this ongoing fight against international money laundering, there are three dimensions involved: consistent policies between national and international efforts, an efficient legal and institutional apparatus, and close cooperation between the public and private sectors.[10]

For an effective and cohesive universal policy against money laundering, participation by and commitment of all States to international cooperation are imperative.

The burden of proof is on the third party to show legitimate possession when the government alleges that the item was transferred to him in order to dodge confiscation, or in the belief that he would deliberately act without due caution. This is how repatriation has been accomplished.

Hence, confiscation and repatriation are two stages of legal proceedings in which the assets of criminals are forfeited on behalf of the victims, communities, or governments. Central to this procedure is the decision that a given asset was acquired as the proceeds of unlawful conduct, and may therefore be confiscated.

The first stage in repatriation is the tracking and identification of goods. This normally involves coordinated efforts on the part of prosecutors and government agencies (revenue authorities, the police, and private collaborators). These efforts also require substantial expertise or skill in dealing with the financial transactions that are sometimes involved. These normally involve communication among the authorities. In the USA, for example, the Asset Recovery Office—ARO in one state will surely provide another ARO with information as to the whereabouts of goods. But once these move into international jurisdictions, court orders are necessary to block or freeze them so that they may then be permanently confiscated. Those cases require cooperation with foreign authorities so that the items may return to their countries of origin.

8.2 International Legal Cooperation

International legal cooperation has been essential to shedding light on the activities of organized groups. It has enabled the blocking of goods and repatriation of assets which, invariably, rely on companies or institutions having their main offices in tax havens or elsewhere abroad.

[10] See Baldwin [6, pp. 47–48].

One approach calls for the application of reciprocity, according to which governments may cooperate with one another in the absence of some previous treaty or international agreement, acting through mutual commitments undertaken in dealing with a specific case.

The UN Convention against the Illegal Traffic in Narcotic Drugs and Psychotropic Substances (Vienna, 1988, Articles 6 and 7), Law No. 11343 dated 08/23/2006 (the Brazilian drug law, Article 65), the Extradition Treaty to which MERCOSUL Member States are party,[11] the UN Convention against Transnational Organized Crime (Palermo, 2000, Articles 16–19), the UN Convention against Corruption (Mérida, 2003, Articles 44 and 46), the Council of Europe Convention on Laundering, Search, Seizure and Confiscation of the Proceeds from Crime (Strasbourg, 1990, Articles 7–35), the Council of Europe Convention on Laundering, Search, Seizure and Confiscation of the Proceeds from Crime and on the Financing of Terrorism (Warsaw, 2005, Articles 15–45), Brazil's Money-Laundering Law (No. 9613, of 03/03/1998, Article 8, as amended by Law 12683 of 07/09/2012), and the Model Regulation promulgated by the Inter-American Drug Abuse Control Commission (CICAD/OAS, Article 20), all contain such provisions of mutual reciprocity.

The Financial Action Task Force—FATF clearly emphasizes in its Recommendations the need to reinforce international cooperation through general exchange of information relating to suspicious transactions. There is the understanding that the various standards relating to the element of intent in criminal conduct should not affect the ability or the will of countries to cooperate on judicial matters. The Recommendations establish: the possibility of freezing and seizure even where the antecedent crime was committed in some other jurisdiction (country), as well as the implementation of specialized multidisciplinary teams or task forces (Recommendation No. 30); international legal cooperation, pursuant to the UN Conventions of Vienna (international traffic, 1988), Palermo (transnational organized crime, 2000), and Mérida (corruption, 2003), by withdrawal of obstacles (Recommendation No. 36); direct mutual legal assistance toward a quick, constructive, and effective solution (Recommendation No. 37); freezing and confiscation even where there is no prior conviction (Recommendation No. 38); extradition (Recommendation No. 39); an attitude favoring the repression of antecedent crimes, money laundering, and terrorism financing (Recommendation No. 40).

International cooperation, however, requires more than just legal cooperation. It also requires the so-called administrative cooperation, not contingent upon indictments. In the latter case, all communication occurs through intelligence channels. Information is exchanged by the so-called Financial Intelligence Units and by direct cooperation among Financial Intelligence Units, the Attorney-Generals' Offices, and police authorities, in many countries.

---

[11] They specifically address International Legal Cooperation and one conclusion arrived at in Rio de Janeiro on 12/10/1998 was promulgated in Brazil through Legislative Decree No. 605 of 09/11/2003, which became effective internationally on 01/01/2004 as a result of the Treaty of Asunción, creating the South American common market, MERCOSUL (signed 03/26/1991).

As Patrícia Núñez Weber explains[12]:

> International administrative cooperation is in the strictest sense not tied to any criminal demands or occurrences, but aimed at technological improvement, exchange of information, creation and maintenance of databases, and the sharing of strategies among the agencies involved. Yet the term is also used to designate cooperation among administrative authorities quite apart from court orders.

This brings us to the possibility of direct exchanges of information, through the aforementioned intelligence channels. Most of the information would originate out of legal cooperation, under the aegis of the Judicial Branch, most notably in cases that require measures such as seizure and lifting of bank or tax record secrecy, that is, whenever a court order is needed.

Brazil's basic institutions for judicial cooperation on criminal matters may be summed up as follows: extradition, transfer of convicts, certification of a foreign criminal sentence, letters rogatory, and direct assistance. These latter two are intrinsically bound up with investigations and information on criminal activity, and for this reason are given greater weight here.

International legal cooperation, generally speaking, may be viewed as active or passive depending on the relative position of each of the States involved. It is active if the requesting State formulates a petition that a measure be taken and passive when a requested State receives a request for cooperation.

They may, in addition, be direct or indirect. In the latter case, it is intrinsically related to the prima-facie evaluation, as in the case of letters rogatory transmitted to Brazil. As for the direct form,[13] this comes about "when the Court of Examination judge is fully apprised. Here we are dealing with direct assistance."

The letter rogatory is the procedural instrument through which the legal authorities in one country request of another the enforcement of an order issued by the judicial branch of the requesting State.

Brazil's Federal Constitution of 10/05/1988 provides, in Article 105, Subsection I(i) that in order for a letter rogatory transmitted to Brazil to be executed, the Superior Court of Justice must conduct a *prima-facie* evaluation before issuing an *exequatur*. After this authorization is given, federal judges would then have jurisdiction to assess and pass on enforcement of the letter rogatory, as set forth in Article 109, Subsection X of the Brazilian Constitution.

The *exequatur* is no more than the authorization given by the Superior Court of Justice to allow within Brazil the enforcement of police inquiries or procedural acts requested by the foreign legal authority.

Pursuant to Superior Court of Justice Resolution No. 09 of 05/04/2005, notably in its Articles 8–10, the *prima-facie* evaluation must be conducted with the participation of the interested parties, as follows:

> Art. 8 The interested party shall be cited to answer the request for certification of a foreign sentence within 15 days, or summoned to impugn the letter rogatory.

[12] *Apud* de Carli [7, p. 589].

[13] Cf. Virgínia Toffoli and Cestari [8, p. 24].

Sole paragraph. The measure requested through the letter rogatory may be set in motion without giving the interested party a hearing whenever such advance intimation could render the international cooperation ineffective.

Art. 9 In the certification of a foreign sentence and in letters rogatory, the defense is only entitled to make a statement on the authenticity of the documents, intelligence underlying the decision, and observance of the requirements of this Resolution.

§ 1 Whenever certification of a foreign sentence is contested, suit shall be filed for judgment by the Special Court, and a Rapporteur appointed and responsible for all other acts relating to and informing the proceedings.

§2 In the event of impugnment of letters rogatory containing judgments, proceedings may, by order of the President, be held over for judgment by the Special Court.

§ 3 Should respondent abscond or be incapable, a special curator shall be named and personally served notice.

Art. 10 The Office of the Public Prosecutor shall have 10 days in which to examine the record in the letters rogatory and enrollment of foreign judgments, and may also impugn these.

Bear in mind that incoming letters rogatory is received in Brazil through diplomatic channels, most notably through the Ministry of External Relations, and all active letters rogatory in Brazil lack the *exequatur.*

The bureaucratic side of processing letters rogatory led to an increase in another mode of international cooperation: direct assistance. This allows us to get around the sending and procedural delays of letters rogatory, for it allows direct transmission. It has emerged as practically the most effective alternative in the fight against international crime.

Through this form of cooperation, authorities other than the judiciary may avail themselves of international requests, and the procedures are much simpler than those involving traditional letters rogatory, and even dispense with the prima-facie evaluation in Brazil.

This brings us back to the observations of Patrícia Núñez Weber, who assures us that[14]:

Direct assistance is cooperation offered by national authorities and likely to satisfy the foreign request, in the performance of their legal duties as though it were a national procedure, when in fact it arises from a request by a foreign State channeled through Brazil's central authority.

(...)

Currently, the most widespread understanding is that direct assistance presupposes the existence of a treaty or agreement with the requesting State, or a promise of reciprocity. Our feeling is that that restriction arises from the relatively recent arrival of the institution on the international scene, compared to letters rogatory.

[14] *Apud* de Carli [7, p. 593, 602].

In direct assistance, once the request is received by the central authority and forwarded to the judiciary authorities, the judge may then examine the facts presented by the foreign nation on their merits, much as in domestic proceedings to which current procedural rules would apply. This is something that does not happen with letters rogatory.

Requests for direct assistance are generally couched in terms of international treaties or agreements. One approach is through the application of reciprocity, according to which governments may cooperate with one another in the absence of some previous treaty or international agreement, acting through mutual commitments undertaken in dealing with a specific case.

For example, José Antônio Dias Toffoli and Virgínia Charpinel Junger Cestari[15] explain that:

> Requests for direct assistance are, as a rule, couched in terms of bilateral treaties or agreements (the so-called Mutual Legal Assistance Treaties or MLATs). Absent any express understanding between the two States, assistance can still be provided based on the requester's assurance of reciprocity. This allows cooperation in many different tax, labor or pensions-related areas. Still, the treaties most frequently encountered in an international setting have to do with criminal and civil subject matter.

How to determine which acts require a granting of *exequatur* (in passive cooperation) and which require issuance of letters rogatory (for active cooperation) for their proper performance is a question that calls for a comprehensive analysis.

The Brazilian Superior Court of Justice did shed some light on how it handles cases of international legal cooperation in its Resolution No. 9 of 05/04/2005, specifically in Article 7, which allows us to make out that the direct assistance mode of cooperation, where it calls for judicial consideration, should be brought to the judicial notice of the court of first instance.

Specifically:

> Article 7 Letters rogatory may request decisional acts or non-decisional acts.
>
> Sole paragraph. Requests for international cooperation which do not involve prima-facie evaluation by the Superior Court of Justice shall—even if classified as letters rogatory—be forwarded or returned to the Ministry of Justice so that all necessary steps may be taken to comply with them by direct assistance.

One can infer, in this provision, that in these cases the granting of *exequatur* may be waived, allowing the central authority to take all appropriate action to provide direct assistance.

The First Panel of the Brazilian Supreme Court has made a declarative statement as to the need for a granting of *exequatur* by the Superior Court of Justice for acting on indictments issued by foreign judicial authorities, as follows:

> Crime—International Cooperation—Enforcement—Investigations—National Territory—Means.

[15] Toffoli and Cestari [8, p. 27].

> Engaging in law enforcement actions within Brazilian national territory to enforce orders issued by foreign judicial authorities presupposes the transmission of a letter rogatory, for purposes of enforcement, to be passed on by the Superior Court of Justice, there being no proper way to bring about international cooperation at the cost of relegating to a lesser role a formality essential to the validity of the acts to be performed.
>
> (STF—Habeas Corpus No. 85.588/RJ, Rapporteur: Minister Marco Aurélio. First Panel. Daily Judicial Gazette, 12/15/2006, p. 95).

Afterward, the Special Court of the Superior Court of Justice was able to have its say in the matter, in Complaint No. 2645/SP, reported by Minister Teori Albino Zavascki, it having been shown that the letters rogatory procedure ought only be followed for requests of a jurisdictional nature formulated by the foreign authority, and that all other solicitations ought to comply with the requirements set by international regulatory bodies.

At an opportune time, amidst allegations of usurpation of jurisdiction of the Superior Court of Justice for the granting of *exequatur* for letters rogatory, the Superior Court of Justice authorized, at the request of the Office of the Federal Prosecutor, the shipment of the hard drive confiscated from the computer in possession of a defendant to the Russian Federation's Attorney-General's Office, in response to a request transmitted by the Russian Assistant Attorney General.[16]

---

[16] Decision of the Superior Court of Justice as following: The Office of the Federal Prosecutor in making the complaint sought to assemble an exhibit with all documents (in Russian and in English) and forward it on to the Attorney General for the Attorney General for the Russian Federation, along with corresponding official translations (folios 163–165). In the opening statement of the acknowledgment of receipt of that exhibit (folios 167/168), the Court ordered that Attachments be compiled to include all documents alluded to, and they were named as follows: "Attachments VII and VIII." The following was granted on an item "c" of the decision set forth on folios 169–214, the petition likewise formulated by the Attorney General's Office for forwarding copy of the hard drives to the Office of the Attorney General of the Russian Federation, as requested by that Authority. The devices in question were at the Federal Police Intelligence Bureau in Brasilia for forensic analysis and were apprehended in May 2006 in the possession of Boris Abramovich Berezovisk, pursuant to a search warrant, as well as a bench warrant naming the suspect, who was then taken to the Office of the Attorney General in this capital city to depose on facts being investigated in Brazil and theoretically related to the racketeering offense (Art. 288 of the Criminal Code), given the suspect's supposed association with other persons for the constant and ongoing purpose of engaging in illegal "laundering" of money, by exploiting the partnership entered into between MSI and Sport Club Corinthians of São Paulo. At the time of the seizure, consideration was also given to the fact that the suspect had entered Brazil using the name Platon Ilyich Yelenin, and was also included in the Red Notice issued by Interpol requesting that the individual be located and arrested for extradition, even though at the time the warrant had not been through proceedings in Brazil for purposes of certification by the Supreme Federal Court (folios 932–934, 1052, 1057–1060, 1061, 1063–1064, 1065–1072, 1082–1084, 1092, 1094, and 1098 of record No. 2006.61.81.005118-0/Attachment VII, admitted in connection with the Criminal Action). The copies in question were forwarded through official communiqué No. 1040/2007-rba dated 09/28/2007 to his Excellency, Russia's Ambassador to Brazil Wladimir Turdenev, for forwarding to the Attorney General's Office in Russia (see folio 75 of the Addendum compiled pursuant to Order No. 18/2005 of this Court). The Russian Federation, like Brazil, is a signatory to the UN Convention against Corruption known as the Mérida Convention, after the Mexican city in which it was signed. It has been signed by 150 countries, 95 of which enforce it internationally, foremost among them

being Argentina, Australia, Spain, the USA, China, France, and the UK. The procedure adopted by this Court in response to the request formulated by the Ministry follows the recommendations set forth in that Convention, notably in the chapter relating to International Cooperation in its Articles 43, and 46, among others, and by the 2000 UN Convention at Palermo on transnational organized crime, in particular in its Articles 18, 27, and 28. And this was accomplished with no deviation from Brazil's own legal proceedings, inasmuch as it also followed the form outlined in Article 7 of Resolution No. 09 of 05/04/2005 by the President of this Respectable Court, to wit: "Art. 7 Letters rogatory may request decisional acts or non-decisional acts. Sole paragraph. Requests for international cooperation which do not involve prima-facie evaluation by the Superior Court of Justice shall—even if classified as letters rogatory—be forwarded or returned to the Ministry of Justice so that all necessary steps may be taken to comply with them by direct assistance." (Emphasis ours). Direct assistance, absent better options, follows from the application of the rules of procedure of the Mérida and Palermo Conventions as from the measure requested by the Office of the Federal Prosecutor, to say nothing of the policy of reciprocity which, in the absence of specific rules, underlies international relations. This is why it was unnecessary to raise the issue of the granting of exequatur as set forth in Article 105, subsection I, clause "i" of the Federal Constitution. In fact, the Palermo Convention stipulates the duty of mutual legal assistance between the Parties when the Requesting State has reasonable grounds to suspect a transnational infraction, and hence the duty to provide all legal cooperation (Article 18, items 1 and 2), to which is added the recommendation that special investigative techniques be used, such as electronic eavesdropping (Article 20, item 1). It further provides an interchange of information to keep the State Parties apprised of trends in organized crime on their territory, of the circumstances in which it operates and of professional groups and technologies involved, and may, to that end, be shared among them (Article 28, items 1 and 2). Furthermore, and in particular, this cooperation is aimed toward detecting and tracking the proceeds of crime, transfer methods, and the dissimulating or disguising of these proceeds in the "fight against money laundering and other financial crimes" (Article 29, item 1, "d"). The international treaty in question, now duly integrated as the law of the land, provides a basis for the investigation, but in addition, urges the State Parties to effectively repress transnational criminal organizations. The UN Conventions against Organized Transnational Crime and against Corruption, it can actually be said, amount to an attempt by all sovereign states to eliminate groups rooted in a certain criminal milieu which systematically resorts to obstruction of justice—in addition to engaging in criminal behavior which affronts the rule of law, and often operates by what amounts to intimidation. What we have here are global legal guidelines. There has been no news yet of forensic analysis of the hard drives, but please note that documented proof by examination was already on the record before this Court, for it was produced on account of the search warrant issued by the Brazilian Federal Justice System in May 2006 in record of proceedings under No. 2006.61.81.005118-0/Attachment VII, as we have seen, and this did not result from any request submitted by a foreign authority, so that the prima-facie evaluation was never an issue. This is simply a case of sharing legitimate evidence produced here. In the Complaint lodged before this Honorable Court, Plaintiff also holds that the official foreign documents were neither translated into Portuguese nor stamped with diplomatic or consular certification required to make them stand up in any court of law, and further postulates renewed application of Code of Criminal Procedure Articles 780 et. seq. [Jurisdictional Relations with Foreign Authorities], as previously submitted on occasion of filing for Habeas Corpus No. 2007.03.00.091069-0. No such argumentation would apply absent additional information, at the heart of a Complaint expostulating only about jurisdiction. In any case, in the aforementioned writ, in proceedings before the Second Panel of the Hon. Regional Federal Court for Region 3, the petition was not granted by the Eminent Rapporteuse for the Habeas Corpus, Her Excellency, Federal High Court Justice Cecília Mello. The foreign language document in question is accompanied by a certified translation, in full compliance with Code of Criminal Procedure Article 236. Hence no taint of irregularity or affront to the law may be ascribed to the admission of those documents, for what we have is a true copy duly forwarded by an agency of the Russian Government. The Court also understands that the provisions contained in

By the understanding set forth in the decision, the Brazilian constitutional requirement contained in Article 105, subsection I, item "i," contains no grant of exclusivity to the Superior Court of Justice to intermediate all international legal cooperation. There must be consideration of its operation in relations among the various judiciary agencies, and, in addition, the various forms of cooperation established in international treaties.

Hence the request for legal cooperation formulated by a foreign authority (in this case, the Office of the Attorney General for the Russian Federation, regarding the sharing of evidence during an ongoing investigation and transmitted to its Brazilian counterpart, Brazil's Office of the Attorney General) shall not be contingent upon issuance of letters rogatory by Russian judicial authorities, thereby obviating the need for an *exequatur* from the Superior Court of Justice.

For a clearer understanding I call attention to an excerpt from the vote cast by the eminent Rapporteur, Teori Albino Zavascki:

> The international system of legal cooperation clearly does not exclude cooperative measures among agents of the judiciary brought about through the use of letters rogatory, within the scope of proceedings already within the jurisdictional sphere. But in addition to these, as pointed out, mutual cooperation encompasses a host of other provisions which may even, where applicable, give rise to future criminal prosecutions. Yet insofar as their scope is restricted to prevention and investigation, they require for their performance no prior approval or judicial intermediation. There is no such requirement in Brazil's domestic law, nor is there any reason for such a requirement in the area of international law.
>
> In Brazilian law, as in most countries, the prevention and investigation of crimes, not jurisdictional by nature, is not the purview of the Judicial Branch, but rather, of police authorities or the Office of the Public Prosecutor, under the Executive Branch.

Articles 780 et seq. of the Code of Criminal Procedure do not apply as claimed in the Complaint, for the instant case does not involve transmittal of letters rogatory. The reasons set forth in the documents comprising the record are beyond reproach, inasmuch as all provisions of the Code of Criminal Procedure which govern the matter have been fully complied with. Observe that the Claimant, in the reasons for filing the aforesaid writ acknowledged that the "… Code of Criminal Procedure contained no specific provision on admissibility of foreign documents intended as evidence in criminal proceedings…" that only being expressly required for letters rogatory (folios 952–953). The admissibility of the foreign documents is in order, in no small part for having been obtained from a foreign authority free of any imputations of illegal behavior given the absolute lack of any grounds for indicating such a thing. There is no denying that international recommendations now seek to simplify procedures and international cooperation, provided there is not, as in this case, any reason to question authenticity, and also provided there is no infringement of our national legal system. Even in the absence of all of the above, one could still argue that the Claimant is a Russian citizen and has resided in the UK for a considerable time, circumstances that warrant the conclusion that both Counsel and Claimant ought to be familiar with the probative material. Indeed, the aforementioned Article 236 of procedural law does not even require the translation where it is patently unnecessary. Although the Court has been unable to discern any irregularity in the documentation forwarded by the Russian Authorities, it has been previously noted that if the Defense so wishes, the Defense could produce a new translation of the documents so as to clear up its misgivings. And so it did, inasmuch as it requested the translation into Portuguese of all documents contained in folios 08, 11, and 12 of Attachment No. 12, which request was met by the order issued on 11/14/2007 (folios 1392 and 1400–1414).

Indeed, the nature of jurisdictional questions—which as a rule are submitted to formal, public, adversarial proceedings—is neither proper to nor compatible with typical police matters, such as these now under consideration, involving prevention and criminal investigation. In our system, only a few such measures require prior judicial approval, such as in the case of those requiring entry into an individual home, or wiretaps (CF, Art. 5, XI and XII).

Aside from these cases, there is no reason at all—even in the case of investigations or preventive measures undertaken during international cooperation efforts—to impose jurisdictional boundaries on these activities, thereby rendering them subject to intermediation or advance prima-facie evaluation by agencies of the corresponding Judicial Branch. Because it takes account of such circumstances, the international legal cooperation system, which includes Brazil, reflects and honors the system of duties and assignments already in place in domestic law, and strictly and fully preserves all of the constitutional duties of the Judicial Branch, including those having to do with jurisdictional considerations affecting the standing of the agencies and authorities involved to take action.

(Rcl. 2.645/SP, Rapporteur Minister TEORI ALBINO ZAVASCKI, Special Court, decided on 11/18/2009, Gazetted 12/16/2009).

Moreover, the subject of actual standing to issue a letter rogatory to Brazil was quite recently raised by the First Supreme Federal Court Panel in the Clarification Requests on *Habeas Corpus* Declaration No. 87.759/DF, reported by Minister Marco Aurélio, in which the Clarification Requests were honored in order to state that the Italian Attorney General's Office did indeed have standing to issue them:

Appeals Requesting Clarification—Omission. Once an omission was found in the judgment, faced with the treaty of cooperation on criminal matters entered into between Brazil and the Republic of Italy—as part of its national legal process—honoring the appeals for clarification would follow, albeit with no power to bring about change, it being recognized that the Italian Attorney General's office does have standing to issue letters rogatory.

(HC 87759 ED, Rapporteur(euse): Min. MARCO AURÉLIO, First Panel, decided 12/13/2011, Unanimous Panel Ruling DJe-053 released 03/13/2012, Gazetted 03/14/2012).

Initially, at the time of the granting of *Habeas Corpus*, it was understood that the letter rogatory had not been issued by judicial authority, which would have violated the provisions of Article 202, subsection I of the Code of Civil Procedure, which regulates the *indication of courts of origin*, so that nationally cooperation through letters rogatory transmitted by a foreign Attorney General's office would cease to exist.[17] In accordance with the precedent set by the Supreme Federal Court in

[17] However, in examining the appeals requesting clarification, the Rapporteur noted that: There was warning of a defect, at the beginning of the voting, in that it had not been issued by a judicial authority per se, which brought up the provisions of Article 202, subsection I of the Code of Civil Procedure. It was deemed apropos to remark on not having taken proper account of the fact that Article 784 of the Code of Criminal Procedure makes reference to letters rogatory issued not from judicial authorities, but from competent foreign authorities. Moreover, consonant with item 1 of Article 1 of the Treaty on Legal Cooperation in Criminal Matters entered into between Brazil and the Republic of Italy—promulgated through Ministerial Decree No. 862 of July 9, 1993—"each of the parties shall, on request, provide to the other party, in the form set forth in this Treaty, ample

examining the Explanatory Restatement of Decisions, account was taken of Article 784 of the Code of Criminal Procedure, which makes provisions concerning *competent foreign authorities*, inasmuch as it allows a broader interpretation than *judicial authority* for purposes of transmitting letters rogatory to Brazil, in that it encompasses agencies clothed in judicial powers.

Legislative Decree No. 501 of March 21, 2012,[18] published in the Federal Official Gazette on 03/23/2012, made provisions regarding the procedures for handling

---

cooperation for criminal proceedings conducted by the judicial authorities of the requesting party." The reference to judicial authorities by the requesting party suggests, initially, agencies clothed in judicial appointments, as in the Brazilian system. However, in Italy, the Attorney General's office is part of the judicial system, per Articles 107, 108 and 112 under the title headed "The Courts" (Italian Constitution, Part II, Title IV). The judicial branch is organized institutionally in a linear fashion, within that same Branch, its duties involving judgment or work traditionally included in the area reserved to the Office of the Public Prosecutor. Briefly, it is a blending of functions, all of them subject to the Superior Council of the Courts. As pointed out by best doctrine, the Attorney General's Office in Italy is an agency for the administration of Justice, and includes all measures that may be taken there for purposes of criminal investigations. See "O Ministério Público na Investigação Penal Preliminar," by Marcos Kac. Hence, the Supreme Court of Justice, in Letter Rogatory No. 998/IT, through a unanimous panel decision authored by Minister Humberto Gomes de Barros, concluded: "The Attorney General's Office together with the Tribunal of Parma does have standing to request Brazilian cooperation in investigations."

[18] Art. 1—This Decree establishes procedures for letters rogatory and both active and passive requests for direct assistance in criminal and civil matters in the absence of any bilateral or multilateral international legal cooperation agreement, and applies only subsidiarily to this case. Art. 2—The following considerations apply for purposes of this Decree: I. Request for passive direct assistance, the request for international legal cooperation which does not require a prima-facie evaluation by the Superior Court of Justice, pursuant to Art. 7, of Superior Court of Justice Resolution No. 9 of May 4, 2005; and II. Passive letter rogatory, a request for international legal cooperation which does require a prima-facie evaluation by the Superior Court of Justice. Sole Paragraph. Definition of the request for active direct support and an active letter rogatory is in accordance with the domestic legislation of the Requested State. Art. 3—In all cases in which the request for passive international legal cooperation does not entail the granting of exequatur by the Superior Court of Justice, and may be handled through administrative channels, not requiring intervention by the Judicial Branch, the Ministry of Justice shall, together with the competent administrative authorities, see to its granting. Art. 4—The Ministry of External Relations shall forward to the Ministry of Justice all requests for passive international legal cooperation, on criminal and civil matters, transmitted through diplomatic channels. Art. 5—In the absence of bilateral or multilateral international legal cooperation agreements, the Ministry of Justice shall forward to the Ministry of External Relations all active requests for international legal cooperation on criminal and civil matters, to be handled through diplomatic channels. Art. 6—The Ministry of Justice shall: I. Provide attachments and opinions to and coordinate the granting of requests for international legal cooperation in criminal and civil matters, by forwarding these to the competent judicial or administrative authority; II. Issue and publish understandings on international legal cooperation within the scope of its powers. Art. 7—Letters rogatory must include: I. Identification of the requesting and requested courts; II. The address of the requesting judge; III. A detailed description of the measure requested; IV. The purpose to be achieved by the requested measure; V. Complete name and address of the person to be cited, notified, served a summons or questioned in the jurisdiction of the requested court, and, if possible, full particulars, specifying the mother's name, date of birth, place of birth, and passport number; VI. Closure, with the judge's signature; and VII. Any other information which might be of use to the requested court for purposes of facilitating compliance with the letter rogatory. § 1—Should a requested measure consist of interrogation of the party

letters rogatory and requests for direct assistance, this after the Ministry of Justice and Ministry of External Relations modernized their rules for handling requests for international cooperation, always to make the procedure move faster. This Decree established that whenever the request can be granted administratively, that is, with

---

or questioning of a witness, it is recommended, under penalty of inability to comply with the measure, that the letters rogatory further include: (a) The text of the questions to be asked by the requested court; (b) Setting up a hearing, beginning with the transmittal of the letter rogatory to the Ministry of Justice, with a lead-time of at least: (1) Ninety (90) days, for criminal matters; and (2) One hundred eighty (180) days, for civil matters. § 2—In the event of civil cooperation, letters rogatory must also include, where appropriate, the full name and address of the person responsible, at the addressee end, for payment of court costs and procedural fees arising from performance of the letter rogatory in the requested country, except for those taken from actions: (I) Handled under the auspices of free justice; (II) For the sending of foodstuffs abroad, for countries bound by the New York Convention, promulgated in Brazil by Ministerial Decree No. 56826 of September 2, 1965, pursuant to Article 26 of Law No. 5478 of July 25, 1968; (III) Coming under the jurisdiction of child and adolescent courts, pursuant to Law No. 8069 of June 13, 1990. Art. 8—Letters rogatory must be accompanied by the following documents: (I) Initial petition, criminal information or complaint, depending on the nature of the matter; (II) Background documents; (III) Court order for its transmittal; (IV) Original copy of the official or certified translation of the letter rogatory and all accompanying documents; (V) Two original copies of the letter rogatory, of the translation and all accompanying documents; and (VI) Other documents or exhibits considered indispensable by the requesting court, in accordance with the nature of the action. Sole paragraph. Where the purpose of the letter rogatory is forensic examination of a document, it is recommended that the original be sent to the requested court, the copy remaining in the record of the requesting court, otherwise the measure may not achieve fruition. Art. 9—All petitions for direct assistance must include: (I) Indication of provision contained in an international bilateral or multilateral legal cooperation agreement or reciprocity agreement; (II) Indication of the requesting authority; (III) Indication of Central Authorities in both requesting and requested States; (IV) Summary containing the number(s) of proceedings or lawsuits in their requesting State, to serve as the basis for the request for cooperation; (V) Complete and accurate particulars on all persons to whom the request makes reference (name, last name, nationality, birthplace, address, birth date and, wherever possible, mother's name, profession, and passport number); (VI) A clear, objective, concise, and complete narrative couched in the actual verbiage of the request for international legal cooperation, of the events which gave rise to it, to include: (a) Place and date; (b) Causal nexus between the ongoing proceedings, all those involved, and measures solicited in the request for assistance; and (c) All documentation attached to the request. (VII) References to and full transcripts of all applicable laws and regulations, especially, on criminal matters, criminal laws; (VIII) Detailed description of the assistance requested, indicating: (a) In cases of tracing or freezing of bank accounts, the account number, the name of the bank, the bank location, and the endpoints of the desired time-frame, along with specific instructions as to how the documents to be obtained shall be forwarded (physical or electronic media); (b) In cases requiring notice, citation, or summonses, full particulars on the person to be served notice, cited, or issued a summons, and the corresponding address; (c) In cases of interrogations and questioning, the list of questions to be asked. (IX) Description of the purpose of the request for international legal cooperation; (X) Any other information which might prove useful to the requested authority, for purposes of facilitating the granting of the request for international legal cooperation; (XI) Other information solicited by the requested State; and (XII) Signature of the requesting authority, location, and date. Art. 10—This Decree revokes Foreign Office/Justice Ministry (MRE/MJ) Interministerial Order No. 26 of August 14, 1990, and the MRE/MJ Interministerial Order of September 16, 2003, published in the Federal Official Gazette on September 19, 2003. Art. 11—This Order shall take effect as of the date of its publication.

no intervention from the Judiciary, action on the part of the Superior Court of Justice may be dispensed with, and the Ministry of Justice shall see to the performance by the competent administrative authorities, as set forth in Article 3.

The institution of Central Authority came about to speed up and facilitate cooperation between countries. As the name itself suggests, the primary role of the Central Authority is to function as a centralizing agency, the focus of all cooperation—requests and investigations alike—whether coming from abroad or transmitted from Brazil. All letters rogatory and requests for legal assistance, whatever their purpose, shall be handled through the intermediation of central authorities.

In Brazil, as in most countries, the Central Authority lies in the Executive Branch,[19] given that it typically represents the State in international relations. The Central Authority is an idea espoused in the Hague Conventions and international conventions on public international law, arising out of the need to have an agency in each country to regulate the administrative procedures for International Legal Cooperation.

Its creation was imperative given the increase in volume and complexity of mechanisms for international cooperation. It imparts uniformity of performance, standardizes all procedures, and provides the necessary specialization for handling such matters, avoiding duplication and waste in the requests.

There are countless advantages to the institution of a single Central Authority: specialization, speed, efficiency, publicity, and affordability of proceedings. It is argued that placing Central Authority in the Executive Branch will also ensure neutrality, transparency, and due process, inasmuch as Executive Branch agencies are subject to oversight by the Office of the Public Prosecutor, their acts subject to review by the Judicial Branch.[20]

It is important to mention that the Central Authority is by no means a *sine qua non* for making international cooperation feasible. Cooperation may occur directly between the competent authorities. However the institution of a Central Authority brings these authorities closer together to eliminate obstacles in the way of rapid realization of shared national interests. Indeed, there is no point to demanding the establishment of a Central Authority unless it is committed to achieving efficiency, simplification and necessary speed of information and action.

---

[19] According to Goal No. 02 of the National Strategy for the Fight Against Money Laundering Report—ENCLA OF 2004 (now the National Strategy for the Fight Against Corruption and Money Laundering—ENCCLA), requests for active international cooperation from the Judicial Branch or the Office of the Public Prosecutor and federal and state police authorities, regarding authorization for direct cooperation on operations (which require an international reciprocity agreement), all go through the Ministry of Justice Asset Recovery and International Legal Cooperation Council Department—DRCI (Art. 13, IV, of Decree No. 4991 of February 18, 2004).

[20] The great challenge at this point is to further popularize the benefits of adopting a single Central Authority for all International Legal Cooperation issues, and broaden the horizon of this institution. With the assistance of the policies of Brazil's Justice Ministry, through the National Anti-Money Laundering Qualification and Training Plan—PNLD, the idea is being spread that, even in the absence of an agreement, it is possible to have requests for active or passive cooperation routed through the Central Authority.

8.3 Confiscating and Repatriating Assets

Legal assistance has allowed the freezing and repatriation of assets, but often requires an affidavit—an internally consistent sworn statement—to enable such measures as freezing assets or bank accounts.[21]

Freezing and seizure operations require a hard sell. It is not enough to simply attach a court order. At times one has to turn over convincing documents to establish a link between assets or a bank account and illegal behavior. It also helps if the goods in question are the proceeds from criminal activity abroad or at least flow (by action or omission) from corrupt practices.

Consider the impact on U.S. asset forfeiture legislation of the case in which Brazil filed for freezing of assets belonging to a Brazilian defendant, and for keeping those assets in the USA. At issue was whether, based on 28 U.S.C. § 2467 (d) (3) Enforcement of Foreign Judgment,[22] foreign assets may only be frozen after a foreign court has definitively ruled in favor of forfeiture, or if it may be done before any final decision on confiscation has been rendered. The United States Court of Appeals for the District of Columbia Circuit, on review of two decisions by the Court in March and April 2009, decided that a final decision by Brazil regarding confiscation was required, according to its interpretation of 28 U.S.C. § 2467 (d) (3).[23] Following this decision, the U.S. Department of Justice requested and obtained from Congress a resolution of the problem because, if upheld and followed, the decision would have compromised international cooperation efforts with other countries.

The disposal of confiscated assets is provided in the 1988 UN Vienna Convention against Illicit Traffic in Narcotic Drugs (Article 5, item 5, clause "b") and in the Convention at Palermo on Transnational Organized Crime (Article 30, item 2, clause "c"), and can stimulate cooperation among authorities in different countries.

---

[21] A bill is being submitted in Brazil (No. 1982, dated September 16, 2003), by national Congressman Eduardo Valverde, to regulate International Legal Assistance on Criminal Matters, irrespective of the transmittal of letters rogatory. It would provide for temporary administrative freezing of proceeds of crime undergoing laundering. It also provides a *Council on International Legal Assistance*, empowered to formulate directives, and serving as a permanent clearinghouse for information among the various government agencies it represents (the Federal Courts, Office of the Federal Prosecutor, Ministry of External Relations, Office of the Attorney General, Brazil's Federal Revenue Secretariat, the Central Bank, the Council for Financial Activities Control (COAF), the Federal Police Department, and the Office of the Comptroller-General), all offering guidance to Brazilian authorities needing to secure international cooperation.

[22] (d) Entry and Enforcement of Judgment—(1) In general—The district court shall enter such orders as may be necessary to enforce the judgment on behalf of the foreign nation unless the court finds that—(A) the judgment was rendered under a system that provides tribunals or procedures incompatible with the requirements of due process of law; (B) the foreign court lacked personal jurisdiction over the defendant; (C) the foreign court lacked jurisdiction over the subject matter; (D) the foreign nation did not take steps, in accordance with the principles of due process, to give notice of the proceedings to a person with an interest in the property of the proceedings in sufficient time to enable him or her to defend; or (E) the judgment was obtained by fraud.

[23] United States v. Opportunity Fund and Tiger Eye Investments, Ltd. [9].

By the principle of specialization, applicable to relations among States and, therefore, to international legal cooperation efforts, no information or documents obtained through legal assistance may not be used with regard to crimes for which International Cooperation is excluded on account of jurisdiction being regarded as an attribute of the State, on which we cite the example of Switzerland, with regard to exchange quota violations.[24]

Insistence on dual criminality, that is, the existence of criminal behavior in both of the jurisdictions involved in the request for legal assistance on criminal matters is, in principle, a common requirement in cooperation cases—with the proviso that the two criminal categories need not be exactly the same, but only similar. Indeed, the UN Convention on Corruption signed at Mérida makes it clear that "in matters of international cooperation, whenever dual criminality is considered a requirement, it shall be deemed fulfilled irrespective of whether the laws of the requested State Party place the offence within the same category of offence or denominate the offence by the same terminology as the requesting State Party, if the conduct underlying the offence for which assistance is sought is a criminal offence under the laws of both State Parties" (Article 43).

The rule cannot, however, be interpreted as an absolute. The Financial Action Task Force advocates international legal cooperation, pursuant to the UN Conventions of Vienna (international traffic, 1988), Palermo (transnational organized crime, 2000), and Mérida (corruption, 2003), by withdrawal of obstacles (Recommendation No. 36) and direct mutual assistance toward a quick, constructive, and effective solution (Recommendation No. 37).

Yet not even the FATF gives the rule the proper crucial weight with regard to money laundering. Failure to honor the principle of *dual criminality*, which is no novelty in international public law, may prove devastating in future requests for cooperation, in specific cases, and completely bar new freezes or obtaining of evidence, among other diplomatic difficulties.

Brazil's Money Laundering Law (Law No. 9613/1998, as amended by Law 12683/2012) does contain provisions on assets located abroad:

> *Art. 8.* The judge shall determine, given the existence of an international treaty or convention and by request of the competent foreign authority, measures to secure assets, securities or amounts proceeding from crimes described in Article 1, and committed abroad.
>
> § 1. All provisions contained in this article shall apply, irrespective of any treaty or international convention, whenever the government of the country whose authorities make the request promise reciprocity to Brazil.
>
> § 2. Absent a treaty or convention, all goods, securities or amounts subject to security measures at the request of the competent foreign authority—or the proceeds from their alien-

[24] Pursuant to ENCLA 2005 Target No. 40, the Justice Ministry's Asset Recovery and International Legal Cooperation Council Department agreed to share *information on the need to keep within limitations on the use of documents obtained through International Legal Cooperation*, and reaffirmed the principle of specialization at the international level.

ation—shall be divided equally between the requesting States and Brazil, following proper provisions for injured or good-faith third parties.

With specific regard to the division of goods, as observed above, the UN Convention signed at Mérida (corruption) made no provisions; however, there was an understanding that there ought to be full restitution of assets to the injured-party-State in view of the legal assets affected (Articles 51–59).

Finally, one notes that with regard to seizure or freezing of assets, there are no obstacles in the way of their international application once the universal rule of reciprocity is in effect, and it is still possible to divide up the goods confiscated or seized, and consequently repatriate them, once the decision awarding forfeiture to the government becomes final.

It is extremely difficult to obtain repatriation of assets based only on an appealable decision, even if reciprocity is invoked.

The authorities of requested States usually wish to be informed regarding:

(a) Evidence that all owners, agents, curators, or others involved with the articles in question are aware of issuance of the order that they be seized, and of its content, including a list of works;
(b) Evidence to show that the Brazilian seizure order was signed prior to the legal sale or transfer of the articles abroad;
(c) Proof of direct association between the artwork and fraud detected in Brazil which would demonstrate that its acquisition does indeed flow from criminal behavior;
(d) Unavailability of the assets (works of art) precisely because such a procedure is public knowledge and one might therefore infer that the interested parties, curators, art dealers, and such had knowledge of the illegal events involving large holdings;
(e) Listing of all legal events (seizure orders, forfeitures, decisions that have become final) relating to the accused, including all corresponding dates.

At the first Judicial Roundtable Meeting between federal judges from Brazil and the USA, attended by several judges from Colombia and Mexico,[25] in Washington DC, October 27–31, 2011, initial conclusions were drawn that the more the evidence, the easier the seizure/sequestering, and that where drug trafficking is concerned, it is easier to secure the granting of the request because the laws are not as difficult to understand. The purpose of this unprecedented encounter was to establish a framework of judicial decisions to render international legal cooperation feasible as quickly as possible.

A glossary was proposed to include the more important expressions encountered in matters of international cooperation, whereupon Brazil presented the following:

[25] Two judges per country, along with U.S. federal prosecutors, attended the meeting organized by the U.S. Department of Justice.

IMPORTANT TERMS AND EXPRESSIONS

I. *Assets:*

Freezing—decision need not be final, a decision of the court will suffice;

Seizure—of everything relating to evidence. A decision of the court will suffice;

Seizure—real estate, assets, securities or cash—of the proceeds of crime. A decision of the court will suffice.

Confiscation or Forfeiture—where there is a final decision. Seek restitution for the State and/or victim or affected third party.

Instrumentalities of the crime—may only be confiscated if their manufacture, use, or possession is itself illegal (e.g. illegal weapon), except in the case of drugs, which are always confiscated.

Proceeds of the crime—economic benefits derived from criminal behavior.

II. *Procedural:*

Investigation—work to be done by the police;

Judicial Proceedings—a generic term for the initial work conducted in the courts by request of the police or the Office of the Public Prosecutor. These may comprise of search warrants or seizure orders; attachment orders; wiretap or electronic surveillance orders; lifting of bank secrecy, etc.;

Police Report—a document summarizing conclusions arrived at by police concerning a crime. Here, instead of the accused, we have subjects of an investigation;

Indictment—initial document which starts the criminal action (filed by the Office of the Public Prosecutor) and which may begin with a Police Report or from a set of informative documents (documents obtained or arising from judicial proceedings). This is the formal accusation before the court;

Parties—1. Defendant, or the accused (represented by a private attorney or State-appointed/public defender); 2. the Office of the Public Prosecutor, or prosecutor.

Judicial Proceedings or Criminal Action—set of documents which begins with the indictment and ends with sentencing if guilty or absolution if not guilty;

Final decision—a judicial decision on the merits which can no longer be appealed.

Citation—notice to the accused or defendant that the indictment (accusation by the Office of the Public Prosecutor) was accepted initially by the court;

Summons—notice served on the accused, the defendant or victim, or a witness, for legal proceedings;

Judicial Decision—a decision issued by a judge regarding some question (for instance, lifting of bank secrecy, wiretaps, placing an examining trial on the docket, requests for restitution of property, etc.). May be appealed.

Sentence—final and conclusive decision on the merits of the charge. May convict or absolve. May occasionally provide relief from a death sentence, statutory limitation, etc.

Final decision—a judicial decision on the merits which can no longer be appealed.

Appeal—attempt to overturn a decision. There are other remedies or constitutional impugnments provided against judicial decisions in general (reviews, appeals in the strictest sense, habeas corpus, writs of mandamus, etc.);

III. *Criminal:*

Illegal Enrichment—not a crime, but may be a fiscal offense;
Money Laundering—requires an antecedent crime;

IV. *Institutional:*

Federal Justice System—handles all cases in which the Union (Brazil's federal government) or its entities, have a stake. Handles international traffic in narcotics, international money laundering, federal tax evasion, crimes against the National Financial System, against Social Security, cybercrime, etc.
Makeup:
1st instance (federal judges);
Appeals (Regional Federal Courts, there are five in Brazil);
Appellate Court (STJ)—unifies understanding of the laws;
Supreme Federal Court (STF)—appeals and constitutional questions.
State Courts—handle everything not handled by the federal court system (ordinary crimes).
Makeup:
1st instance (state judges);
Appeals (State Courts of Appeal);
STJ;
STF;
There is also the Military Justice System, the Electoral Courts and the Labor Courts.

V. *International Legal Cooperation:*

Direct Assistance—requires an indictment or decision in the requested country;
Rogatory—not subject to judicial review, but is merely a service to public order and sovereignty, since it amounts to enforcement of a judicial decision already made abroad.

With regard to the content of judicial decisions, Brazil made the following proposals:

STANDARDIZED DECISIONS (CONTENT)

I. *Request for Legal Assistance (direct assistance)*

1. *Regarding Assets, Securities or Cash:*

- *Identification;*
- *Location or request to identify the location, or notification through some national information network for purposes of future repatriation;*

- *Causal connection (between asset and criminal or suspected criminal behavior) or relevant information (illegal enrichment).*

Record of a JUDICIAL DECISION (not necessarily final), but for REPATRIATION, A FINAL DECISION (that has become final, that is, unappealable), excepting only such crimes as corruption and the like (UN Convention, Mérida, Art. 57) or a special interest case, such as artworks.

2. *Bank Secrecy:*
   - *Identification of account holders;*
   - *Name, address, and branch location;*
   - *Description of requested documents (signature cards, transfers, statements);*
   - *Dates or timeframe (delimited);*
   - *Causal connection (between asset and criminal or suspected criminal behavior) or relevant information (illegal enrichment).*

JUDICIAL DECISION (may be appealable).

3. *Citation and subpoenas (defendants, victims, witnesses, affected third parties);*
   - *Questions.*

DECISION OF THE COURT.

II. *Legal basis for its grounding (for ease of understanding and to verify dual criminal liability):*
   - *A clear, objective and complete narrative.*

III. *Literal transcription of all provisions to be able to verify a similar crime in the requested State.*

The document summing up the importance of Judicial Round Table Meeting reads:

JUSTIFICATION FOR LEGAL DIALOGUE AIMED AT ESTABLISHING CASE LAW PRECEDENT

WHEREAS there is a need to facilitate International Cooperation;

AND WHEREAS the fight against organized crime must not be defeated by lack of understanding regarding the various international legal systems;

AND WHEREAS explanation of domestic legal systems has converged on the stripping away of assets from criminal organizations from small conceptual changes;

AND WHEREAS standardization of judicial decisions to facilitate cooperation among all countries involved in the fight against organized crime is important;

AND WHEREAS there is a need for States to unite behind the seizure, confiscation and repatriation of goods, securities and money,

BE IT RESOLVED THAT WE ESTABLISH THE FOLLOWING TO ENSURE BETTER UNDERSTANDING TOWARD PROPER INTERNATIONAL COOPERATION WITH NEEDED STANDARDIZATION OF JUDICIAL DECISIONS:

1. *The fight against crime is independent of the place where the crime was committed, and confiscation is indispensable;*
2. *Cooperation through Letters Rogatory is not recommended because it is slow and bureaucratic, and because analysis in the requested country is limited to checks on public policy and affronts to sovereignty;*
3. *Cooperation by Direct Assistance is a response to be followed by States because it is faster, based on mutual trust and conveys to the requested State a proper analysis of the requests;*
4. *The simplified Mutual Legal Assistance Treaty (MLAT) approach is recommended, and must be objectively clear;*
5. *Central authorities have placed no obstacles in the way of direct contact between magistrates or competent authorities, and channels of communication must be opened up to ease unnecessary bureaucratic burdens (Article 18.13 of the UN Convention against Organized Crime at Palermo does not prohibit such understandings);*
6. *The regular legal systems of countries involved must be respected (requesting and requested States), and it is no bar to cooperation if the request originated with or was addressed to the police, the Office of the Public Prosecutor, or the courts;*
7. *If Extradition is refused, on grounds of citizenship, then the persons believed to be involved ought to be promptly submitted to authorities in their own country (Art. 16.10, Palermo). However, if extradition is accepted, it is recommended that the sentence be served out in the requested State (Art. 16.11, Palermo), otherwise, require serving the sentence or part of it in the requesting State (Art. 16.12, Palermo);*
8. *Possibility of joint prosecution or transfer of criminal proceedings (Art. 21, Palermo) for final disposal of assets and joint measures (cooperative debriefings with effects in both countries) and to achieve better administration of Justice;*
9. *International Cooperation ought not to be blocked while the whereabouts of an asset are unknown. The requested State should try all available measures for tracing or seizure for future confiscation or repatriation;*
10. *As a condition for restitution to the interested party, the requested State should provide proof of the legality of the asset, security or pecuniary amount whenever the requesting State requires seizure with an eye to confiscation or repatriation, but which request was mooted by legal decisions setting aside the merits as to its legal origin;*
11. *Invocation of absence of dual criminality cannot justify failure to cite or subpoena defendants, victims, witnesses or affected third parties once criminal proceedings have been initiated in the requesting State;*

12. *Information gained for criminal proceedings may be used in other such proceedings if the requested State so authorizes, even if retroactively;*
13. *Assets, securities or pecuniary amounts shall be restituted for indemnification of victims or to be turned over to the United Nations Fund for technical assistance among countries or even for reimbursement of the State. A division might be arrived that to deduct only expenses, except for such crimes as corruption and the like, and also with regard to cultural goods, which should be so disposed of as to give priority to public access;*
14. *Reimbursement of States lies outside the reach of the statute of limitations, which does not nullify International Cooperation;*
15. *What does negate International Cooperation is invocation of a need for a court order for a mere citation, subpoena or copies, and it is incumbent upon States to simplify their legal system to make Direct Assistance workable;*
16. *Defense witnesses ought to be heard in the country filing charges or, otherwise, by teleconference from embassies or consulates, with International Cooperation not being invoked except where the evidence is accepted by the prosecution;*
17. *International Cooperation does not require the attachment of proof, but rather, a presentation of arguments leading to the decision to see that measures be taken abroad;*
18. *No specific Mutual Legal Assistance Treaty is required for each asset, security or pecuniary amount if the requesting State attaches to its request a list of assets and gives grounds.*

Artworks seized in the USA at the request of Brazil's Federal Courts in Criminal Action No. 2004.61.81.008954-9 (involving the former Banco Santos) filed at the Sixth Federal Criminal Court in São Paulo, specializing in Financial Crime and Money Laundering, among them, paintings by Jean-Michel Basquiat (Hannibal), Joaquin Torres Garcia (*Figures dans une Structure*), Roy Lichtenstein (*Modern Painting With Yellow Interweave*), and Helen Frankenthaler (*Sea Strip*) and a Togatus romano (XIV-IX B.C.).

On September 17, 2010, the Federal Court announced bankruptcy proceedings and the importance of preserving public access to repatriated works of art:

> The Judge at Law for the No. 2 Special Court of Bankruptcy and Recovery for Precinct 2 of the County of São Paulo, through Communiqué No. 65/2010-DIR, received at this Court on 09/16/2010, all necessary steps having been taken (logistical planning for transporting the works, among them, inspection, crating, insurance, transportation and allocation of space at the University of São Paulo Museum of Contemporary Art) for repatriation of Modern Painting With Yellow Interweave, by Roy Lichtenstein, and Figures Dans Une Structure, by Joaquin Torres-Garcia.
>
> These works of art were traced to the United States of America through the operation of a Request for Legal Assistance on Criminal Matters transmitted by this Court on 05/25/2006, in record No. R005.61.81.900396-6, on account of seizure ordered for artworks of unknown whereabouts belonging to defendant Edemar Cid Ferreira listed in bank records on a CD-ROM of the Cid Collection (belonging to the accused), and duly listed in the "LIST OF MISSING ARTWORKS," prepared by the staff of this Court.

On that same occasion an order for its repatriation, if located abroad, was also transmitted to INTERPOL for full enforcement.[26]

There are times, in particular now, in which the authorities must go beyond the mere protection of capital. To the contrary, they are expected to reinforce values, primarily cultural values in harmony with universal unity.

To speak of repayment in kind will only make sense when all of us—even potential private interests—are included, and the repayment is accomplished by positive actions that allow public access to global heritage to the public at large (and not just to the few) that it may influence future generations. Half-measures are not consistent with his view.

If everyone comes out ahead, so do the creditors of the bankrupt estate. So that there are no losses whenever the people as a whole are the great beneficiaries.

It is also expected that judgment of the bankrupt estate, in keeping with the handling up until then of the holdings by the Federal Criminal Justice System in the sense of enforcing the Convention Concerning the Protection of the World's Cultural and Natural Heritage formulated at the UNESCO General Conference (held in Paris, 1972, and passed, in Brazil, by Legislative Decree no. 74 of 06/30/1977),[27] it is indeed incumbent upon all to preserve the cultural heritage of mankind.

It is only in this spirit, after the criminal sentence issued by this federal court became final (consonant with the findings of 06/15/2009 and of 12/07/2009 in Conflict of Jurisdiction No.76.740/SP of the Honorable Appellate Court), that Brazilian society awaits future decisions from the Bankruptcy Court quite apart from any interest which the Government may have in the acquisition of that wealth of holdings, inasmuch as it behooves all of us, as pointed out above, to bring about the conclusion of this story through our commitment to the common good.

Observe that in the decision of the Hon. Superior Court of Justice the exclusion of archaeological and ethnographic works is clear. Their final disposal is up to the University of São Paulo's Museum of Archaeology and Ethnology as of 08/30/2005 (decision on folios 373–376 of record No. 2005.61.81.900396-6, not subject to appeal), in view of the constitutional and legal ban on commercial sale of the art as, indeed, was never in doubt, not least because any act in violation of fundamental provisions likewise set forth in special legislation would render it subject to immediate seizure.

---

[26] Folios 3587, 3588, 3590 of record No. 2005.61.81.900396-6.

[27] Notably, in its Articles 4 and 5 described below:

Article 4: Each State Party to this Convention recognizes that the duty of ensuring the identification, protection, conservation, presentation and transmission to future generations of the cultural and natural heritage (...) and situated on its territory, belongs primarily to that State. It will do all it can to this end, to the utmost of its own resources and, where appropriate, with any international assistance and co-operation, in particular, financial, artistic, scientific and technical.

Article 5: To ensure that effective and active measures are taken for the protection, conservation and presentation of the cultural and natural heritage (...) each State Party to this Convention shall endeavor (...) (d) to take the appropriate legal, scientific, technical, administrative and financial steps necessary for the identification, protection, conservation, presentation and rehabilitation of this heritage...

> I congratulate the initiative of the Bankruptcy Court in unveiling a particular view of works of art, instituting cautionary measures aimed at their safe repatriation to Brazil and provisionally placing the works in the Museum of Contemporary Art (inasmuch as prominent placement is still contingent upon the sentencing decision of this Court becoming final). All of this signals to us that that Court also recognizes the importance of the issue and the questions involved. These are no simple matters of economic satisfaction, but rather, they give substantive form to the UNESCO Convention referenced above, both in Brazil and in other countries signatories to the Convention.
>
> There is confidence, then that the magnanimous treatment that the issue requires, in the certainty that all of the commitments assumed by Brazil before the international community will prevail, indeed, to the satisfaction of deeply-held beliefs which our constituted authorities ought no longer to trespass upon.
>
> Brazil's Federal Justice System will, in the ceremony to be held next week in New York, receive all of the aforementioned works and pass them along to the failed estate of Banco Santos, making it all the more important to press forward with the criminal sentence and make that decision final. Then there is the appeal as to the bankrupt estate and the assignment of these works to the Union, and the decision of the Hon. Superior Court of Justice, which held that only this criminal court had jurisdiction to decide on measures necessary for all the situations involving repatriation of goods, whether in the simplest cases or in those in which the procedure for recovery of assets requires negotiations with the requested State Party.
>
> Thus, notify the Bankruptcy Court of this decision and also inform them that the Federal Criminal Court has agreed to the measures taken, up to then, in that specific case, with regard to the works indicated above, repatriation efforts for which were accomplished through the Federal Courts, with the cooperation of the Justice Ministry's Asset Recovery and the International Legal Cooperation Council Department (DRCI/MJ) and of the Office of the Federal Prosecutor, in hopes timely notice will be given of future measures.
>
> Serve notice to the Office of the Federal Prosecutor and the University of São Paulo Museum of Archaeology and Ethnography (MAE/USP).
>
> São Paulo, September 17, 2010.
>
> Fausto Martin de Sanctis
>
> Federal Judge.

On June 18, 2015, in the U.S. Attorney's Office, in New York City, the author made a statement about the importance of the repatriation based on mutual trust and the need to preserve public assets from exclusively private interests, as following:

> This ceremony of repatriation of two artworks, Hannibal (from Jean-Michel Basquiat, estimation $10 million), and Roman Togatus (Before Christ, $773,000), exemplifies the confidence of Brazil in the International Justice System, especially in the United States. Artworks were forfeitable as property imported into the U.S. by means of false and fraudulent statements or practices in violation of U.S. Customs Laws. According to American authorities, both artworks were shown as valued $100 with false invoices to circumvent laws.

The Brazilian Federal Court, which I represent here, believed in the efficacy of INTERPOL and foreign authorities, and sought the help of friend states. Our work aimed to address the need for redressing the crime by repatriation of works of art.

These works deserve destination for which they were requested: meeting the social interest through people's access to works that, although allegedly acquired with the proceeds of crime, have undeniable culture value which should not be economically measurable.

Artworks represent history, aesthetics, reflection, creativity. They reveal a society, a moment, a feeling, the nature, a place. They never should be seen in their monetary aspect because it would diminish something that transcends this vision, which would be simplistic and selfish. There is only compensation of victims when all the people are included because art protection for public purposes benefits society in general. 2010 was the first and historical result of a huge Bilateral Mutual Legal Assistance in Criminal Matters.[28]

Due to a meticulous work of many civil servants, it was possible to identify artworks that were missing, supposedly concealed from the Court, in order to be possible to deal them here, in the U.S. That could perform an illegal interest allowing sell and/or buy them through a front person, a shell company or an intermediary. Money laundering should not be committed again.

I remember coming to the U.S. to deal with American authorities about the best treatment and destination of artworks forfeited by the Brazilian Federal Trial Court. Although a formal mechanism for Criminal International Cooperation, we had to use an informal method, talking eye-to-eye in a very respectful way. I contacted the U.S. Attorney Sharon Levin who did a wonderful job here.

I am grateful to the federal civil servants, to the Federal Police and INTERPOL, to the Brazilian Central Authority – DRCI, and to the U.S. who understood the importance of those facts, expressed in this ceremony. We are materializing the UNESCO Convention Concerning the Protection of the World Cultural and Natural Heritage (Paris, Nov. 16, 1972), ratified by the U.S. on Dec. 07, 1973, by Brazil on Sept. 01, 1977, and by France on June 27, 1975. It entered into force on Dec. 17, 1975.

I congratulate the U.S., who was the first country that ratified this Convention and helped us to make it real. Finally, I would like to give special thanks to Seth Taylor, special agent from Immigration and Custom Enforcement—ICE (Department of Homeland Security), David Rogath (owner of an art gallery and communicated the attempt of selling them), Sharon Levin (U.S. Attorney) and the Department of Justice—DOJ for the outstanding and diligent work in this historical and important International Cooperation.

These artworks are being delivery today, not to the Judiciary branch, but to the People of Brazil, and must remain with Them.

Fausto Martin De Sanctis

Federal Appellate Judge at the Federal Appellate Court/Sao Paulo

---

[28] In 2010, there was the repatriation of *Modern Painting With Yellow* (from Roy Lichtenstein) and *Figures dans une Structure* (Torres-García); in 2014, *Composition Abstracte* (Serge Poliakoff).

8.4 Virtual World

The exercises of personal and prescriptive jurisdiction can been seen as problematic in the case of absent of physical contact between the defendant and the forum. So, states may well be tempted to create new rules of substantive liability for third parties who do have a physical presence in the state's territory.

For example, a state unable to compel a nonresident merchant to collect sales tax on sales to its residents might insist that a resident financial institution collect that tax if credit cards issued by it are used by the resident.

The Internet, being the face of globalization, resists the imposition of borders and requires a regulatory system that does not spillover. But, while the use of a website may have effects beyond a user's own territory, these effects result from the technology that allows easy access to a website from everywhere.

Modern geolocation technologies offer an automatic, accurate, and affordable means of identifying an Internet user's geographic location. Because every website operator now has, according to Kevin F. King, "the ability to screen users by jurisdiction, the chief obstacle to the constitutionality of many of these law is gone. That new technological order shifts the focus to a new question: when are lawmakers free to compel sites to adopt geolocation technologies? The mere fact that such technologies exist does not mean that a mandate for their use would be constitutionally permissible."[29]

Imaging that a government agency suspects that someone in the USA is involved in a conspiracy to plant a bomb in a café in Paris. Law enforcement officials, seeking to gather information about the suspect as quickly as possible, rush to a web portal and online service provider, and ask its local data security manager voluntarily to disclose all information related to the suspect. The provider cooperates and reveals all information related to the suspect. Usually, law enforcement officials needed a judicial order authorizing search and seizure of the information. It should be convinced by a Court about reasonable suspicious based upon a probable cause. State intervention is justified in this field just as any other human activity that could affect public welfare, limiting intervention to protect civil rights. Facilitating cooperation between law enforcement agencies and the private sector requires close attention avoiding the concentration of power and the threat of human rights. It is up to democratic governments and their citizens to work together to strike a balance between the most basic and necessary levels of intervention and the inherently democratic rights of citizens.

To Renee Keen, "citizens and organization fighting against regulation, and governments seeking to protect their citizens through regulation, must come together and recognize their common objectives in order to effectuate the changes they want to see through mutual sacrifice. Citizens must accept that a minimum level of

[29] See King [10, p. 109].

Internet filtration may be necessary for the government to effectively perform the task of preventing and punishing illegal activities conducted online."[30]

Assertions of jurisdiction based on physical presence are not implicated by changed technology. Acts outside the state, which in one way or another could be said to target residents of this state, permit the assertion of jurisdiction if such could be said to target residents of the state, as long as it could be a reasonable statement. To facilitate international cooperation in combating money laundering, the USA, and other nations have ratified Mutual Assistance Treaties—MLATs. MLATs "expedite the process of uncovering and prosecuting international money laundering by, for example, by extracting binding obligations between nations to provide key evidence despite domestic privacy laws."[31]

In fact, a company that maintained a website could be subject to jurisdiction anywhere, because the Internet is widely accessible in many foreign jurisdictions. So, "mere maintenance of a website cannot subject a defendant to global jurisdiction if the new technology is to be capable of meaningful use. If each website subjected its sponsor to global jurisdiction, many would forego use of the technology for fear of its secondary costs. If these costs were in practice nonexistent because judgments rendered by distant courts were not enforce by courts that could seize the person or assets of the defendant, an evolving and necessary system of internationally accepted jurisdictional principles would be undermined."[32]

The central issue is where acts occurred rather than what choices a defendant has made. Interactivity would be relevant only in determining whether, for example, a transfer of digital property was "performed" at the seller's or buyer's terminal. The contacts the defendant has with the forum or certain acts there are sufficient to permit jurisdiction to be asserted.

On one hand, the maintenance of a website outside the forum, even when coupled with sales into the forum, is insufficient to sustain an assertion of general jurisdiction. On the other hand, foreign companies that conduct business in a country on a continuous base should register a place of business and a representative. Because the company's principal place of business is outside the country, this residence would suffice for an assertion of general jurisdiction.

There is always a risk for a strong regulation if it is not made globally. As stated by Michael M. Mostyn, talking about privacy and anonymity, "if strong regulations are passed that vicariously threaten the remailer operators for the actions of remailer users, then operators may begin setting up shop elsewhere."[33]

According to John Hunt, criminal organizations would attempt to exploit loopholes in outdated legislation to further their aims by committing old crimes using modern methods. Utilizing the Internet and cyberlaundering techniques, criminal enterprises are able to transfer legal and illegal funds across the globe in seconds.[34]

---

[30] Keen [11, p. 381].

[31] Hoffmahn [12, p. 800].

[32] *Ibidem,* p. 1850, 1855.

[33] Mostyn [13, p. 86].

[34] See Hunt [14, p. 145].

A framework of binding can be flexible since there are precise rules based on protocols or annexes. Precise rules are possible later in time when the sovereignty concerns of states are reduced and uncertainty about the state of scientific research less acute.

It is imperative that both developed and developing nations share in the dialogue equally and harmonize their interests, having a global consensus on what is and is not illegal activity on the Internet and a mandate for cooperation between law enforcement agencies of different nations. Specifically, investigation and access, including questions over seizure of information as opposed to tangible objects, must be resolved. So, on the national level, agreements and treaties must be updated to respond to the issues being created by new technology, including transnational character of the offenses. Current laws in many nations are inadequate to deal with illegal online activity, and once made efficient, attempts to effectively enforce laws online will lead nations into conflict with one another.[35]

To Molly Beutz Land, citing Laura Thoms, "the primary advantage of such 'incremental policymaking' is flexibility; states can adapt strategies specific to the conditions existing in their countries, agree to an international regime before scientific certainty is established, and revise the structure of the regime as needed."[36]

Talking about European law, Richard Eccles reveals that the Article 101 of the Treaty on the Functioning of the European Union—TFEU "treats selling on the Internet as 'passive' as opposed to 'active sales'. Generally, under the EU competition law regime for vertical agreements, restrictions on active sales can be permitted under the exceptions criteria of Article 101 (3) whilst restrictions on passive sales are almost always prohibited."[37] This means that a restriction on passive selling, including a restriction on Internet selling, is treated as by its nature infringing the competition rules, without needing to demonstrate that it actually has anti-competitive effects. So, a regulatory international system over the Internet must be deemed limited.

Cooperation requires mutual trust among the cooperating bodies, and also a two-way communication that complete each other necessity of the transfer of information, so a need for cross-institutions cooperation is a logic consequence of this last statement. A problem this large can fail to offer solutions since it touches different jurisdictions, with different levels of protection of the Internet, forcing the existence of a cooperative body like the Financial Action Task Force – FATF, or under the auspices of the FATF, an ideal forum to implement an international solution to a problem that is international in scope and requires a high degree of mutual cooperation.

To Todd M. Gardella, "regulation of this medium-which relies on its users to construct the architecture, provide the content, and organically improve the state-of-the-art is tricky and potentially destructive."[38] So there must be caution that regula-

---

[35] French and Zahralddin [15, p. 127].

[36] Land [16, p. 28].

[37] See Eccles [17, p. 4].

[38] Gardella [18, p. 691].

tion does not reach the point of reaping the freedom of thought and expression that has been the force-matrix of the Internet.

The solution for cross-border electronic commerce issues must be challenged by online resolutions, facilitating communications through states to have as fast as possible the needed international cooperation. This would be a way to keep costs low and affordable.

References

1. Weaver, S. J. (2005). Modern day money laundering: Does the solution exist in Na expansive system of monitoring and record keeping regulations. *Annual Review of Banking & Financial Law, 24*, 443–465.
2. Henriques, D. B. (2009, June 30). Madoff, apologizing is given 150 years. *New York Times*, A1.
3. The United States Department of Justice, Asset Forfeiture Program, Annual Financial Statements, FY 2011 Report no. 12-12. Retrieved 25 May, 2018, from http://www.justice.gov/jmd/afp/01programaudit/index.htm
4. McCaw, C. E. (2011). Asset forfeiture as a form of punishment: A case for integrating asset forfeiture into criminal sentencing. *American Journal of Criminal Law, 38*, 181.
5. European Commission. (2012). Confiscation and asset recovery: Better tools to fight crime. *States new service*, Brussels. Retrieved May 26, 2018., from www.lexis.com
6. Baldwin, F. *Art theft perfecting the art of money laundering (Jan. 2009 for the 7th Annual Hawaii International Conference on Arts & Humanities)*. An unpublished work, sent to the U.S. Library of Congress on 04/20/2012 by University of Florida College of Law Professor Emeritus Levin, by request of the author (pp. 47–48).
7. de Carli, C. V. (2011). *Lavagem de dinheiro: prevenção e controle penal*. Porto Alegre: Verbo Jurídico.
8. Toffoli, J. A., & Cestari, V. C. J. (2009). *Mecanismos de Cooperação Jurídica Internacional no Brasil. Manual de Cooperação Jurídica Internacional e Recuperação de Ativos – Matéria Civil* (2nd ed.). Brasília: Asset Recovery and the International Legal Cooperation Council Department, National Secretariat of Justice, Ministry of Justice.
9. United States v. Opportunity Fund and Tiger Eye Investments, Ltd. *United States District Court for the District of Columbia* (No. 1:08-mc-0087-JDB). Decided 07/16/2012. Retrieved June 14, 2018, from http://www.cadc.uscourts.gov/internet/opinions.nsf/1B9DC0B1D05DB6D5852578070070EC9C/$file/09-5065-1255619.pdf
10. King, K. F. (2011). Personal jurisdiction, internet commerce, and privacy: The pervasive legal consequences of modern geolocation technologies. *Albany Law Journal of Science and Technology, 21*, 61–124.
11. Keen, R. (2011). Untangling the web: Exploring internet regulation schemes in western in western democracies. *San Diego International Law Journal, 13*, 351–381.
12. Hoffmahn, C. D. (1998). Encrypted digital cash transfers: Why traditional money laundering controls may fail without uniform cryptography regulations. *Fordham International Law Journal, 21*, 799–860.
13. Mostyn, M. M. (2000). The need for regulation anonymous remailers. *International Review of Law Computers & Technology, 14*(1), 79–88.
14. Hunt, J. (2011). The new frontier of money laundering: How terrorist organizations use cyberlaundering to fund their activities, and how governments are trying to stop them. *Information & Communications Technology Law, 20*(2), 133–152.

15. French, J. A., & Zahralddin, R. X. (1996). The difficulty of enforcing laws in the extraterritorial internet. *Nexus, 1*, 99–127.
16. Land, M. B. (2009). Protecting rights online. *The Yale Journal of International Law, 34*(1), 1–46.
17. Eccles, R. (2015). Online sales and competition law controls. *International Journal of Franchising Law, 13*(3), 3–10.
18. Gardella, T. M. (2006). Beyond terrorism: The potential chilling effect on the internet of broad law enforcement legislation. *St. John's Law Review, 80*, 655–692.

Chapter 9
Conclusions

It is known the traditional physical placement methods of criminals: cash smuggling, casinos and other gambling venues, insurance policies,[1] hawalas or "doleiros" or the black market currency exchange,[2] money service businesses—MSBs,[3] shell corporations, nonprofit organizations—NPOs, cryptocurrencies, cryptoassets, and so on. But there is also a number of online crimes (it is more a means for traditional crimes) currently being used by criminal enterprises to pass illegally received funds through legitimate accounts, and new ones are popping up all the time.

There is no doubt that digitalization and artificial intelligence, big data, and the Internet of things have impacted our lives rapidly changing all facets of our societies and economies. The scale of the technology transformation is causing uncertainty, and a clear framework approach is needed to make sure this transition can help to build more innovative and inclusive economies and prepare all sectors of society for these changes. So this is just part of the issue. Another is the use of this heightened pace of digital transformation for wrongdoing activities forcing governments to debate the issue and consider that this important tool deserves updating for the proper social-protection. It must take into account the rise of inappropriate use of irregular employment of the Internet.

Technology can be considered a new frontier of crime with the increasing virtualization of the world and the dramatic growth of currencies, challenging authorities to prosecute criminals hided in cyberspace.

Global marketplace has been revolutionized by the advent of the Internet. Products and services once offered only at the local store are now available in any corner of the planet. For instance, a funding portal is defined as a crowdfunding intermediary that does not: (1) offer investment advice or recommendations, (2) solicit purchases, sales, or offers to buy securities offered or displayed on its website

[1] Launderers, for instance, purchase policies and redeem them at a discount, paying fees and penalties but receiving a clean check from the insurance company.

[2] An informal value transfer system.

[3] A formal value transfer system.

F. M. De Sanctis, *Technology-Enhanced Methods of Money Laundering*,
https://doi.org/10.1007/978-3-030-18330-1_9

or portal, (3) compensate employees, agents, or other persons for such solicitation or based on the sale of securities displayed or referenced on its website or portal, (4) hold, manage, possess, or otherwise handle investor funds or securities, and (5) engage in such other activities as the SEC, by rule, determines appropriate.[4]

It is a new type of SEC registrant created to facilitate crowdfunding transactions. Compared to broker-dealers, funding portals enjoy a streamlined SEC registration process and have pared down regulatory compliance burdens. A funding portal must: (A) register with the SEC as a funding portal, and (B) gain membership in a national securities association (i.e., FINRA). Funding portals register with the SEC by filing Form Funding Portal. The Form Funding Portal requires the disclosure of information consistent with, but less extensive than, the information required for broker-dealers on Form BD. In summary, the Form Funding Portal includes information concerning the funding portal's principal place of business, its legal status and disciplinary history, business activities, and the type of compensation that the funding portal would receive.[5]

Talking about AML Requirements for Funding Portals of the JOBS Act,[6] Zachary Robock mentions specific requirements like the implementation of an effective customer identification program, CI program, which itself has three components: "(a) collecting identifying information about the investor, issuer, and the issuer's directors, officers and 20% or more shareholders; (b) taking reasonable steps to ensure this data is genuine (not a false identity); and (c) conducting a background check on the issuer and its significant personnel to determine potential fraud or terrorism risks. Second, a funding portal must maintain a program to monitor and report suspected money laundering activity to FinCEN, SAR Program. Specifically, a transaction (or series of transactions) requires reporting if it is conducted or attempted through the funding portal, it involves at least $5000, and the funding portal 'knows, suspects, or has reason to suspect' that the transaction (or series of transactions): involves funds derived from illegal activity; is designed to evade a mandatory reporting requirement; has no apparent business or lawful purpose based on available information; and/or is in furtherance of criminal activity or terrorism. In other words, if a transaction (or a series of transactions) involves at least $5000 and looks suspicious or has no apparent legitimate purpose, then it should be reported to FinCEN."[7]

In fact, the goal should not prohibit higher risk activities, but rather to ensure that appropriate risk mitigation strategies are implemented when necessary. Containing costs are an important aspect of keeping the system as a whole financially viable and AML requirements were conceived to avoid that funding portals do not become an obvious target for potential criminals.

---

[4] See EquityNet [1].

[5] Foster Swift Attorneys [2].

[6] It was passed on April 5, 2012 with a stated goal of improving access to the public capital markets for emerging growth companies.

[7] See Robock [3, p. 121].

Digital money represents the future of trading and banking. By allowing individuals to transfer money fastly and anonymously without triggering any reporting requirements, digital payment systems provide the ideal mechanism for laundering money. Virtual currency entity must provide for the effective investigation of fraud and other wrongdoing by providing effective procedures and controls to protect against identified risks and allocating responsibility for monitoring risks. The entity must submit to an enforcement department a report stating all pertinent details know at the time of the report, and, as soon as practicable, a further report or reports of any material developments relating to the originally reported events.

New York State Department of Financial Services—DFS has issued guidance reminding all virtual currency entities licensed by New York State, including those that hold a money transmitter license, that they are required to implement measures designed to effectively detect, prevent, and respond to fraud, attempted to fraud, and similar wrongdoing.[8]

Some banks are not accepting accounts related to cryptocurrency because they don't know to handle them and they are worried about the risk involved with uncertain regulatory expectations, transferring the risk elsewhere, because the customer will simply take its business to a less regulated non-bank financial institution. Eventually, banks could end up with the cryptocurrency risk they tried to avoid if they transfer or receive funds from non-bank financial institutions, especially if the sources are from a country deficient in customer compliance policy.

Cecily Raiborn, Chandra Schorg, and Christie Bubrig state that "the Internet is probably the best thing to come along since terrorists discovered plastic explosives. Banking on the Internet and its attendant possibility of money laundering will not stop and cannot be precluded: access is available and performance is fast. Paper currency is being supplanted with smart cards, E-cash, and instant funds transfers using personal digital assistants. Internet banks will not disappear: they are likely to survive as low-cost providers because performing a transaction online costs approximately 10% of the cost incurred by traditional bank employees. Under these conditions, money laundering using cyberspace will continue to occur and may even increase in volume. Fortunately, banks and other financial institutions (both brick-and-mortar and Internet) have numerous resources to combat money laundering on the Internet,"[9] basing its correspondent supervisory function on solid internal control procedures, by reflecting new technologies of infiltrating and analyzing data, and relying on international cooperative efforts regarding transaction legality and information sharing.

Out-of-state retailers who sell products over the Internet avoid collecting sales taxes on behalf of their customers by not having a physical presence in their customers' states. Attributional nexus will likely change this, netting online retailers in the attributional nexus taxability net.

According to Andrew W. Swain and Nathaniel T. Trelease, taxing authorities developed attributional nexus from the US Supreme Court's decisions in *Scripto v.*

[8] See Finextra [4].

[9] See Raiborn et al. [5, p. 39].

Carson, in which the Court upheld Florida's imposition of its use tax on a Georgia retailer based on the retailer's use of independent contractors (jobbers) to solicit sales in the taxing state. In *Tyler Pipe Indus. V. Dep't of Rev.*, "to establish the requisite connection between the in-state entity and the remote retailer, the in-state entity's activities must establish and maintain the remote retailer's market. Taxing jurisdictions traditionally have used attributional nexus as a technique to subject remote mail-order retailers to a state's taxing jurisdiction." In *Border Online, LLC v. State Bd. of Equalization,* "a limited liability company ('LLC'), sells books, CDs, videos, magazines, and other tangible goods over its Internet website. The LLC was formed under Delaware law and is headquartered in Michigan. Online sold its products to customers throughout the nation, including California, delivering its products to customers using a common carrier. During the tax years in question, Online did not maintain a place of business in California, own or lease property in the state, locate employees in it, or hold bank accounts there. Online did not collect sales taxes associated with its sales to California customers." In order to attribute an agent's in-state physical presented to an out-of-state retailer, the company's in-state activities must be significantly associated with online's ability to establish and maintain a market in California.[10]

Many issues arise when utilizing electronic commerce and the attendant payment systems. Talking about credit card use for payments, security and cryptography, methods of insuring necessary authenticity, non-repudiation, and information privacy or secrecy is an important topic that impacts all of the Internet payment methods. Although theoretically there is no need for particular software to effect a credit card transaction since the information may be simply transmitted over the computer network between the buyer and seller, in practice, some security measures must be taken to deter the unauthorized interception of this information. In this way, Janine S. Hiller and Don Lloyd Cook state that "a buyer may use encryption to directly forward credit card information over the Internet, but this process may not be practical if the seller does not have the same encryption, and it does not protect the buyer against the fraudulent, impostor merchant."[11] So, it is important to provide a means of payment in response to the development of the new technology methods.

Cyberspace must be an environment where people rights, specially personal data, can be protected from all sort of criminals. This contemplates a rich source of opinions and comments and regulation must consider the role of users and providers balancing protecting freedom of speech and citizens' rights. Could the creators of the Internet, intending to guarantee freedom of thoughts and expressions, have imagined such abuse of their intentions?

On one hand, online gaming poses regulatory and technical challenges denoting the need of protection of consumers from fraud, gambling addiction, tax evasion, and money laundering. On the other hand, since the growth of online sales, the need of a supervisory and legal system assuring, at least, following the money is needed

[10] Swain and Trelease [6, pp. 37 and 40–42].

[11] See Hiller and Cook [7, p. 76].

due to many issues arise when utilizing electronic commerce and the attendant payment systems.

Add the fact that a unified regulatory tax regime should be welcome, especially similar to physical transactions but adapted to the new form of doing them: the Internet. The simple use of it for illegal purposes must be prevented.

When Internet service providers allow the remittance of large sums of funds to foreign countries without properly notifying authorities, it becomes necessary to inquire into the existence of profitable activity that will eventually collide with the institution of tax regimes.

The traditional view of criminal jurisdiction (territorial principle, extradition, and mutual assistance) is now challenged since this new era requires efficient transnational enforcement mechanisms. That is why international intelligence gathering must be emphasized. The technological aspects of globalization bring greater exchange of information among governments. Each of us, in the modern global world, must be even more vigilant and on our guard.

Tensions between free land cyberspace and the need for regulations are at an all-time high and are especially evident in tax exempt lobbying restrictions and disputes over the use of Internet. The freedom of speech is not sufficient reason in and of itself to be considered tax free or free from government supervision. When adjudicating crimes related to the Internet, judges must consider the nature and purpose of the crime, the character of the offender, the circumstances in which the crimes was committed, as well as the need to preserve liberties rights. Magistrates must also take into account the seriousness of the offense and the need to protect public and its values. The purpose of sentencing is not only to punish the wrongdoer but also to protect the public by deterring others of like mind from breaking the law.

One solution would be to find a way to track and monitor money flows. Another one would be to verify accurately the merit to have tax misapplication and the need to respect the freedom rights by recognizing special benefits upon public utility of cyberspace.

So, the Internet must play an important role in ensuring and maintaining conformity to social norms through stronger individual and institutional connections and not the opposite. The cybercrime phenomenon intensifies the competition among the safety, security, technology, and the technical knowledge of the authorities, and implementing any plan, freedom of the Internet, and the benefits of dealing online must be considered. The task of reconciling traditional values and public interest on the regular use of the Internet is difficult and deserves constant reflection. Deterring the commission of money laundering through the Internet must be a high order priority.

References

1. EquityNet. *Funding portal definition*. Retrieved September 2, 2018, from https://www.equitynet.com/crowdfunding-terminology/funding-portal

2. Foster Swift Attorneys. *Biztec Law Blog, Title II crowdfunding: What is a funding portal?* Retrieved September 2, 2018, from https://www.michiganitlaw.com/Title-III-Crowdfunding-Funding-Portal
3. Robock, Z. (2014). The risk of money laundering through crowdfunding: A funding portal's guide to compliance and crime fighting. *Michigan Business & Entrepreneurial Law Review, 4*, 113–129.
4. Finextra. (2018, February 6). *NYDFS sets out new cryptocurrency fraud guidelines.* Retrieved September 3, 2018, from https://www.finextra.com/pressarticle/72539/nydfs-sets-out-new-cryptocurrency-fraud-guidelines
5. Raiborn, C., Schorg, C., & Bubrig, C. (2003). Guarding against e-laundering of dirty money. *Commercial Lending Review, 18*, 36–39.
6. Swain, A. W., & Trelease, N. T. (2006). Online retailers netted by Nexus: The borders online case. *Intellectual Property and Technology Law, 35*(1), 37–42.
7. Hiller, J. S., & Cook, D. L. (1997). From clipper ships to clipper chips: The evolution of payment systems for electronicd commerce. *Journal of Law and Commerce, 17*, 53–98.

Chapter 10
Proposals to Improve the Efforts Against Online Crimes (Money Laundering)

International treaties, supplemented by recommendations from foreign multilateral organizations, along with recurring discussion meetings, have all sought to improve the global system of enforcement to curb serious crimes. Now we turn to effective enforcement in the sector under study: the Internet as a means to online crimes.

The subject is one of the constant concerns, for much is said about the need to improve the efforts against them, yet in practice, few effective has been the prevention of crime. If not duly regulated, there is little enforcement and crime-fighting efforts are left up to stakeholders. Traditionally, only when the financial system is resorted to can we detect suspicious transactions. There is no significant record of reporting on the part of Internet service providers, or related people, and they only can limit themselves to occasional cancellation of the online transaction.

Furthermore, preferred methods of payment were at least brought into focus. This is important in any business environment, and could make things easier for money launderers. Hence the need for the study of this method.

It is hard not to notice that major drug traffickers, among other criminals, look to the Internet industry as a way of investing the profits from their deals or as currency to use in the illegal drug market. Cyberspace has been targeted for use for illegal ends.

The concern has emerged in several debates, but still in a timid or incipient form, so that the real work ahead is to get all government agencies to put some teeth into the prevention and punishment of online crimes, including money laundering through the recovery of dirty money and of illegal goods.

There is no word of important advances in this area, and that may explain the fact that organized crime, in principle, finds there an extraordinary array of techniques to put a legal face on the proceeds of crime using the Internet.

What is called for is an immediate rereading of all mechanisms of enforcement and prevention of money laundering as a general proposition, and all of its myriad forms of expression, but notably in this very important area where enforcement is the reaffirmation of cultural and social traits.

F. M. De Sanctis, *Technology-Enhanced Methods of Money Laundering*,
https://doi.org/10.1007/978-3-030-18330-1_10

There will be proposals to reflect upon, not necessarily the last word, rather more like the beginning of a new debate over our forms of cultural expression. It is hoped that these proposals will prove useful to deal with this issue, but also, as a means of better handling prevention and enforcement in the war on online crimes.

Current anti-crime policies must be reviewed since they often rely on the same prescribed instruments and sectors. For risk-based policies, it is important to know in which business sectors and instruments money laundering risks are relatively higher. This work built upon as part of identifying and assessing the existent environment focused on Internet, specifically on online crimes, due to the huge use of it in day-to-day life.

Attempting to stop or reduce online crimes is a herculean task, unless there is an improvement in efforts already made to help control the problem. The proposed solutions include stricter penalties for rogue businessmen (rather than placing more requirement on legitimate online websites), more resources devoted to informing both consumers and sellers about online crimes and off-label marketing (reducing the illegal black market), and creating a database with links to certified Internet business companies or websites that operate online depending on the nature of the products.

10.1 An International Perspective

10.1.1 Technological Action Task Force: TATF

Explanation The TATF or a group under the auspices of FATF should express particular concerns regarding the cyberspace due to the significant number of cases discovered so far.

001 Include Internet Service Providers and Cryptoasset or Cryptocurrency Trading Brokers in the Suspicious Transaction Reporting Recommendation for Designated Non-Financial Businesses and Professions (DNFBPs) or Companies alongside casinos, real estate brokers, dealers in precious metals or gemstones, attorneys, notaries, and accountants (Recommendation No. 22, together with 18 through 21).

002 Authorities must meet each other in a forum similar to the Financial Action Task Force—FATF, here called Technological Action Task Force—TATF, or a group under the auspices of the FATF, to have an ideal forum to implement a solution across borders to a problem that is international in scope. It must uncover the facilitation of online crimes and the networks and schemes here involved due to a lack of prescriptive international standards in order to endeavor to ensure a more efficient and coordinated approach to deal with the issue.

10.1.2 *Financial Action Task Force: FATF (if the technology group is under the auspices of FATF)*

003 The Financial Action Task Force establishes transparency requirements for beneficiaries of companies, with countries required to obtain reliable and timely information (Recommendation No. 24), including information on trusts, settlors, trustees, and beneficiaries (Recommendation No. 25). Financial Information Units (FIUs) must have timely access to financial and administrative information, either directly or indirectly, as well as information from law enforcement authorities in order to fully perform their functions, including analysis of suspicious statements on operations (Recommendations Nos. 26, 27, 29 and 31). It recommends restricting or banning the physical transportation of currency (Recommendation No. 32), but says nothing about the cards and forms of payment mentioned here. So, it ought to include cards as instruments that should reveal information about the transactions and its parts.

004 The FATF must clarify how its standards apply to virtual currency providers and related businesses, including customer due diligence, fund transfers, supervision, and enforcement. The mere fact that even e-money could be electronically traceable does not preclude its being successfully used for illegal ends while it has the potential to remove the existing impediments of the traditional payment mechanisms like lack of immediacy, security, and anonymity. As more of these types of services become available online, the transactions become more complex and there is greater opportunity for apparently unrelated, off-the-grid value exchanges. Both encryption and electronic money make it almost impossible to prevent serious crimes via the Internet.

005 Business relationships or transactions involving high-risk third countries should be limited when significant weaknesses in the AML/CFT regime of the third countries concerned are identified, unless adequate additional mitigating measures or countermeasures are applied.

006 Determine that the final beneficiaries be published on official public pages.

10.1.3 *Tax Havens, Offshore Accounts, and Trusts*

Explanation The advantage of offshore accounts is that they enable the free movement of capital, which is only taxed in negotiations taking place in-country, with exemptions for transfers to other offshore or nonresident accounts, corporate income taxes, and income tax withholding on payments made to nonresidents. Arnaldo Sampaio de Moraes Godoy has apropos observations on these, especially concerning

Barbados, Panama, the Bahamas, and Vanuatu.[1] Moreover, there are treaties to avoid double taxation, and which allow governments to establish unilateral measures domestically (such as, exemptions for fiscal credits at a reduced proportional rate, and deduction of taxes paid abroad from domestic taxable income), which is why they are referred to as tax havens. The author cited also adduces that there is a draft being circulated by the Organization for Economic Cooperation and Development (OECD), called the *Model Tax Convention on Income and on Capital* (comprising of 31 articles distributed over seven sections) aimed at eliminating obstacles relating to double taxation. It provides, for example, that dividends paid by a company having its home office in one State Party to someone living in another State Party to the Convention will be taxed by the latter, and their remuneration taxed by the State in which the services are rendered.[2] It is true, as they say, that they facilitate the circulation of goods, services, and capital, but they are also an effective instrument for evading taxes with considerable legitimacy. They lend themselves to legal uses of arguable utility, but also to illegal practices. There are considerable advantages to be had by using them as conduits, especially by those interested in laundering ill-gotten money, on account of defective or nonexistent government control, but also because they make it easy to generate false trails, and also handle international wire transfers. Offshore bank accounts make it possible to disguise their real controllers, since ownership is—according to the legislation in the countries in which they are located—evidenced by bearer paper, and partners or officers are simply proxies, often proxies for hundreds of companies of the same pattern. All of this amounts to creating a veil for the actual owners to hide behind. Their paper cannot be traded on the domestic market, nor cashed in without considerable expense and questions, about possible complicity in money laundering, directed at anyone who converts it. It is argued that these accounts are advantageous in that owning one does not involve liability to taxes, unless one were to actually invest in the country. Loan agreements are often written so as to lay hold of funds from offshore accounts without exposing them to tax liability. There are transparency requirements for beneficiaries of companies, with countries required to obtain reliable real-time information (FATF Recommendation No. 24), including information on trusts, settlors, and trustees or beneficiaries (Recommendation No. 25), which would preclude anonymous accounts. This is why the customer and actual beneficiary must be identified (i.e., know-your-customer duties, often called Customer Due Diligence) along with a requirement to collect enough information about the institution to which service is rendered, so that the trustee, who administers the assets, is accountable for turning in suspicious transaction reports. Observe that the FATF takes a clear stand against the invocation of banking secrecy or professional privilege as a means of obstructing its recommendations (Recommendation No. 9).

007 Require tax havens to comply with all provisions whereby information must be provided to proper international authorities. This amounts to placing ethical and

[1] In Godoy [1, pp. 83–84].

[2] Cf. Id. Ibid., pp. 166–170.

legal considerations above financial considerations, all the way down to obtaining information about the ownership (beneficial or ultimate beneficial ownership) and identifying the controllers. Indeed, the controllers merit special attention, and their very existence ought to be looked into to check whether they might be providing services to criminal enterprise. The hurdles in the way of their suppression are closely related to the Janus-faced discourse of many States which rely on tax havens to conduct non-transparent transactions purportedly having connections to "reasons of State" or for the management of assets belonging to their political elite.

10.1.4 International Legal Cooperation

Explanation As already put forth by the Financial Action Task Force—FATF, there is a need to make it possible to bring about freezing and seizure, even if the antecedent crime occurred in another jurisdiction (country). There is also a need for deployment of specialized multidisciplinary teams, task forces if you will (Recommendation No. 30). It also recommends International Legal Cooperation, pursuant to the UN Conventions of Vienna (international traffic, 1988), Palermo (transnational organized crime, 2000) and Mérida (corruption, 2003), by withdrawal of obstacles (Recommendation No. 37) and direct mutual assistance toward a quick, constructive, and effective solution (Recommendation No. 38). The fight against organized crime must not be defeated by lack of understanding regarding the various international legal systems. Consider the impact on US asset forfeiture legislation of the case in which Brazil filed for freezing of assets belonging to a Brazilian defendant, and for keeping those assets in the USA. At issue was whether, based on 28 U.S.C. § 2467 (d) (3) Enforcement of Foreign Judgment,[3] foreign assets may only be frozen after a foreign court has definitively ruled in favor of forfeiture, or if it may be done before any final decision on confiscation has been rendered. The United States Court of Appeals for the District of Columbia Circuit, on review of two decisions by the Court in March and April 2009, decided that a final decision by Brazil regarding confiscation was required, according to its interpretation of 28 U.S.C. § 2467 (d) (3).[4] Following this decision, the US Department of Justice requested and obtained from Congress a resolution of the problem because, if upheld and followed, the decision would have compromised international cooperation efforts with other countries. The Internet, being the face of globalization, resists the imposition of borders

[3] (d) Entry and Enforcement of Judgment. (1) In general. The district court shall enter such orders as may be necessary to enforce the judgment on behalf of the foreign nation unless the court finds that (A) the judgment was rendered under a system that provides tribunals or procedures incompatible with the requirements of due process of law; (B) the foreign court lacked personal jurisdiction over the defendant; (C) the foreign court lacked jurisdiction over the subject matter; (D) the foreign nation did not take steps, in accordance with the principles of due process, to give notice of the proceedings to a person with an interest in the property of the proceedings in sufficient time to enable him or her to defend; or (E) the judgment was obtained by fraud.

[4] United States District Court for the District of Columbia [2].

and requires a regulatory system that does not spillover. But, while the use of a website may have effects beyond a user's own territory, these effects result from the technology that allows easy access to a website from everywhere. A problem this large can fail to offer solutions since it touches different jurisdictions, with different levels of protection of the Internet, forcing the existence of a cooperative body like the Financial Action Task Force—FATF or under the auspices of the FATF an ideal forum to implement an international solution to a problem that is international in scope and requires a high degree of mutual cooperation. Improving international cooperation also provides repatriation of assets and lends substance to the administration of justice, which ought to be considered universal, through the following measures and national policies, mindful that the fight against crime is independent of where the crime occurred, and that confiscation is essential.

008 Cooperation through Letters Rogatory is not recommended because it is slow and bureaucratic, and because analysis in the requested country is limited to checks on public policy and affronts to sovereignty.

009 Prioritize cooperation by direct assistance as the response followed by States because it is faster, based on mutual trust and conveys to the requested State a proper analysis of the requests.

010 Give preference if at all possible to the clear, simplified standard Mutual Legal Assistance Treaty format. Specific, separate MLATs are not required for each asset, security or pecuniary amount if the requesting State attaches to its request a list of assets and gives grounds.

011 Consider that central authorities have facilitated matters, for they placed no obstacles in the way of direct contact between magistrates or competent authorities, and channels of communication must be opened up to ease unnecessary bureaucratic burdens (Article 18.13 of the UN Convention Against Organized Crime at Palermo does not prohibit such understandings).

012 The regular legal systems of countries involved must be respected (requesting and requested States), and it is no bar to cooperation if the request originated with or was addressed to the police, the Office of the Public Prosecutor, or the courts.

013 If extradition is refused, on the grounds of citizenship, then the person believed to be involved ought to be promptly submitted to authorities in their own country (Art. 16.10, Palermo). However, if accepted, it is recommended that the sentence be served out in the requested State (Art. 16.11, Palermo), otherwise, require serving the sentence or part of it in the requesting State (Art. 16.12, Palermo).

014 Possibility of joint prosecution or transfer of criminal proceedings (Art. 21, Palermo) for final disposal of assets and joint measures (cooperative debriefings with effects in both countries) to achieve better administration of Justice.

015 International Cooperation ought not to be blocked while the whereabouts of an asset are unknown. The requested State should try all available means for tracing or seizure for future confiscation or repatriation.

016 As a condition for restitution to the interested party, the requested State should provide proof of the legality of the asset, security or pecuniary amount whenever the requesting State requires seizure with an eye to confiscation or repatriation, but the request was mooted by decisions setting aside the merits as to its legal origin.

017 Invocation of absence of dual criminality cannot justify failure to cite or subpoena defendants, victims, witnesses, or affected third parties once criminal proceedings have been initiated in the requesting State.

018 Information gained for criminal proceedings may be used in other such proceedings if the requested State so authorizes, even if retroactively.

019 Assets, securities, or pecuniary amounts shall be restituted for indemnification of victims or turned over to the United Nations Fund for technical assistance among countries—or even for reimbursement of the State. A division might be arrived at to deduct only expenses, except for such crimes as corruption and the like.

020 Reimbursement of States lies outside the reach of the statute of limitations, which does not affect international cooperation.

021 What denies international cooperation is the invocation of a need for a court order for a mere citation, subpoena or copies, and it is incumbent upon States to simplify their legal systems to make direct assistance workable.

022 Defense witnesses ought to be heard in the country filing charges, or else by teleconference from embassies or consulates, with international Cooperation not being invoked and requested except in cases of evidence being clearly disguised by the charges.

023 International cooperation does not require the attachment of proof, but rather, a presentation of arguments leading to the decision to see that measures be taken abroad.

024 Both developed and developing nations ought to share equally in the dialogue in order to harmonize their interests, having a global consensus on what is and is not illegal activity on the Internet and a mandate for cooperation between law enforcement agencies of different nations. Specifically, investigation and access, including questions over seizure of information as opposed to tangible objects, must be resolved. So, agreements and treaties must be updated to respond to the issues being created by new technology, including transnational character of the offenses. Current laws in many nations are inadequate to deal with illegal online activity, and once made efficient, attempts to effectively enforce laws online will lead nations into conflict with one another.[5]

025 States ought to adapt strategies specific to the conditions existing in their countries, agree to an international regime before scientific certainty is established, and revise the structure of the regime as needed.

026 Cross-institutions cooperation must be encouraged because cooperation requires mutual trust among the cooperating bodies, and also a two-way communication that complete each other necessity of the transfer of information.

10.2 A National Perspective

10.2.1 Institutional Measures (Executive and/or Legislative Branch)

Explanation The hazards of globalization may be minimized if, with globalization, our notions of law draw authority from social and philosophical—as opposed to just economic—considerations. The subject cannot be dealt with from a purely economic view. Criminal organizations must be throttled by denying them what gives them their mobility and power, affording them continuous and unprecedented illegal wealth. The subjective collective degradation afoot in the world today, which regards economics as the standard of value, can never so bind our numbers together as to gloss over such indispensable critical thinking. Legitimate social movements and individuals ought to assume a stance for ethical values to compel obedience to basic rules of coexistence. Standing these rules at defiance by parallel paths amounts to the real breakdown of rights both de facto and *de jure*. There is a duty to perform Customer Due Diligence for all financial and non-financial activity, whether with natural or artificial persons, to ban anonymous accounts or those bearing fictitious names, and require identification of their beneficial owners, with records to be kept for at least 5 years (FATF Recommendations Nos. 10 and 11). There are, at times, requirements to make suspicious transaction reports on non-financial companies engaged in domestic or international cash transfer services, obliging them to record the amounts transferred, form of payment, transaction date, purpose of the wire transfer, name, individual, or corporate taxpayer ID, where applicable, of both sender and receiver and addresses for both. These requirements give a false impression that any money laundering occurring in that sector could actually be detected. There is also a need to make Internet service providers and cryptocurrency trading brokers liable to these rules, inasmuch as they may have knowledge or probable knowledge of criminal behavior (willful blindness doctrine).

[5] French and Zahralddin [3, p. 127].

027 Allow administrative freezing and seizure to be accomplished quickly, so as to prevent disappearance or acts of terrorism.

028 Allow confiscation of assets when transferred to an outside party which may have been aware that the assets were illegal, or that they were transferred solely to avoid confiscation.

029 Allow confiscation of illegal assets when a conviction cannot be obtained on account of death, statutory limitations, or grant of immunity. Adopt civil actions to terminate ownership.

030 Even after a decision has become final, allow further financial investigations to enforce prior confiscation orders covering all of the proceeds of crime.

031 Once criminal proceedings are instituted, the statute of limitations ought to stop running, for there is no reason to count government inertia, nor lack of interest in criminal prosecution.

032 Compelling sites to adopt geolocation technologies since they offer an automatic, accurate, and affordable means of identifying an Internet user's geographic location because every website operator has the ability to screen users by jurisdiction. A company that maintains a website could be subject to jurisdiction anywhere, because the Internet is widely accessible in many foreign jurisdictions. However, mere maintenance of a website cannot subject a defendant to global jurisdiction if the new technology is capable of meaningful use. If each website subjected its sponsor to global jurisdiction, many would forego use of the technology for fear of its secondary costs.

033 Make failure to comply with data protection regulation, report, or delays in reporting suspicious operations, or incomplete or false reporting, or making public the required reporting, or structuring transactions or operations to circumvent reporting requirements should render those perpetrators liable of criminal prosecution.

034 Authorities should create a centralized monitoring and enforcement division in order to track online activities and identify illicit operations and threat nodes that require immediate enforcement action, also having the power to take any measurable action against noncompliant providers, as well as imposing fines for negligent providers, also establishing a consolidated blacklist of individuals and entities banned from using, benefiting, or profiting from the Internet alerting people about bad users, and a database with links to certified Internet business companies or websites that operate online depending on the nature of the products.

10.2.2 Regulatory Agencies

Explanation Obtaining information has been hampered considerably by a lack of channels of communication with the competent authorities—to say nothing of timely notice—in the conduct of international and national cooperations.

035 Establish a regulatory agency, if it is not be feasible for the Financial Information Units to provide proper oversight so as to timely obtain direct or indirect access to financial and administrative information, and information from law enforcement authorities in order to fully perform their functions, including analysis of suspicious transaction reports (thereby fully complying with FATF Recommendations Nos. 26, 27, 29, and 31). The agency must be fully empowered and supplied with human and material resources to monitor and supervise in order to spot artificial inflation of online prices, as is done for real estate. It must also inspect for fraudulent sales or acquisitions, forged documents, financing of nonexistent objects, loans taken out in the name of third parties or trustees, and the involvement of offshore accounts to disguise the true identity of a buyer or seller.

036 The regulatory agency shall be empowered to demand secure records with profound and specific evaluations of Internet user transactions: photo ID, ID number, proof of domicile, bank statement, beneficial owner if not it is a public information, purpose of transaction, form and structure of the transaction, price, payment, involvement of intermediaries, source of funds.

037 Broadening access to information on beneficial ownership, improving transparency in the ownership of companies and trusts through public sites. For that, a database must be created, with access by the law enforcement authorities, as well as the public. Public access to beneficial ownership information allows greater scrutiny of information by civil society, including by the press or civil society organizations, and contributes to preserving trust in the integrity of business transactions and of the financial system.

038 Financial Intelligence Units—FIUs or the new agency should have access to information and be able to exchange it without impediments, including appropriate cooperation with law enforcement authorities. In all cases of suspected criminality, information should flow as directly as quickly possible without undue delays, by defining and clarifying the powers of the FIUs and cooperation among them. Rules that apply to trusts and similar legal arrangements with respect to access to information relating to their beneficial ownership should be comparable to the corresponding rules that apply to corporate and other legal entities.

039 Delayed access to information by FIUs and other competent authorities on the identity of holders of bank and payment accounts and safe-deposit boxes, especially anonymous ones, hampers the detection of transfer of funds relation to online crimes. It is therefore essential to establish centralized automated mechanisms, such as a register or data retrieval system, as an efficient means to get timely access to information on the identity of holders.

040 Establish regulations, irrespective of any obligation arising in law (provided there is a basis in the reasons for which they are created), as to the requirement of suspicious activity reports by individuals or Internet service providers and cryptocurrency trading brokers that sell, import, export, or intermediate a currency or a business (sale)—whether on a permanent or temporary basis, in a principal or accessory role, and cumulatively or otherwise, to prevent the laundering of money through cyberspace. In the absence of a regulatory agency, oversight shall be performed by the FIUs, so that no one may be induced to believe that online crimes are less risky than committed through other means.

041 Require Suspicious Activity Reports—SARs on the part of Internet service providers and cryptocurrency trading brokers, most notably when cryptoasset or cryptocurrency is used, or attempted of it occur, or payments are made through overseas accounts.

042 Require punishment of the offense of business practices that violate the good faith or the loyalty contract which are protected by consumers' rights. They are supervised by, in Brazil, the National Consumer Protection System, formed by Procon, Public Attorney, and Prosecutor, in the USA, at the federal level, by the Federal Trade Commission and the US Department of Justice.

043 Financial Intelligence Units—FIUs or the Treasury Department ought to treat virtual currencies as equivalent to real currencies and it would treat some users of virtual currencies as money transmitter, but not considering virtual currency users as providers or sellers of prepaid access or dealers in foreign exchange. Once the user provides money transmission services, that user becomes a virtual currency exchanger, and administrator, or both and must comply with MSB requirements. So, users that merely use the virtual currency for real or virtual goods are not subject to money transmitter regulation, unless that user sells virtual currency for real currency or its equivalent.

044 Create special licenses for digital currency providers work to strengthen the soundness of virtual currency schemes and increase public trust in the products, as some may refrain from investing in or using digital currencies due to a perceived legal uncertainty and/or lack of consumer protection.

045 Financial Intelligence Units—FIUs or the Treasury Department ought to create a virtual database for issuing electronic money, in which users may check the coins once issued. So instead of withdrawing an amount in bills from a bank, a financial institution could be asked to coin (renew) a block of records identified by a hash value, which can be used for identification and integrity verification, and occasional returns to the bank. It is important to use cryptographic techniques to prevent duplication, complicating the transfer of funds to the point of making it difficult to ensure security in order to avoid the different addresses, with one of them used only once for a single transfer.

046 Standardize licensing requirements at the Financial Intelligence Unit or directly to the Treasury Department, by acknowledging e-money as forms of international legal currency (which requires cryptocurrency exchangers to abide regulations); including entities dealing in digital currencies as subjects to MSBs' regulations; maintaining identifying records of customers (personal registration through identifying information); detecting the occurrence of an electronic money transfer through tokens programmed to notify law enforcement bodies every time an amount transferred exceeded a certain threshold; programming electronic tokens to keep track of the transactions in which they are used; limiting the number of transactions or its transferability could be used to prevent online crimes, and law enforcement authorities must have access to cryptographic keys because without access to the content of ciphertext, law enforcement bodies cannot determine the transmission's origin, destination, or whether it includes digital money, requiring virtual wallet providers to gather and share information about account holders in order to stop tax evasion.

047 Implement a universal encryption key, or create a key escrow agency to hold duplicates of active cryptographic keys and subject e-money transfers to reporting regulations and law enforcement officials, which should have access to decryption keys because they are unable to determine who or what is involved in the transaction since they do not have access to the key used to decode the transmission. The regulation of cryptocurrencies ought to stem from the process of tracing cash flows in encrypted mode and this is difficult and more confusing because of the lack of communication between people in the real environment and virtual currency accounts, the existence of obstacles to tracing, such as encryption and anonymizing mixers, and possibilities of creating an unlimited number of accounts.

048 The regulation must ensure a strong encryption technology. The encryption must have authentication through digital signatures that ensures the link between the payor and the payee in order to facilitate every phase of money-laundering cycle, since it is possible to avoid financial transaction reporting system, and without the assistance or intervention of third parties such as banks or financial institutions.

049 In order to prevent or restrict offshore tax evasion by using cryptocurrency, require virtual wallet providers, specialized storage service for cryptocurrency, to report foreigner account or virtual wallets to the enforcement body as it does banks or credit unions. Therefore, the IRS should define cryptocurrency as being subject to the Foreign Account Tax Compliance Act—FATCA or the Common Reporting

Standard—CRS restrictions to avoid tax evasion using offshores virtual wallet providers.

10.2.3 NGOs and Trusts

Explanation There ought to be a complete record by type of business and types of NGOs. NGOs should be required to keep records on all transactions entered into within the country and/or abroad. This would comply with FATF Recommendation No. 08, in the spirit of clearly delimiting the rights and responsibilities of directors and employees of NGOs. It would encourage countries to establish good policy whereby information on their activities, size, and other important characteristics such as transparency, integrity, openness, and best practices can be had in real time for purposes of supervision and monitoring (FATF Recommendation No. 8).

050 All cash payments should be banned because they are practically untraceable and usually are the result of some sort of tax evasion or illegal act. Cash payment should therefore be banned for purchase of vehicles, boats, airplanes, real property, shares of stock, lottery tickets, bets in excess of $10,000, artworks, and luxury items. One thus tries to cut off the illegal flow of money and its entry into the legal market. This shifts us away from dereliction with regard to measures to curb money laundering and the financing of terrorism.

051 Payments by third parties should also be deemed illegal, unless under certain conditions, so as to preclude their use for purposes of masking real ownership of the goods and resources, with the potential for tax fraud that entails.

052 Licensing should be required from NGOs for operation under tax exempt status, and continuation of this status ought to be contingent upon regular reporting to revenue authorities of all relevant information, in an official document duly dated and signed under penalty of perjury, listing the name and telephone number of the person in charge of the books and records of the organization or foundation.

053 Even if a license is granted, it must be required of the entities so benefited, with relevant information entered—under penalty of being closed down—on a form for that purpose, dated and properly signed on penalty of perjury, and containing the name and telephone number of the person who keeps books and records for the organization. These records must contain a detailed list of the organization's activities and management, of all revenues and expenses, and liquid assets, to include: the name and purpose of the institution; whether it has on hand more than 25% of its liquid assets; number of voting members listed within and outside of the organization; number of employees; number of volunteers; unrelated business revenue and amount paid in taxes; contributions and donations; amounts invested; benefits paid to and for members; total assets and liabilities; basic description of all assistance programs; whether any loans or benefits were granted to employees, directors, a trustee or any other person; name, number of hours worked, and job description of all employees and former employees (including directors, trustees, and key personnel); earnings had by these individuals; expenses claimed (including travel and entertainment); and names and particulars of all donors.

054 The organization's books and records ought to include a detailed list of NGOs activities and management, all revenue and expenses, and liquid assets, to include: the name and purpose of the institution; number of members; whether they have on hand more than 25% of their liquid assets; number of voting members listed within and outside of the organization; number of employees; number of volunteers; unrelated business revenue and amount paid in taxes; contributions and donations; resources invested; benefits paid to and for members; total assets and liabilities; basic description of all assistance programs; whether any loans or benefits were granted to employees, directors, a trustee or any other person; name, number of hours worked, and job description of all employees and former employees (including directors, trustees, and key personnel); earnings had by these individuals; expenses claimed (including travel and entertainment); and names and particulars of all donors.

055 An external audit should be required above a given gross revenue ceiling (more than $100,000, for example), as the state of New York so capably provides.[6]

056 Include in their bylaws requirements for distribution of financial reports and outside audit reports for all directors and management personnel (president, manager, and financial department), for easy review.

057 Universal access to all NGOs, associations, or foundations (electronic addresses), containing important information on records and reporting requirements.

058 In the case of a temple, church, mosque, educational institution, or trust, even if registered as an NGO, association or foundation, all sources of funding must be provided in sufficient detail.

059 Barring receiving cash donations, or at least a cap above a certain amount (say, $3000), which would, above that amount, restrict donations to banking instruments.

060 Review accounts of all such entities to reinforce due diligence and check whether they actually perform the purposes for which organized. Allow only the opening of accounts in their own names and in accordance with the documentation turned in.

[6] Cf. NY Charities [4].

061 If announcements are made that a given account will be receiving donations or something similar, banking institutions must monitor this to check on the beneficiary of wire transfers made from that account, and promptly make out a suspicious activity report to the Financial Intelligence Unit if the published account is different from the account owned by the NGO or foundation.

062 Check that all donations and contributions received for specific purposes are being properly recorded and faithfully accounted for.

063 Provide clear procedures for board membership, thus to ensure diversity among the members.

064 See to it that all board members act in good faith to avoid any conflict of interest between the entity, its purposes, and themselves.

065 To check the profits earned by auction houses and art galleries one must take into account of the cost of goods sold, their inventory of works (stocks and consignments), their accounting and sales all matching the business done by them and the artist, with special attention to earnings from consignment sales. Some artists pay their own personal expenses in cash and prefer that form of payment from auction houses or galleries for their works sold on consignment.

066 Secure independent and exempt financial evaluation of them.

10.2.4 Payments: Black Market, Wire Transfers, Cards, and Cryptoassets or Cryptocurrencies

Explanation It is relevant, talking about virtual assets as legal subjects of taxation, to well define concepts of sales and use taxes and games taxation when considering the cyberspace. The Internet challenges the way that they have been levied and collected.

067 Credit/Debit card payments should also be subject to stricter controls. Lax controls have been exercised by card issuers, often with no prior relationship, exacerbated by failure to disclose credit limits, changes of address, name, date of issue, and expiration date. “Know your client” or due diligence rules must be enforced. Such cards must be listed among monetary instruments and otherwise subject to customs declarations.

068 Cards, although closely resemble traditional credit cards, but provide access not to credit at a financial institution, but to a sum of money stored on the card, on a chip, or simply in an account accessible using the card (which sometimes even dispenses with the chip), must be capable of holding digital wallets and programmed to allow for different levels of online transaction authentication, or using a secure PIN number or Token connection.

069 Ban all wire transfer payments which do not allow the money to be tracked. There is always a separation between the non-financial remittance company and the financial institution receiving the investor's money whenever these come from individuals or companies unrelated to the negotiations (cash deals negotiated by factoring companies or companies having home offices in tax havens). Currency brokers or hawala systems are often resorted to, as are wire transfers from and to secret banks or banks in tax havens—often by people having no connection whatsoever to the institution receiving the resources. Either they are not account holders, or are unconnected with the account holder receiving the wire transfer, or even transfer the amount which is actually the sum of many small deposits. Allowing this sort of practice would amount to having no preventive measures whatsoever. In wire transfers, detailed information should be obtained on the sender, as well as the beneficiary, with monitoring made possible, and there should be an option to prohibit transactions by certain people pursuant to UN Security Council Resolutions 1269 of 1999 and 1373 of 2001, for the prevention and suppression of terrorism and its financing (FATF Recommendation No. 16). Reportability of suspicious operations on the part of designated non-financial businesses and professions (DNFBPs) such as casinos, real estate offices, dealers in precious metals or stones, and even attorneys, notaries, and accountants, requiring internal controls and protection of whistleblowers from civil or criminal liability (FATF Recommendation No. 22, in combination with Nos. 18 through 21). Transparency requirements for beneficiaries of companies, with countries also required to timely obtain sufficient information (FATF Recommendation No. 24), including information on trusts, settlors, and trustees or beneficiaries (Recommendation No. 25).

070 Establish clearly defined categories for stored value cards (be they debit cards or prepaid access cards), so as to make it easier for government agencies to identify suspicious cards, given that it is not easy to distinguish between traditional debit cards and prepaid access cards. Identification should be demanded of their customers, so as to enable comparison of identities of those individuals and wanted criminals. Hence the need for a top-down compliance program to include customer identification, storage of records, and reporting of suspicious operations. Prepaid stored value cards have, with their explosive growth, become a perfect tool for money laundering whereby illegal money may be moved, with no documentation, identification, suspicion, or seizure. They are poorly (or sloppily) regulated, which ensures their anonymity, even when purchased or reloaded. Their daily limits are the same as the face value. They offer advantages over physical transfers because they are easy to carry and may be sent through the mail, and hence even replace the cross-border transportation of cash. Regulations alone will not suffice if they are issued by non-financial institutions. Their issuers' obligations must therefore be clearly established, and they ought to be classified as monetary instruments and, therefore, be subject to declaration when going through customs. These cards, then, possibly in combination with cash or other monetary instruments, once aggregating the $10,000 limit, ought to be subject to customs declaration.

071 Tighten controls on remittance companies, so as to have real knowledge of situations which might allow clandestine wires or wires not subject to suspicious operation reporting requirements (poor or borderline tracking by authorities). One example would be requiring a declaration by the bank accredited by the Central Bank to handle the conversion whenever called upon by the government (say, of Brazil) to appear for settlement of the currency exchange operation. The requirement, in wire transfers, that detailed information be obtained on the sender, as well as beneficiary, with monitoring made possible, and the option of prohibiting transactions by certain people pursuant to UN Security Council Resolutions 1269 of 1999 and 1373 of 2001, for the prevention and suppression of terrorism and its financing is FATF Recommendation No. 16. Reportability of suspicious operations on the part of designated non-financial businesses and professions (DNFBPs) such as casinos, real estate offices, dealers in precious metals or stones, and even attorneys, notaries, and accountants, requiring internal controls and protection of whistleblowers from civil or criminal liability (Recommendation No. 22, in combination with Nos. 18 through 21).

072 There has to be some form of electronic tracking of payments over the Internet, possibly even easier than for cash money, which simply passes from hand to hand. This would enable detection, for example, of payments made using cryptoassets or cryptocurrencies, like Bitcoins, even though considered a transparent method of conducting transactions inasmuch as the system allows identification of its users, albeit in aliases or nicknames. Hence, if a trafficker has a given cryptocurrency address, it ought to enable the download of all data on the person using that address and download the entire graph of parties with whom that trafficker has dealings. It might be possible to access all his clientele. Although the medium is not as anonymous as would appear first blush, there is no denying the possibility of someone setting up channels on the Bitcoin system to conceal transactions behind anonymity. As more services like this come online, the more complex the transactions, and the greater the opportunity for apparently unrelated, off-the-grid offsets—especially when it is possible to use a number of different addresses, with each one used for only a single transfer.

073 Cryptoexchanges should be included as financial activities because they transmit money or representations of monetary value by any means. Over-regulate virtual currency is clearly not welcome and regulators must work to understand it before they regulate. It is important to keep in mind that traditional money laundering schemes and cryptoassets or cryptocurrencies laundering schemes, however, are similar in their intents, but are clearly different in their regulations. So, this discrepancy creates a *legal blind spot* that must be not easily exploited. The responsible for accepting and transmitting anything of value that substitutes for currency makes him or her a money transmitter under the regulations implementing the Bank Secrecy Act—BSA. The mere fact that the value transmitted is not represented as physical media, nor issued by a sovereign entity, is not sufficient to exempt of being valuable and substitutable for conventional currency, and that suffices to bring it under the scope of any regulation.

074 Design and implement requirements that must be well described to avoid an invitation to fail. The private sector should report certain client profiling data and records of all financial transactions (photo ID, ID number, proof of domicile, bank statement, beneficial owner if not it is a public information, purpose of transaction, form and structure of the transaction, price, payment, involvement of intermediaries, source of funds). Financial intelligence should be required to use, to the extent possible, empirical analysis. The governments should keep in mind the possibilities of limiting the value of electronic cash that can be put on smart cards and Internet-based accounts and limiting the number of peer-to-peer transactions. So the governments should work to be sure (1) that electronic cash systems are engineered to produce an audit trail; (2) that the trail can be decrypted on a showing of probable cause by use of the Clipper Chip; and (3) that the trail can be followed by continuing efforts toward international cooperation.

075 As an alternative form of currency, e-money products, including crypto ones, must be addressed by regulators in order to avoid becoming a substantial threat to anti-money laundering worldwide efforts. The essence of financial technology is the integration of emerging technologies and financial services, and need to adopt classified and differentiated management in the regulatory environment and adopt a "control of neutrality" and "principle-based supervision" model, in order to not limit market participants' intention of investing in financial technology and the market competition.

076 Virtual currencies should not to be confused with electronic money, although included in the definition of funds. The anonymity of virtual currencies allows their potential misuse for criminal purposes. Prepaid cards and virtual currencies have legitimate uses and constitute an instrument contributing to social and financial inclusion. However, they are easy to use in financing criminal enterprise activities and criminals' logistics. These tools must be used if they are considered to comply with standard requirements defined by international authorities in consensus.

077 Full particulars absolutely must be obtained over all actual investors, even if they belong to companies chartered abroad, provided they do business and are represented in the country. A simple listing of proxies or stockholders is not enough. Complete identification must also be required of partners and administrators concealed within offshore accounts or trusts domiciled in tax havens. A listing of all Partners and Administrators ought to be required for being listed or removed from the tax rolls (which in Brazil is the Treasury Ministry's National Corporate Register or CNPJ).

10.2.5 Dark Web: Cybercrimes and Cyber-Attacks

Explanation The communications system for reporting suspicious transactions is the key to effective suppression of money laundering. It turns up a number of shady deals. Many others go unnoticed when there is no cooperation from those whose legal duty it is to report transactions. Certainly the failure of one of the methods of control held to be essential in the fight against online crimes, namely reportability, can give rise to misleading statistics. Moreover, making one liable to criminal charges for incorrect notices of suspicious transactions is clearly aimed at protecting privacy and image on the one hand, and the effectiveness of early investigations on the other, for the danger is that future freezes on accounts and other confidential security measures might be rendered inoperative. Also giving people rights with regard to the protection and control of their personal data is fully recommended. So, people can have direct knowledge of whether their data will be used to generate advertisements, if the information will be generated to build profiles or if the companies that collect data will sell this data to third parties.

078 Implement and issue a guidance with measures designed to effectively detect, prevent, and respond to fraud, and similar behavior, essentially through written policy in order to avoid cyber-attacks made by hackers (who work for fun) and crackers (for profit). Cybersecurity standards on owners and operators in critical infrastructure industry sectors must be imposed through compliance requirements. It must be disseminated and published on websites, in a way that small business may use voluntarily to help reduce their cybersecurity risks. The resources must be: (1) technology-neutral, (2) based on international standards to the extent possible, (3) able to vary with the nature and size of the implementing small business and the sensitivity of the data collected or stored on the information systems, and (4) consistent with the national cybersecurity awareness and education program.

079 Regulation on data protection and privacy for all individuals must aim primarily to give control to citizens and residents over their personal data and to simplify the regulatory environment for international business by unified regulation.

080 This regulation should contain provisions and requirements pertaining to the processing of personally identifiable information of data subjects, such as name, address, email, age, marital status, and financial position, obtained by any means: paper, electronic, computer, sound, and image are considered personal data. No personal data may be processed unless it is done under a lawful basis specified by the regulation, or if the data controller or processor has received explicit, opt-in consent from the data's owner. The data owner has the right to revoke this permission at any time.

081 A processor of personal data must clearly disclose any data collection, declare the lawful basis and purpose for data processing, how long data is being retained, and if it is being shared with any third parties or outside of the country.

082 Users must have the right to request a portable copy of the data collected by a processor in a common format, and the right to have their data erased under certain circumstances.

083 Public authorities, and businesses whose core activities center around regular or systematic processing of personal data, are required to employ a data protection officer, who must be responsible for managing compliance with authorities. Businesses must report any data breaches within 72 h if they have an adverse effect on user privacy.

084 An independent supervisory authority must be established to hear and investigate complaints, sanction administrative offenses, etc.

085 Pseudonymization as a process should be required when data is stored (as an alternative to the other option of complete data anonymization) to transform personal data in such a way that the resulting data cannot be attributed to a specific data subject without the use of additional information. Encryption, which renders the original data unintelligible and the process cannot be reversed without access to the correct decryption key, must be used. For the additional information (such as the decryption key), it must be kept separately from the pseudonymized data. So, pseudonymization is fully recommended to reduce the risks to the concerned data subjects and also to help controllers and processors to meet their data protection obligations. Business processes that handle personal data must be built with data protection by design and by default, meaning that personal data must be stored using pseudonymization or full anonymization, and use the highest-possible privacy settings by default, so that the data is not available publicly without explicit consent, and cannot be used to identify a subject without additional information stored separately.

086 The data controller must be under a legal obligation to notify the supervisory authority without undue delay unless the breach is unlikely to result in a risk to the rights and freedoms of the individuals. It is recommended a maximum of 72 h after becoming aware of the data breach to make the report.

087 The following sanctions might be imposed: (1) a warning in writing in cases of first and non-intentional noncompliance; regular periodic data protection audits; (2) a fine up ten million or up to 2% of the annual worldwide turnover of the preceding financial year in case of an enterprise, whichever is greater.

088 Both consumers and business should be aware of the potential uses and misuses of personally identifiable and location information. It must be developed wireless applications and business plans that not only comply with current and future legislation relating to privacy and security, but also assuage consumer fears and apprehensions. For this, it is important to communicate the terms and conditions of wireless transactions to the customers, to obtain customers' assent to such terms, and authenticate that assent by developing a suitable solution for retention of electronic records.

10.2.6 Online Gaming

Explanation It is important to identify public policy challenges and market issues referring to the differing regulatory models of online gaming or gambling needs in different countries since they are today widely available and used. The economic significance of the sector is growing at a very high speed. The advent of the Internet and the growth of online gaming opportunities are posing regulatory challenges as these forms of gambling services are subject to national regulatory frameworks that vary rather significantly. These frameworks can be broadly categorized into either licensed operators operating within a strictly regulated framework or strictly controlled monopolies. Furthermore, the growth of online gambling opportunities has given rise to the growth of an unauthorized market, which consists of unlicensed illegal gambling and betting activity, including from third countries and operators licensed in one or more Member States offering gambling services in other Member States without having obtained the specific authorization in those countries.

089 As a global phenomenon, an effective international regulator should be formed to monitor the management, accountability, efficiency, and sector proportionality of the stakeholders involved in order to sustain market confidence in trading by promoting public understanding in addition to maintaining an appropriate degree of protection for consumers.

090 Licensing must be required; the licensing jurisdiction ought to include players to hold an account and/or be registered by the licensed provider; in order to open an account and be registered, players should be required to provide proof of identity, age, and place of residence; licensed providers are to require the identification of players each time a player attempts to access the site, using such methods as a personal identification number or password and challenge questions.

091 Require gaming operators or providers to obtain and verify accurate client information. For this, it will be necessary all systems must incorporate a method to confirm identity, age, and location of the player which complies with the legislation in the licensing jurisdiction.

092 Control gambling websites and the flow of money involved to combat fraud.

10.2.7 Online Sales

Explanation Although much of the concerns are related to financial transactions, online sale communications on the Internet must be secure and its users must have confidence in that security. E-commerce regulations should be harmonized to assure (1) the principle of non-discrimination with respect to the recognition of data messages as writings; (2) technology neutral recognition of signatures; (3) flexible, commercially responsive and uniform public key infrastructure provisions with respect to certification authority—CA qualifications, binding procedures, certificate lifespans, certificate revocation lists, cross-jurisdictional certificate recognition standards, and the privacy related duties and liabilities of CAs and subscriber; and (4) party freedom to establish transaction specific agreements regarding, inter alia, writings, signatures, and certificates.[7]

093 In spite of encryption must be unbreakable and should not be exported, key recovery techniques should be required because of the danger that criminals, like pornographers, pedophiles, terrorists, drug dealers, money launderers, and others will use this technology as a means to evade detection.

094 An important set of rules in terms of avoiding anti-competitive effects is fully recommended and will bring legal certainty for sellers and buyers in the legal regulation rules and thus help businesses expand their activities to foreign online markets and increase consumer trust through a high level protection. By collecting data on a user's behavior on the Internet including browsing habits, search queries, and website viewing history, authorities are more concerned about the need for intensive regulation. It must be developed, by introducing online sales, in order to uniform application of future acts, taking into account consumer preferences, business practices and that online sales can affect competition, by the reduction of the documentation costs and the impact on distribution costs, the geographical extent of activity area, and the asymmetric information.

095 Foreign companies that conduct business in a country on a continuous basis should register a place of business and a representative. Because the company's principal place of business is outside the country, this residence would suffice for an assertion of general jurisdiction.

096 Prescribe mandatory terms, being suspicious of terms of sellers with market power, or requiring increased contract disclosures, and being aware about the risks imposed by online payments are concerns to be addressed by all actors: sellers,

[7] In this way, see Kossick [5, pp. 281–283].

consumers, and government bodies. The purpose here is making consumers well informed about contract terms and less vulnerable to seller exploitation.

10.2.8 Social Media

Explanation A good social media policy is important with goals for its usage, and all the actors must agree to comply with these goals, using it on behalf of the publication and for personal purposes. In this process of modifying existing laws and creating new ones, it is relevant to maintain a delicate balance between protecting freedom of speech and protecting citizens from online crimes on social media, taking advantage to the growing of criminal nexus by tracking criminals rather than crimes.

097 A law review's social-media policy should be tailored to suit the needs of the particular publication, but the overall framework should remain similar to the typical framework used by other entities. The policy should include the designation of who has authority to use social media on behalf of someone and provisions about harassment, and discrimination, with sanctions.

098 Users must be aware that the anti-discrimination and anti-harassment provisions apply to their social media usage as well as when on behalf of someone.

099 A regulation should enforce registration disclosure and develop mechanisms to reveal the true personal identity, by (1) implementing an user ID system, that is, establishing an universal Internet user identification, a unique identification number for each individual upon completion of a brief registration process by an applicant; (2) providers must store user traffic data for a long period although the cost and privacy concerns; (3) the user account must be barred from establishing a new account after a predetermined number of violations; (4) authorities should create a centralized monitoring and enforcement division in order to track online activities and identify illicit operations and threat nodes that require immediate enforcement action, also having the power to take any measurable action against noncompliant providers, as well as imposing fines for negligent providers; (5) it should be established a consolidated blacklist of individuals and entities banned from using, benefiting, or profiting from the Internet alerting people about bad users.[8]

[8] Ideas taken from Benjamin R. Davis (see Davis [6]).

10.2.9 Tax Misapplication

Explanation Virtual assets are legal subjects of taxation in case of business transactions in which they have real-world values, especially of undeniable accessions to wealth, clearly realized, and over which the taxpayers have complete dominion (what is called "realization"). It is prudent for many countries, and especially for those with high tax burdens, to begin preparing themselves for what could prove to be significant downward pressures on tax levels in futures years, making policymakers and tax administrators to face a challenge in the coming years that might change the way in which taxes have hitherto been levied and collected. As the Internet has rapidly evolving borderless global forum consisting of a multitude of anonymous users, it contributes to one of the core problems of enforcing tax laws with respect to e-commerce: asymmetric information. Another aspect is countries, so far, have no solution to prevent or restrict offshore tax evasion by using cryptocurrency.

100 The tax authorities must adapt concepts, in order to align the general legal rule and the digital environment, considering the existence of a new model to preserve and not interfere in the values of cyberspace, in order to avoid failing to develop tax rules that can effectively tax e-commerce transactions. They should adopt a hybrid approach to basis accounting in virtual worlds, where basis is traced for virtual items and pooled for currency, thus taking the best of both approaches and balancing administrative concerns with the conceptually accurate result for both nonfungible and fungible assets.

101 It is relevant to improve international tax systems, by eliminating tax preferences and considering that there are trade-offs to be made on virtually every margin in the design to tax systems and ignoring them is a recipe for dysfunction.

102 Policymakers should develop measure to design, test, and implement sales and use tax system that simplifies sales and use taxes for all out-of-state or remote commerce, including Internet transactions, in order to avoid underreporting and tax evasion.

103 Taxes should not be levied against sources which are not considered income; so, game or virtual worlds (computers simulated 2D or 3D environment, ranging from the simple to the complex) should not be taxed for being a game when the purpose of it is the game itself; taxing income when it can be acquired in the game. So, instead of focusing on finding and prosecuting the wrongdoers, policymakers should put more emphasis on trying to tax them.

104 Establish the similar requirements as outside virtual word transactions for operations performed inside Internet in a way to avoid domestic or international cash transfer services and tax evasion, obliging them to record the amounts transferred, form of payment, transaction date, purpose of the wire transfer, name, individual or corporate taxpayer ID, where applicable, of both sender and receiver, and addresses for both.

105 A unified system of taxation of all income from whatever source derived should include, but not limited to: (1) compensation for services, including fees, commissions, fringe or additional benefits, and similar items; (2) gross income derived from business; (3) gains derived from dealings in property; (4) all income from auctions, traditional or online, and consignment sales unless certain exceptions are met. It must take into account the need for simplifying the administration of the tax laws and reporting income through effective information, eliminating the risk of compliance cost growth. Also, there must be caution that regulation does not reach the point of reaping the freedom of thought and expression that has been the force-matrix of the Internet.

106 Increase in the legal liability of the online administrators for their irresponsibility as the primary method by which to balance anonymity concerns with personal accountability, and tax compliance.

107 Online resolutions are the solution for cross-border electronic commerce issues, facilitating communications through states to have as fast as possible the needed international cooperation.

10.2.10 Internet Service Providers and Cryptoasset Trading Brokers

Explanation There is a need to avoid wrongdoings on the Internet what makes important to issue guidance to implement measures designed to effectively detect, prevent, and respond to fraud, and similar behavior, essentially through written policy. This policy must provide effective procedures and controls to protect against identified risks; identify and assess the full range of fraud-related and similar risk areas, including as applicable, market manipulation; and allocate responsibility for monitoring risks. It is essential the clarity of the government's need to be able, under certain circumstances, to gain access to the identities of the people who are behind Internet transactions.

108 A code of conduct must be implemented to see if one practice taken up does not involve conflict of interest, and check on whether illegal behavior is being detected and proper sanctions applied. All sensitive information ought to be analyzed and duly reported to the directors of Internet service providers and cryptocurrency trading brokers.

109 Provide Customer Due Diligence—CDD, with identification requirements, with records must be kept for at least 5 years. If they are found to be Politically Exposed Persons, that is, persons in prominent positions, such as politicians and their relatives, and hence more readily able to launder money, or businessmen from countries known to be large producers or consumers of drugs, they ought to be more closely monitored. This brings to the establishment of a compliance job description or department, for the occasional work done by peers (especially when located outside of the country of negotiation), frustrating sales or closing the door to fraudulent transactions, forged documents, unconvincing or nonexistent identification, negotiations made in the name of outside parties or trustees, or the involvement of offshore accounts to conceal the true identity of buyer or seller.

110 Cancel transactions from businesses that cannot provide enough financial justification to make it possible to check on the investor's financial strength. Cancel sales if there is any suspicion of money laundering or that the funds arose from financing of terrorism, and notify the competent authorities irrespective of whether or not there is some specific regulation requiring Suspicious Activity Reports.

111 Refuse payments on behalf of outside parties or trustees, or which involve offshore accounts that mask the true identity of the buyer.

112 Require justification when there is a use of third parties in order to avoid concealing the actual ownership of the resources, and possibly for tax fraud.

113 Inform to the competent authorities or regulatory agency, if any, and to the Financial Intelligence Unit, of any negotiation based on suspicion of fraud, forgery, illegal sale, money laundering, and financing of terrorism—even if confidential.

114 Provide information to Federal Revenue Authorities, or, whenever required, and to the Financial Intelligence Unit, including detailed records on clients (photo ID, ID number, domicile, beneficial owner if not it is a public information, purpose of transaction, form and structure of the transaction, price, payment, involvement of intermediaries, source of funds name, address, profession, deals made), under penalty for noncooperation.

115 Submit all personnel to required training on prevention of online crimes, with rewards for managers who properly enforce all compliance obligations.

116 Providers and cryptoasset or cryptocurrency trading brokers engaged in exchange services between virtual currencies and fiat currencies (that is to say coins and banknotes that are designated as legal tender and electronic money of a country, accepted as a medium of exchange in the issuing country), as well as custodian wallet providers, are under obligation to identify suspicious activity. Therefore, although criminals may be able to transfer money into the international financial system or within virtual currency networks by concealing transfers or by benefiting from a certain degree of anonymity on those platforms, risks can be reduced.

117 Providers and cryptoasset or cryptocurrency trading brokers deemed as obliged entities must deliver to authorities required information to be able to monitor the use of virtual currencies, providing a balance and proportional approach and safeguarding technical advances and the high degree of transparency attained in the field of alternative finance and social entrepreneurship addressing the issue of anonymity attached to virtual currency transactions. This obtained information must allow authorities to associate virtual currency addresses to the identity of the owner of virtual currency, as well as the possibility to allow users to self-declare to designated authorities on a voluntary basis. They must report e-money transfers in order to create an audit trail that leads to an anonymous transferor.

119 Providers and cryptoasset or cryptocurrency trading brokers must implement a universal encryption key and provide to enforcement bodies or to a special agency to hold duplicates of active cryptographic keys in order to facilitate the discovery of every phase of money-laundering cycle.

120 Provide, when requested, all Internet service providers and cryptocurrency trading brokers—as ought to be required of all financial institutions—detailed records of profits, profit-sharing, or other transactions.

121 Require licensing to work as a provider or a cryptocurrency trading broker, so as to lend some transparency to dealings. The regulation and supervision of all activities of them, with required licensing or special authorization (personal and nontransferable), is relevant to the extent that they might represent interests more inclined toward the financial exploitation of the misuse of the Internet.

122 Providers and cryptoasset or cryptocurrency trading brokers should turn in Suspicious Activity Reports—SARs upon acceptance of such illegal transactions as may be detected (applying the willful blindness doctrine).

123 Providers and cryptoasset or cryptocurrency trading brokers must store user traffic data for a long period (at least 5 years) although the cost and privacy concerns and feed a virtual database for issuing electronic money, in which users may check the coins once issued, by a hash value, which can be used for identification and integrity verification, and occasional returns.

124 Virtual Wallet providers and cryptoasset or cryptocurrency trading brokers must report virtual wallets to authorities, as being subject to the Foreign Account Tax Compliance Act—FATCA or the Common Reporting Standard—CRS.

References

1. Godoy, A. S. M. (2005). *Direito tributário comparado e tratados internacionais fiscais*. Porto Alegre: Sergio Antonio Fabris.
2. United States v. Opportunity Fund and Tiger Eye Investments, Ltd. *United States District Court for the District of Columbia* (No. 1:08-mc-0087-JDB). Decided 07/16/2012. Retrieved September 14, 2018, from http://www.cadc.uscourts.gov/internet/opinions.nsf/1B9DC0B1D05DB6D5852578070070EC9C/$file/09-5065-1255619.pdf
3. French, J. A., & Zahralddin, R. X. (1996). The difficulty of enforcing laws in the extraterritorial internet. *Nexus, 1*, 99–127.
4. NY Charities. Retrieved September 10, 2018, from charitiesnys.com or www.charitiesnys.com/pdfs/statute_booklet.pdf
5. Kossick, R. M. (2011). The internet in Latin America: New opportunities, developments & challenges. *Florida Journal of International Law, 13*, 263–288.
6. Davis, B. R. (2006). Ending the cyber Jihad: Combatting terrorist exploitation of the internet with the rule of law and improved tools for cyber governance. *Commlaw Conspectus, 15*, 177–184.

Index

F. M. De Sanctis, *Technology-Enhanced Methods of Money Laundering*,
https://doi.org/10.1007/978-3-030-18330-1

CPSIA information can be obtained
at www.ICGtesting.com
Printed in the USA
LVHW080725240619
622154LV00007B/89/P

9 783030 183295